D0077992

JACKI WILLSON is a Cultural Studies lecturer in
Fashion, Textiles and Jewellery at Central Saint Martins,
University of the Arts London. She is the author of
*The Happy Stripper: Pleasures and Politics of the New
Burlesque* (I.B.Tauris, 2008).

'Makes an important, timely and provocative intervention into debates about performance and objectification. [...] Jacki Willson has a way of making hugely original statements that make sense of what have felt like intractably complex and polarised debates.'

DEBRA FERREDAY
author of *Online Beginnings*

Being Gorgeous

*Feminism, Sexuality
and the Pleasures of the Visual*

J ACKI W ILLSON

I.B. TAURIS
LONDON · NEW YORK

First published in 2015 by
I.B.Tauris & Co. Ltd
London • New York
www.ibtauris.com

Copyright © 2015 Jacki Willson

The right of Jacki Willson to be identified as the author of this work has been
asserted by her in accordance with the Copyright, Designs and Patents Act 1988.

Every attempt has been made to gain permission for the use of the images
in this book. Any omissions will be rectified in future editions.

References to websites were correct at the time of writing.

International Library of Cultural Studies: 27

ISBN: 978 1 78076 284 5 (PB)
978 1 78076 283 8 (HB)
eISBN: 978 0 85773 999 5

A full CIP record for this book is available from the British Library
A full CIP record is available from the Library of Congress
Library of Congress Catalog Card Number: available

Typeset by Tetragon, London
Printed and bound by CPI Group (UK) Ltd, Croydon, CR0 4YY

FSC
www.fsc.org
MIX
Paper from
responsible sources
FSC® C013604

CONTENTS

List of Illustrations

Audacity Chutzpah
© *Photograph by kind permission of Terry Mendoza,*
www.retrophotostudio.co.uk

INTRODUCTION

Being Gorgeous and Feminism

In 2006 I first saw the film *Marie Antoinette*. It was full of enticing imagery: impossibly tall wigs as well as gorgeous colourful food which women gorged on with gusto. It was sensual and highly visual, like a performing painting or sculpture. There was a sense of fun, exuberance and anarchic play. It was a visual treat, and signposted something at play in culture at large. This film was set against a popular culture where bodies were being defined and controlled in a particular way; the women in *Marie Antoinette*, however, were acting indifferently and having a ball. This cinematic painting appeared at a similar time to other visual feasts such as new burlesque and, in the world of music, Lady Gaga. This was an indulgent display of revealing flesh, decadent dress and confident gestures.

There was something going on here that I needed to explore in more depth; something that I touched upon in my last book, *The Happy Stripper: Pleasures and Politics of the New Burlesque*, but did not fully elucidate. The main thrust of my argument in *The Happy Stripper* was that performers used flamboyant sexual display as an ironic means of challenging stereotypes, stereotypes that they hammed up and performed with a smile, a wink and a shimmy. This was a politicized display that was both pleasurable and 'knowing'. The performances were signposting a different relationship to the audience, where 'being-looked-at-ness' was neither passive nor vacant, and 'looking' was neither hostile nor sexist. In fact, what was being created was a different kind of politics, which challenged assumptions about power hierarchies in terms of spectatorship and objectification. The power dynamic of the 'male gaze' identified in Laura Mulvey's seminal essay, 'Visual pleasure and narrative cinema' (1975)[1] is one where the spectator identifies with an active male posturing himself as 'the bearer of the look'.[2] The manner in which the camera frames the 'woman as image'[3] into passive 'to-be-looked-at-ness'[4] creates a 'world ordered by sexual imbalance'[5] that drives the narrative forward.

However, I would like to revise scholarly assumptions about visual pleasure, feminized performance and objectification to forward a different model of spectatorship that is collective and empathetic. What happens if visual pleasure becomes a shared politicized narrative? If we dispense with academic feminist assumptions regarding the 'politics' of the gaze and allow ourselves to be pulled into the whirligig of vibrant colour, lip gloss, carousel horses and false eyelashes, what happens then? This becomes the key question and premise for this book. For many young women performing in the cultural arena, a highly visual surface is being used to express and experiment with a diverse range of identities and sensual experiences. And it is intriguing that this focus on surface appeal, objectification and 'a different kind of politics' is happening at a time when there is a pronounced sense of feminist urgency.

In both the UK and USA, 'new feminism' stresses the worrying increase in sexism in such books as Kat Banyard's *The Equality Illusion: The Truth about Men and Women Today* (2010) and Natasha Walter's *Living Dolls: The Return of Sexism* (2010). Banyard narrates a story of sexism throughout the day of one young woman, and Walter discusses the damaging sexualization of young women today. In 2014 Laura Bates added to this discussion with her book, *Everyday Sexism* (2014). Jessica Valenti's books *Full Frontal Feminism* (2007 [and a revised edition in 2014]) and *He's a Stud, She's a Slut*, (2008) also pushed these issues to centre stage in the USA. Indeed, when the furore broke out in September 2014 regarding leaked naked images of high-profile female actresses, Valenti spoke out about how viewers like to 'revel in the humiliation' of young beautiful female celebrities, and that 'looking at naked photos of someone who doesn't want us to goes beyond voyeurism; it's abuse.'[6]

What does it now mean, therefore, that running parallel to this wave of frustration and sexism regarding objectification, female liberation is now seemingly being played out through this very spectacle of 'being gorgeous'? Perhaps this is a different kind of politics, a politics that does not relate to existing antagonistic perceptions young women have of 'feminism'.

This is what I found extremely provocative about *Marie Antoinette*. Even though the film is set against the upheaval of the French Revolution, the female characters behave as if they are oblivious to this and carry on with their pleasurable shenanigans despite (or in spite of) the politics. The film was booed when it was first shown at the Cannes Film Festival because of this disregard for what was going on outside the palace. However, the erotic visual exuberance and behaviour narrates a different and non-linear story of appetites, pleasure, pain, sexuality, desire and liberation played out through costume, colour, texture and objects. The style is the content; the surface is the substance. The clothes, the colours and the textures speak to us from a different angle. This is not overtly about politics per se, but about women performing female experience by way of an erotic visual surface.

This is a sensual aesthetic narrative where seeing becomes an experience which is felt throughout the body. Communication happens by way of all the senses: seeing is also feeling, and being seen is also being felt. Emotions, desires, fears, pleasures and yearning are expressed through colour, pattern, shapes, objects and composition, like a painting. This 'painterly' aesthetic is discussed in a compilation of essays edited by Rosemary Betterton.[7] Through the medium of paint the spectator not only sees a naked female body but also experiences what that body feels. Through the materiality and expressiveness of the paint – the brushstrokes, layering, texture and hue – something else is evoked of that woman's creativity and sensuality.

This book will be exploring this idea of a sensual surface in conjunction with photography, performance, art, fashion, cinema, popular culture and subcultural cabaret. I will look at the question of objectification in relation to today's feminist politics and argue that surface appeal, or 'being gorgeous', can be a means by which women can express themselves as subjects more pleasurably and more meaningfully.

So, let us turn firstly to the question of objectification.

In Berlin in 2006, I was taken, reluctantly, to see an exhibition of works by fashion photographer David LaChapelle. On the way up the staircase to the gallery, life-sized photographs of six naked women loomed intimidatingly over me. I felt incredibly embarrassed. It all felt wrong but strangely compelling. I could see every pore and every hair follicle. Tanned and oiled, their skin sizzled like sausages. They were astonishingly and extraordinarily visible: magnified and objectified. This – Helmut Newton's 1981 image of powerful Amazonian women entitled *Sie Kommen (Here They Come)* – is obviously a fitting product of 1980s feminism and power dressing. Yet for me the image opened up scholarly concerns, which are still pressing now. The way in which these performing female bodies as subjects and as objects met and mingled with my spectatorial position flagged up a potentially positive, embodied and celebratory resistance to the gaze. However, an antagonistic feminist perspective regarding the spectacle of female nakedness and objectification should rightly temper any intervention into debates around objectification, spectatorship and performance.

And this antagonist perspective has an historical context. Within the discipline of art history, feminists such as Griselda Pollock, Lynda Nead, Linda Nochlin and Rozsika Parker have critically explored the nude tradition where women have predominantly been the passive models, not the artists; the objects, not the subjects. There was an imbalance of power. The male artist was using the woman's naked body to construct his idea of artistic beauty and aesthetic appeal. The model's erotic desires, thoughts, feelings and emotions were irrelevant. In the 1960s and 1970s, second-wave feminist artists were highlighting this discrepancy. Martha Rosler created collages of half-naked women from adverts she had cut out of magazines to question the sexual objectification and 'sale' of these bodies. And Carolee Schneemann spliced a film of her and her husband making love in order to make positive rather than gratuitous images of female eroticism. Many artists and art historians like Lynda Nead, Linda Nochlin and Griselda Pollock have thus questioned why it was that naked images of women were solely objectified as either pornography (sexualized, not sexual) or the nude (idealized).

These feminist politics are still relevant in popular cultural debates. In the *Woman's Hour* radio programme 'Women on Italian television'[8] in May 2010, filmmaker Lorella Zanardo argued that since Silvio Berlusconi had come to power in Italy television had become saturated from the early hours of the morning into the late hours of the evening with overly sexualized images of women. She argued that sexism had become routine and she wanted to see images of 'real' women. By showing this film in schools she was trying to politicize children and highlight the problem of daily repetition normalizing the objectification of women.

The negative result of objectification and sexism was also debated in 2011 in relation to street harassment. The London Anti-Street Harassment (LASH) campaigns against the manner in which women are sexually objectified in the streets, sometimes to the point of physical harassment.[9] Abundant display has, it seems, created in some instances a dangerous public free-for-all.

Though I also saw nakedness when I looked up at Helmut Newton's photograph, I feel this is a different kind of objectification which does not equate to powerlessness or abuse (this topic will be explored in more depth in Chapter 5). It would be useful for now to explore this different kind of objectification and spectatorship further by way of another example, an extraordinary scene from Jane Campion's 1990 film about the New Zealand writer Janet Frame, *An Angel at my Table* (1990). The character depicting Janet in this film is not traditionally pretty – she is plump and self-conscious about her teeth. But in one scene of her skinny-dipping with her boyfriend, the sensitivity in which her sexual awakening is evoked is breathtaking and achingly beautiful. Ripples of water move concentrically away from her naked body like a pencil line tickling the surface. This is an image of nakedness that is sensuous and positive. It is representation that evinces empathy, not shame, and is wholly reliant on visual pleasure and the gaze.

However, the visual pleasure forwarded in this scene is not the variation Laura Mulvey endeavoured to destroy when she stated: 'It is said that analysing pleasure, or beauty, destroys it. That is the intention of this article'.[10] The pleasure in the Janet Frame narrative is not just driven by our identification with male desire and a male masculine perspective. We see Janet through her lover's eyes, but the narrative and desire are shared and affirmative and embodied in female pleasure, which invites the look. This gaze is intersubjective and celebratory. We can hear her lover's appreciative comments as he looks on. It is about an erotic embodied encounter with another. By way of this pleasurable surface, of cinematic goosebumps – the

sun beating down on naked flesh, warm waves lapping over the
body – we as the onlookers feel and share the confidence, liberation, desire and pleasure of this sexual subject. In this scene the
spectator can see female naked flesh depicted in a positive, erotic
and liberating manner.

I walked into photographer David LaChapelle's exhibition affected;
Helmut Newton's image had got under my skin. Feeling these emotions, I looked around at LaChapelle's photographs. They were visually
gorgeous: shocking pinks and lime greens, objects of pure pleasure
such as topiary mazes, crinoline dresses and decadent languishing
poses. I felt hostile towards his work but found it strangely soothing
in a similar way to when viewing the glossy images that one sees in
Vogue or *Elle*. These were guilty pleasures, and as with Newton's
images there was a heightened sense of surface. It was decadence
for decadence's sake, and felt excessive and frivolous. These pictures
were unashamedly superficial.

… And yet I could not get these delicious images out of my head.
The more I thought about it, the more I realized that this was highly
significant, and that annoyed me. This was a visual experience that
was felt throughout the whole body. The lush surface, the colour and
the objects made this imagery accessible; the style was everything.
Ideas were being communicated aesthetically. In a similar way to artist
Matthew Barney's film *The Order*, from *Cremaster 3* (2003), which
will be discussed in Chapter 1, the experiences of pain, shame, joy,
exuberance and freedom were being conveyed through the texture
and hue of crumbling paint, the rustle of a skirt or the visually audacious eroticism of a glass leg or pink tartan. This is the evocation of
a creative spectacle that brings out the glint and twinkle in our eyes
and goads and stokes our anarchic spirits and identities. It pricks the
senses and awakens our rebelliousness, sensuality, unfettered thought
and raw feeling. We are not passive viewers. These are not didactic
images. We feel alive. The surface speaks to us and connects with
us on an emotional level.

This book champions these aesthetic, sensual surfaces. It may
seem to be flighty and frivolous with its narration of false eyelashes
and shoes, cakes and powder puffs, and to some extent it is. But this
does not make the imagery unimportant or insignificant. That most

fabulous of storytellers Roald Dahl was once reported to have said that invention was far better than fact. The imagination, he concluded, was far more fun. The imagination does not speak of hard facts, of sexism and inequality, but it does speak about liberation through visual freedom. The imagery in this book creates a sensual fantastical landscape of dressing up, of fairgrounds and absinthe, of wigs, lip gloss and masquerade balls, of chocolate fountains, high fashion and glamorous *Vogue* front covers. It is about poetic self-invention, about identities and possibilities and potential. It is about feeling and seeing using the whole body. Like the ebb and flow of warm seawater over naked flesh, a sip of absinthe, a taste of coffee, a walk through the park, it is about living and feeling intensely.

This spectacle of being gorgeous is about women's movement in visual culture from being sex objects to self-determined art objects. And it is this key transformation that I shall lay out in the last part of this introduction.

BEING AN ART OBJECT

In an article in *The Sunday Times Magazine* on 12 September 2010,[11] pro-sex-objectification feminist Camille Paglia argued that Lady Gaga's performance signalled the death of sex: 'For Gaga, sex is mainly decor and surface; she's like a laminated piece of ersatz rococo furniture [...] Can it be that Gaga represents the exhausted end of the sexual revolution?' Paglia argued that Lady Gaga was not sexy: every movement was contrived, even her arrival at an airport. She was 'stripped of genuine eroticism'. Her fans, she concluded, were 'marooned in a global technocracy of fancy gadgets but emotional poverty'. For Gaga, according to Paglia, was a performer who was 'calculated and artificial, so clinical and strangely antiseptic'. On the other hand, Kathy Burke had spoken about her admiration for Lady Gaga and her performance style on *Desert Island Discs* on 20 August 2010. Lady Gaga represented something different for Burke, and she drew parallels with her own youthful identification with punk. As a young woman, Burke stated, she felt ugly and awkward and punk gave her the freedom to accept herself. When she found punk, she was finally able to be herself and be happy in her own body, skin and big boots.

For me, this discussion of Lady Gaga in 2010 highlighted another exciting rebellion in relation to self-determination. Her admiration for fashionistas such as the late Isabella Blow and the similarly glamorous Daphne Guinness – and her modelling of Alexander McQueen's now infamous twelve-inch heeled Armadillo shoes and milliner Philip Treacy's outrageous hats – points to an identity that resides at the surface via artifice and 'dressing up'. In her performance she is clearly in control of how she appears and takes great pleasure in the theatricality of her own objecthood: her body as spectacle. This represents not the exhausted end of the sexual revolution (which perhaps is illustrated in the hyper-sexualization of the pre-pubescent) but the beginning of something much more anarchic and transformative. What is being acknowledged at the moment within certain corners, niches and subcultural pockets of both low and high aspects of cultural production is a different slant and control over the spectacle of women's sexual bodies – a move from sexual passivity to aesthetic extravagance.

Contemporary artists and artistes are choosing to frame their own sense of adventure and flamboyance by asserting artistic control over and above the 'feminine' and glamour. At an event in Bethnal Green's Working Men's Club in London one extremely cold and snowy November evening, I took part in a *Question Time*-type panel on burlesque, 'Art or bust', organized by *Time Out* and the Blue Stocking Society. After arriving, I sat down at a table with burlesque dancer Kitty Bang Bang and writer and former burlesque dancer Lucille Howe. Our discussion moved quickly to the affect and impact of clothing. Howe was debating whether she should wear her faux fur coat on stage and then throw it off for dramatic effect at a key point in the discussion. This tongue-in-cheek comment had a disarming charm, a self-conscious dandyism, which was evident in the room at large. The audience was embellished with glamorous adornment: glossy red lipstick, feathers, tattoos, beauty spots, berets, leopard print, false eyelashes and thick eyeliner. They were conscious of the aesthetic narrative of vintage 'bricolage': of fabric, colour, texture, pattern and gesture. This vintage spectacle was deliberately stylized and fun, and self-consciously beautiful.

Stella Bruzzi's idea of 'clothes-language'[12] is useful in relation to this. Bruzzi uses this term to describe the 'eroticization of clothes'[13] in the Jane Campion film *The Piano* (1993). The concept is used to describe the way in which costume has a 'narrative purpose' but also can 'exist independently of that dominant discourse'.[14] The 'clothes-language' of the vintage costume worn by the audience at Bethnal Green's working men's club was a reiteration of the dominant tradition of feminized styles, but it was also a subversion of that same tradition. They were using these styles to create a frame within which a range of ideas, emotions and politics could be played out, from the close encounter of soft faux fur as we brush by a spectator to the harsh distancing effect created by cheesecake Betty Page's severe fringe and tattoos. It is also useful to weave into this discussion Judith Butler's concept of performativity: 'The effect of gender is produced through the stylization of the body and, hence, must be understood as the mundane way in which bodily gestures, movements, and styles of various kinds constitute the illusion of an abiding gendered self.'[15] The audience at the 'Art or bust' event were performing the sensual and sexual pleasures of this gendered 'illusion' – which is of course a rich, embodied, cultural and historical experience – but they were also acknowledging that this process of engendering is an 'illusion' which is not beyond parody, critique or play.

And this sense of parody and play, this camp delight in appearance and delectable surface, was also apparent in the dress code for the vintage cabaret and burlesque evening *Bête Noire* at Soho's Madame Jojo's, which stated: 'Cads, Dandies, Vixens, Pinstripes, Furs & Feathers, Bête Noire operates a relaxed dress code policy – we won't force you to be beautiful.' This was a nod both to drag performance in its sexual ambiguity and to the dandy in its flirting with a heightened sense of gender identity and potentiality. And it is relevant and useful to refer to the literature on the dandy to help make sense of what is taking place in many quarters of women's performance today. Jessica Feldman[16] describes dandyism as 'the practice and impersonation of the act of self-creation and appearance.'[17] Erotic motifs of femininity are being embraced in order to self-consciously impersonate the erotic lexicon of glamour whilst simultaneously using this visual vocabulary to assert creative personality and agency.

It is significant from this perspective that the *Bête Noire* evening also included in its listing of entertainment tricksters, thespians, magicians and flâneurs. This presented us with something intriguing in relation to gender theory and sexual politics, for what was being performed was a collective and experimental play with gender and identity. In her conclusive remarks in *Gender Trouble* (1990), Judith Butler comments:

> In what sense, then, is gender an act? As in other ritual social drama, the action of gender requires a performance that is *repeated* [...] Although there are individual bodies that enact these significations by becoming stylized into gendered modes, this 'action' is a public action.[18]

With the *Bête Noire* example, and various examples that will be put forward later in this book, there is a playful endeavour to reiterate and stylize bodies and identities differently as a shared political and pleasurable action. It is a collective interplay, exchange and dialogue between the experiential, the embodied and the experimental.

But let's go back to that snowy November evening in Bethnal Green's Working Men's Club. During the evening, various performers strutted their stuff, including a performance by the Blue Stocking Society's Audacity Chutzpah with her signature striptease act *A Complete History of Women's Liberation in the 20th Century in Six and a Half Minutes*. This is a tongue-in-cheek survey of 'women's liberation' played out via gendered stereotypes of femininity: fashion, hairstyles, underwear, red lipstick, seamed stockings and stilettos. There is the notion, though, that this performance of femininity, this gendered spectacle, is embodied and linked to physical pleasures and politics. It is lived through the private interiority of a woman's physical body with her appetites, emotions, needs, wounds and confidence, but it is also simultaneously lived through a social, public body, as a commodity fetish, as 'ideal' and as a gendered stereotype. This is a woman who takes a glorious delight in being gorgeous. She is a sexy spectacle but with agency, debunking myths and assumptions about 'sexiness', 'feminism' and 'liberation' as well as enjoying the camp and outré irony of putting powder puffs

and world affairs on an equal footing. But more about this later in
Chapter 4.

For now what needs to be said is that creative, intelligent, articulate women are in the process of taking to task assumptions relating
to the affective (political and performative) potential of aesthetics
and visual pleasure. The artists and artistes – and indeed spectators – discussed in this book are initiating, creating and performing
contemporary twenty-first-century incarnations of feminism. Much of
the practice explored is current or has been created since the turn of
the new millennium. It is therefore indicative of a continual desire
and urgent need to engage with representations of woman's sexual or
sexualized body, or 'woman-as-image' with its ingrained conventions
and assumptions, as Sally O'Reilly states: 'And yet today, the passive
totem of sexualized womanhood is still visible in pornography and
advertising, suggesting an ongoing need for artists to engage with the
nude and to challenge ingrained conventions.'[19] However, the problem that has persisted has been how to do this effectively without, as
O'Reilly rightly comments, 'compromising the aesthetic remit of art'.[20]

This is difficult and problematic territory. But it is also an arena
which is rich for exploration and experimentation. There are several
female artists who have set a precedent here, artists such as Cindy
Sherman, Pipilotti Rist and Vanessa Beecroft, who have used glamorous bodies in and as their art. It could be said, however, that by using
stereotypically feminine, white, attractive, young, thin bodies these
women create imagery which fails to differ from the commodified,
flat, sexualized imagery that surrounds us; that by taking pleasure
from their delectable bodies as objects we do not empathize with the
subject. These artists, however, have set a precedent and created a
significant stepping stone for our understanding of what is taking place
in our contemporary cultural arena. They have opened up questions
and debates, most importantly being how artists and artistes can use
their sexually attractive bodies without being co-opted back into the
representational economy as purely a commodity fetish. This book sets
out the various ways women are tackling this paradox, whether that
be from within the underground cabaret scene, the 'high' art arena,
or the 'pop' industry of fashion, music and modelling.

*   *   *

My discussion in this book will be divided into four sections.

In Part I, I will look at how aesthetic sensuousness and visual opulence in 'low' and 'high' female performance has been used in relation to gender and sexuality as a strategy for undermining stereotype and convention through an almost politically indifferent sense of play, excess and self-absorption. Fashionistas, fashion designers, drag queens, fashion photographers, artists and filmmakers have used colour, style, glamour, texture and exquisite surfaces to create a different visual erotic, bringing identities, sexuality and lived gender into play.

In Chapter 1, 'Drop Dead Gorgeous', I will explore Camille Paglia's statement that Lady Gaga's appearance on the scene signalled the 'death of sex'. For Paglia, there was nothing sexy about her performance; it was contrived and artificial, with the sex 'mainly decor and surface'. I will firstly explore this 'decor and surface' in relation to pleasurable, playful, even anarchic identities. I will give this sense of surface a context by exploring the flamboyant spectacle of fashionistas such as Isabella Blow and Daphne Guinness, drag queens, carnival and masquerades, costume drama, and artists such as Matthew Barney. Fantastical surfaces allow women to be inventive and rebellious and push boundaries in terms of the rules of play. This is a sensuous aesthetic narrative.

However, this discussion is not without its problems. By discussing a frivolous and self-indulgent femininity, this could be seen to be falling regressively back on stereotypes aligning women with the senses rather than the mind, with surface rather than depth. With reference to fashion photography, the *Next Top Model* series and photography from *Vogue*, I will argue that this surface appeal and visual excess offers up a different perspective on pleasure, fun, play, self-invention and creative objectification.

Chapter 2, 'Skin Deep', will look at the spectacle of the naked female body and issues revolving around objectification, sexuality and sensuality. In her book *Living Dolls: The Rise of Sexism*, New Feminist Natasha Walter discusses the hyper-sexualization of young women and girls. Indeed, this sense of sleaze has recently come to a head in popular culture over the flaunting and cavorting of knicker-clad female bodies on prime-time television and the banning of a

Tom Ford advert which figures a naked, shaven, greased-up pubis that is only just covered by a perfume bottle. In 2003 the pressure group OBJECT was set up to challenge the objectification and commodification of women's bodies. These are pressing issues. Women want to (and indeed are beginning to) take back control of their objecthood as commodity and as spectacle. The two films on burlesque that were released in December 2010 demonstrate both the packaged commodified sexiness as well as the more renegade sexuality, physicality and personality of experiencing life through a thinking, feeling, sensual body.

Being an object, experiencing our skin and surface appeal, is important. We live through our sexualized, gendered skin. Part of our sense of self comes from looking and feeling good as objects. Our thingness, how we take up space – how we are seen, validated, recognized, admired and made visible – is how we count socially and sexually. The second section of this chapter will examine 'being looked at' from a more positive perspective.

Part II will explore female spectacular performance in popular culture. This flamboyant spectacle crosses fashion, theatre, performance art and popular culture with the female body, sexuality and femininity. The section will question what this spectacle tells us about young women's current position vis-à-vis bodies, visual pleasure, identity, spectatorship and politics.

In Chapter 3, 'Crinoline and Cupcakes: Dangerous Identities', Sofia Coppola's *Marie Antoinette* and new burlesque cabaret performers such as Imogen Kelly and Gwendoline Lamour will be discussed in relation to more 'dangerous' apolitical young female identities. In *Marie Antoinette* I was struck by the opposition set up in the film between the vibrant use of colour, texture and form, and the 'politics'. What did this seemingly apolitical revelry of the senses tell us? Was a rebellious gendered experience being expressed through an anarchic sense of pleasure in food, fabric, wigs, texture, shapes, colour and ostentatious costume?

The UK's new burlesque scene will then be further discussed in Chapter 4, 'Powder Puffs and Beauty Spots: Spectacular Objecthood', in relation to art, objecthood, objectification and feminism where 'high art' aesthetics and sensibility cross into popular culture's sense of spectacle and spectatorship. I will explore Audacity Chutzpah's cabaret performance *A Complete History of Women's Liberation in the 20th Century in Six and a Half Minutes* in conjunction with two beauty manifestos from the popular women's magazine *Psychologies* and from the Blue Stocking Society's online blog in order to investigate the politics of 'powder puffs and beauty spots'. The second section of this chapter will look at *Dr. Sketchy's Anti-Art Class* in order to discuss subcultural models who challenge the traditional ideas of the 'gaze' and instead offer up an experience which is more communal and shared.

Part III will explore how contemporary female performance artists and 'high' art have looked at woman as spectacle and how our culture has framed the female body in terms of fashion, femininity and sexuality.

Chapter 5, 'The Paradoxical Body', will focus on fashion and art and the 'ideal' commodification of the female body. It will explore how art has been seduced by the glamour and cool chic of fashion, but with an edge. This could perhaps be described as subversive conformity. When Lady Gaga turned up to an award ceremony in 2010 with a meat purse and her 'high' fashion dress and shoes made from a dead carcass, it obviously caused a furore. However, this marriage of blood and glitter has a context. It highlights many intriguing issues which relate 'beauty' with flesh: beauty which chooses to ignore the fact that women bleed, that they age, give birth, change and die; that being gorgeous does not have to mean that we edit women and annihilate personality. However, there is a desire to conform to the 'ideal' standard and court the fashion world even though we know it is problematic. Vanessa Beecroft highlights this desire for beauty in her work, which captures the frozen moments of modelling and allows us to gaze at these naked 'ideal' bodies. But perhaps this desire to be glamorous and court the gaze can also open up alternative possibilities which do not undermine the female as a subject.

Chapter 6, 'The Sexual Body', will explore the sexual female body and its rate of exchange as a pornographic body. Artist Alex McQuilkin's video *Fucked* (2000) showed the then 19-year-old being taken from behind whilst she tried to apply lipstick. This piece brought to the fore many interesting current questions related to our sexual bodies as objects and our sense of identity and pleasure as subjects. We are surrounded by imagery which commodifies women and marks out youthful, usually white, female bodies as objects of exchange. These issues will be discussed by way of Marc Jacobs' Autumn/Winter 2013 'prostitute chic' promotional video for Louis Vuitton entitled *Love* (directed by James Lima), as well as Terry Richardson's fashionable soft-porn photography in *Purple* and Larry Clarke's film about pornography, *Destricted* (2006). These questions of a 'pornographic' body are contrasted in the second half of this chapter with the erotic female subject as represented by Tracey Emin in her drawings, photography and animation of masturbation, and the paintings by Marlene Dumas such as *Exposure* (1999), *Fingers* (1999) and *High Heel Shoes* (2000). I will also discuss Sam Taylor-Wood's *Death Valley* (2004), where a male actor is filmed masturbating hard in the Nevada desert.

The final section, Part IV, will explore how the female body can create an aesthetic revolt and a different kind of sensual, sensate and sensitive feminist politics full of colour, texture, taste, objects, flamboyance and extravagance.

Chapter 7, 'Pleasure, Violence and the Sensual Spectacle', will look at the female spectacle in relation to pleasure and pain, violence and glamour, masochism and beauty. I will firstly focus on Karla Black's sculpture and her girly palette of crumbling dissolving bath bombs and foundation smears in relation to Ben Highmore's ideas about aesthetics. In a cultural arena where all imagery is picture-perfect, Black's objects create a much more unstable and unfinished 'feminine' experience, where aesthetics is not just about fixating on Photoshopped 'beauty' but also about how the world affects us in a rich variety of ways. Black's work reveals an aesthetic which embodies 'feminine' experience more holistically. This is a visceral materiality which deals more with real, physical, messy, not-quite-beautiful everyday encounters and interactions between objects and bodies. The smears and goo of these encounters leave a residue and trace of an unfinished, more grotesque body in process. The chapter will then explore how glamour can be used to violate the pictorial in the video work of Pipilotti Rist including *Sip My Ocean* (1996), and in Sigalit Landau's *Barbed Hula* (2000). The radical juxtaposition between 'beauty' and violence creates an aesthetic which registers in the body as an opposition to established thought. The trace that this artwork leaves in the body feels subversive.

The final chapter, 'Creative Spectatorship and the Political Imagination', will look at the decadent imagery of the fashion show and new burlesque with its anarchic visual combination of absinthe, false eyelashes, fairgrounds, masked balls and extravagant costumes, as well as Marisa Carnegie's *Ghost Train* with its weird and wonderful performers. This chapter will explore how this could possibly translate into the political, into rebellion by way of visual pleasure. Our contemporary pornified visual culture disallows mystery. It wants us to reveal all, expose everything, and thus leaves nothing to the imagination. It has demystified sexuality, sensuality and the pleasures of the visual. This chapter dwells on vision as a facility for opening up rather than closing down possibilities, and how in that way it can move us beyond limited ideals and stereotypes. The performances politicize the visible by evoking the invisible through dance, puppets, dressing up, trapdoors or magic. This is a political revolt of the imagination, a positive celebration of what has been lost and what has literally 'disappeared' from our cultural landscape. In the act of looking, the magical and the fantastical sensations of the unseen, the unrepresented, the ignored and the unknown are brought to life, conjured up, reimagined.

Being Gorgeous brings our attention to the technicoloured erotic presence of the subject by way of a heightened seductive spectacle of colour, texture, costume, fabrics, objects, interiors and landscapes: what I would like to call a 'performative painting'. This is eye candy, but it is also a transformative honeytrap which reconstitutes the gaze in the act of seduction. The examples in this book reframe politics through aesthetics. Various conventional codes of 'glamour', beauty or femininity are being used as a styling mechanism for self-invention and intervention. The excess of the spectacle is therefore a stylized theatrical assertion of female subjects who have been edited out of the flat, lifeless imagery which surrounds them, imagery which offers up limiting visual cultural expectations. The play on the visible and the seen is used in a tantalizing manner to play with the invisible, the concealed and the unseen. This is expansive rather than limiting. As such the intention of this book is to bring together examples of 'low' and 'high' performers and performance that seek to create and energize a politics of empathy through the aesthetics of visual pleasure.

Part I

Sexuality, Gender and the Art and Erotics of Visual Extravagance

1

Drop Dead Gorgeous

EXQUISITE SURFACES

Back in 2003, I arrived jetlagged in New York at 4 a.m. my time. I looked in *What's On* and noticed that an exhibition of artist Matthew Barney's work *The Cremaster Cycle* was opening at the Guggenheim, showcasing the culmination of eight years of work. I got on the subway and joined the queue. Snaking away from the gallery was a camp array of drag queens, flâneurs, fashionistas and impresarios: men in ostentatious wigs, platform shoes and thickly made-up faces, and long-legged beauties à la Folies Bergère, littered the pavement.

I was in for a treat.

Once inside the building I wandered up a swirling staircase, which contained in its centre a large-scale five-channel video installation of *The Order*, the sequence from *Cremaster 3* which had been filmed in the Guggenheim. This contains a visual extravaganza of Busby Berkeleyesque synchronized hypnotic dancing, fixed smiling faces and seductive sparkling women. In the background we can hear twinkling, glittering music as if emanating from a fairy godmother's wand. This feminine fairytale poise is punctuated by masculine aggression, with loud throbbing punk splintering our brains as we try to take in the succulent visual imagery. As the smiling lovelies bathe and frolic in a pool of bubbles at the centre of the atrium, this jarring hateful cacophony issues from a band playing on a stage from one of the floors.

Then there is the protagonist, Barney himself, pink tartan, pink wig, strong muscular body climbing up the insides of the Guggenheim, athletic and determined. The female protagonist is the gorgeous, fascinating Aimee Mullins, with glass legs sculptured into a stiletto-heeled finish. This spectacle is hypnotic: it attracts yet also repels with its glitter and ear-splitting thundering. Nancy Spector, in her essay on Barney's work, argues by way of Glen Helfand that: 'Gender is raw material for Barney. He molds it much as he molds space. The feminine and the masculine, or some combination thereof, become zones of articulation within the narrative.'[1] If we consider gender in this artwork as 'zones of articulation', then what is being articulated?

In *The Order*, masculinity and femininity are expressed by way of exquisite haptic surfaces. They carve out the outer boundary of signifiers, which culturally express the sexual differentiation between the biological male and female body. By virtue, however, of their extreme differentiation, these binary constructions become the extreme positions in between which the main character can construct his own narrative. We see Barney's muscular toned body in a pink kilt and pink busby (a military headdress). This is an intriguing combination and creates a very masculine shape with the added female sartorial 'pink' element. The kilt and the busby are the flamboyant chinks in the armour of what is normally classed as female territory. Within the culturally guarded categories of 'the skirt' and 'wigs/headdresses', the kilt and the busby become limited, culturally permitted outlets for masculinity, and create another vocabulary which is exempt from usual culturally guarded rules.

This is not 'drag'. What this extravagant display is doing is exploring the cultural parameters of being male and finding other outlets for expression which enmesh opposing gendered signifiers – such as the colour pink with a muscular heterosexual male body, or 'to-be-looked-at-ness' with physical exertion – to create new meanings and significance. Barney is using his erotic male body to challenge corporeal and social boundaries. Barney's work is, as Francesco Bonami argues, 'a celebration of desire and its repression'.[2] And this, Bonami states, is made tangible through the physical exertions of the protagonist, who tosses a heavy caber-like object and climbs up the inside of the atrium. By doing this, Barney continues his own obsession with the 'hypertrophy of the muscles', a 'process that allows muscles to expand when subjected to strain or resistance'.[3]

This hypertrophic process is also applied to gendered signifiers and stereotypes. He uses pornographic excess in his imagery to the point where this excess moves the body and its meanings beyond the conventional, much like when a word is repeated over and over again until it becomes nonsensical and therefore morphs into another sense. With Barney's performance, we see this in the way the diegetic bubble of smiles and bare breasts – light and fluffy and vacuous – creates a visual wonder full of electric energy when these bodies break into a dazzling display of synchronized tap dancing. Here, feminine 'to-be-looked-at-ness', which represses the female body into passivity, is given an electric energy expressed through the collective unity and skill of these female bodies.

We also have this play off in relation to hyper-masculinity with Barney's masculinity set in motion next to the more destructive 'conqueror and vanquished' masculinity, as represented by the over-powering violence of the band. The male protagonist exerts his body, pushing against his physical, environmental, architectural and cultural boundaries to allow for more expansion and growth. The *Cremaster Cycle* explores the process by which we become sexually differentiated and ultimately finds creativity in the sexually undifferentiated, as Nancy Spector argues in 'Only the perverse fantasy can save us'.[4] There is therefore an energy and growth of these bodies in motion, which expands the body's significance and meaning. We see this with the female protagonist Aimee Mullins. Being both model and athlete with no legs, she challenges numerous categories and stereotypes for her sex. Her body is lean and 'drop-dead gorgeous', her body supported by glass prosthetics, which makes seemingly fragile material appear solid. This is a powerful perversion of elegance and visual charm demonstrating potentiality and vigour.

This fusion of the artificial and the natural is also demonstrated in Barney's use of 'showgirls'. Throughout the film we see a synchronized display of women's bodies dancing and smiling in theatrical head-dresses and sparkling revealing costumes. In one scene of half-naked female flesh, submerged and playful in bubbles, the self-conscious voyeuristic spectacle prevents this pornographic visual pleasure from imploding into a 'wet dream'. The scene is still visually pleasurable, but the pleasure remains on the highly constructed surfaces – it seems natural, all of the expected elements are there – yet the excessive play of femininity disturbs the natural. What we watch is compelling yet strange. This artificial scene makes the 'naturalness' of femininity and poise feel awkward. There is a sense of wonder and a playful sensual pleasure of bubbles on flesh, yet this is also constructed, also acted out. The feminine surfaces are as fictive as the cinematic surfaces – they are 'acting acting': they are playing the part of themselves.

This idea of fiction and acting in relation to gender can usefully be explored by way of Jessica Feldman's discussion of the dandy. The key idea that Feldman forwards that is pertinent to Barney's conceptualization of gender relates to the idea of impersonation. Feldman argues that the dandy 'is the figure who practices, and even impersonates, the fascinating acts of self-creation and presentation'.[5] The showgirls in Barney's narrative are playing with the construction of femininity by way of two surface interfaces. First, they are playing with the artifice of being a woman, taking pleasure from acting out the self-creative practice of femininity; and second, they are also impersonating that act of self-presentation by way of their role as showgirl in the narrative. As a result their feminine behaviour seems strange and otherworldly.

Femininity is therefore seen to be self-consciously constructed. This is a 'painstakingly presented body'[6]. The fixed smiles reveal someone who is acting smiling. The conventional 'norms' are played out as expected, yet the utter artifice makes these norms feel simultaneously familiar and strange, delightful and disturbing. This performative spectacle delights in its delightfulness, and as a result contradictions are perceived that reinvest gendered bodies with new significance.

Feldman's idea of analogy with regard to dandyism would also therefore be relevant here. She argues that it is by way of analogy that the dandy slips out of categorization; one can be like something or someone whilst not actually being that thing or person. To live *like* a king is to live in the world of the imagination, not in the world of reason.

This is the power of dressing up and presentation in relation to self-creation. To be like a 'man', yet not; this is how the dandy evades essentialism, for he isn't anything solid. He slips between fact and fiction; he retains yet evades stereotypes. He is male, but the manner in which he presents himself so carefully and painstakingly prevents clear categorization. The dandy is a mercurial figure who opens up rather than closes down possibilities for gendered expression.

We see this use of analogy with regard to dandyism in the way Barney plays with masculine display. Culturally, for women the art of display and spectacle is taken as read; it is 'natural' to collapse womanhood with the spectacle of femininity. This is not expected from the heterosexual male body. Yet Barney reconfigures gendered signifiers to express the sexual male body creatively and in a more undifferentiated manner. He reshuffles binaries, and reconstitutes and re-presents a male identity in flux.

Lorraine Gamman speaks about the contradiction between display and masculinity in her discussion of dandyism in relation to the gangster in her article 'If looks could kill'.[7] The peacock-like 'masculine display'[8] of the gangster invites voyeuristic opportunities, yet this seems at odds with the gangster's tough-guy masculinity. Barney uses the 'feminine' spectacle of the body – which bids for attention, which wants to be looked at and admired – to ironically reinforce masculinity and the male silhouette. The overemphasis on appearance and spectacle provides pleasures for the gaze and a display that, ironically, reinforces masculinity. The sensual painterly surface detail is compelling and intentionally attracts the voyeuristic gaze in order to bring the eye back to the male silhouette and its creative possibilities. This allows the body to be willingly acted upon, to be willingly at the mercy of the gaze. This is a body that doesn't just act upon its environment but is also acted upon. And this process of display allows for a relationship of expression and reciprocity.

The audience members who queued up to see the Matthew Barney show were also expressing gender as undifferentiated creativity. They were participants and collaborators in the imaginative act and impersonation of self-presentation. Their painstakingly constructed looks conjured up a fantastical kaleidoscope of glittering eyelashes, tattooed bodies, showgirls, carnival divas, masquerade balls and men in unwieldy platforms, thick make-up and huge wigs. This was the aesthetics and erotics of visual extravagance. These are painters of our contemporary life. Their painterly textures, colour, flamboyance and sensual abandon absorb and express male and female bodies within a gendered landscape.

In his essay 'The painter of modern life', Baudelaire discusses the painter of modern life as artist, poet, philosopher and man of the world. He is a 'passionate spectator'[9] – a flâneur – who paints the world, the 'moral and aesthetic feeling of their time'[10] by way of his creative presentation. The surface of the world can be played with in a painterly fashion, *like* an artist. Baudelaire describes this painter as drunk on life, for whom 'no aspect of life has become *stale*.'[11] There is therefore a sense of wonder and curiosity about the world in which this painter lives, and he uses his clothing and bodily comportment as his paintbox, his 'excessive love of visible, tangible things, condensed to their plastic state'.[12]

In his book, *The Changing Room: Sex, Drag and Theatre*, Laurence Senelick argues that this idea of being 'beyond gender' is 'the boast of the theatrical cross-dresser, because the eradication of binaries seems to provide a wider range of moods and genres for the performer.'[13] Barney's spectacle of undifferentiated gender is not necessarily though pushing beyond gender, but is using gender to embellish and enhance the creative expression of sexed bodies. The male and female bodies in Barney's work utilize and pervert cultural expectation; they push against the constraints of gendered boundaries and reshuffle binaries to permit the body to expand. In this way they reinvent the 'natural' by way of artifice.

To go 'beyond gender', therefore, would be to ignore a rich cinematic panorama of exquisite surfaces and an established set of conventions and norms which could be used to resist and then expand. To ignore these is to lose some of the pleasures culturally made enticing for erotic play. An established 'version' gives us the possibility for 'subversion', and for expansion beyond the expected. This flamboyant play makes us look at male and female sexual bodies differently, and gives greater creative freedom for expression within established cultural parameters. The exquisite surfaces painted by these passionate spectators offer us an opportunity for gendered play within our cultural palette. They make us look at 'natural' versions afresh – with curiosity. And by performing and acting out these versions, they reveal a 'given' that can in fact be embellished, reinterpreted and reinvented through impersonation.

EYE CANDY

In one of the episodes of the *Australia's Next Top Model* series a ballerina says to one of the competing models that being a model is a
lot like being a ballerina – every single move has to be drop-dead
gorgeous. Indeed, much of the modelling, props, style and fashion
photography in the episodes we watch from various countries' *Top
Model* episodes are fantastical in their appeal. The desire to nail
the right mood, emotion, concept and fantasy is paramount to the
photograph, and the model is the centrepiece of this aesthetic. It is
all about the styling, the composition, the textures and the narrative.
We want to look at this model; the image has been created in such
a way as to keep us looking. We are like bees to a honeypot. And of
course this is the intention. The images are selling clothes, perfume
or some other object of desire.

But do the models count beyond their role as eye candy – as a
honeytrap for the fashion industry? Do they have any other significance other than their 'prettiness' – their pretty vacancy? And if that
is their significance, can we pursue this further? What does it mean
to be (and to want to just be) idolized in this way? Is there more to
this that we can explore? In her book, *Wet: On Painting, Feminism,
and Art Culture* (1996) Mira Schor argues that the visual pleasure of
paint and the painterly act 'not as "eye candy" but as a synergetic
honey-trap' for ideas about the 'now'.[14] The visual pleasure and the
'seductive potential'[15] of oil paint – the lush colours, textures and
brush strokes – are a way of seducing us into the painting so that we
can then consider another aspect of the artwork that 'glimmers around
the paint' or that 'flicker[s] in and out of representation'.[16] This is, she
argues, the 'subversive potential of visual pleasure.'[17]

But what ideas are being trapped within a fashion image that
bristles with youth, photogenic and Photoshop-enhanced 'perfection'? Can Schor's seductive ideas apply to fashion photography?
She argues that the politics of the 'male gaze' prevents us (as female
painters and critical spectators) from realizing the subversive potential
of visual pleasure. The pleasures of the painterly, she argues, can
be in and of themselves challenging. The French word *peinture* has
been used pejoratively about paintings to insinuate a pleasure which

is vacuously sensual – a craft, even. This pejorative use of *peinture* certainly applies to fashion – it is seen as frivolous and lightweight – yet for many woman this 'secret vice' is very much alive in their daily dosages of pleasure when they flick through women's magazines at break, over lunch, on the bus, before lights out. As I flick through the September 2013 edition of UK *Vogue*, very young white women gaze directly into the camera, making a connection with the reader through its lens. These are images which communicate on the whole with a female readership and cannot easily be dismissed as purely scopophilic.

The fashion image is visually gorgeous – it is painterly, and aesthetically evocative. But what is it saying? Certainly the aim is to make us want to linger over the image that speaks beyond text and visualizes contemporary aesthetics. It does not operate in the world of politics or morals but reflects the current mood, *ambiance*, sensation or 'ideal'. It reflects. It is not self-conscious. The image stylizes what is 'in' and what is 'now' – the aesthetics of the body's pose, of the shapes and pleasure of fabric, pattern, make-up, wigs, fantasy and composition. The young models are selected because of their 'perfect' and 'ideal' beauty. The same facial features on every page blur into an homogenized landscape of the same: the same faces, the same complexion – same, same, same – beautiful people, beautiful lives – beautiful, beautiful, beautiful – lips slightly opened, skin on the whole pale and blemish-free, features balanced, eyes large, lips full, noses small, body thin.

In *The Face of Fashion* (1994), Jennifer Craik states that Cecil Beaton would charm models to their faces but in their absence would call them 'silly cows'. In 1938 he exclaimed that he had finished taking fashion photographs of 'young models who survived just as long as their faces show no sign of character.'[18] The model is the muse, the idol, one of the many shimmering surfaces which inspires. Baudelaire similarly argued that woman 'is a kind of idol, stupid perhaps, but dazzling and bewitching, who holds wills and destinies suspended on her glance.'[19] In this description there is an idea of being lured in by a devastating beauty, yet this attraction is also akin to the vertigo induced by looking over a sheer sensual cliff and seeing one's own empty and decadent annihilation.

I feel this sense of vertigo, of drowning in surfaces that are at once seductive yet terrifyingly empty, when I look at the glossy fashion photography by David LaChapelle. Amongst the images in *Hotel LaChapelle* is one photograph of fashionista Isabella Blow and designer Alexander McQueen, *Burning down the House*[20] (1996). This is a vision of decadence; it makes tangible that terrifying emptiness below the surface. In the background a castle burns to the ground, with Blow and McQueen in the foreground resplendent in dresses. McQueen is holding a flaming torch with an expression of satanic madness and glee on his face. Blow has an expression of indifference; she is looking picture-perfect in an extravagant Philip Treacy hat. In this image, two iconic figures from the fashion world dance at the gates of the immoral and the apolitical.

What this image expresses is an anarchic destruction of the old and a statement of the new, heralded by two fashion revolutionaries. It feels a hollow victory. This is a spectacle of burning down the old, yet in its place is a hollow sense of beauty and emptiness, a horrifying sense that they are, as Gianni Mercurio argues, 'prisoners of things and seduced by goods to the point of becoming one with them.'[21] This Dionysian pleasure is almost dangerously vacant, for it celebrates the victory of the superficial, inconsequential and the insubstantial. The beauty they represent induces a terror that comes from looking over a chasm into vast, absurd nothingness. Mercurio argues that LaChapelle's photographs are about both 'beauty and terror' and the nausea one feels 'from feeling oneself just an object amongst things when the absurdity and emptiness of the world has been sanctioned'.[22] This is the nausea that comes from looking at and being looked at purely as an object, as a purely indulgent, debauched surface.

The phoenix of a new modern identity born out of this fire is concentrated in the face of the model as object of our contemporaneity. She represents this vision of heaven and hell condensed on to the surface of her beauty, her femininity as reflection of the exterior. In her article 'The enchanted spectacle', Caroline Evans argues that the model acts like a prism for modernity; she represents the ideals of the 'now'.[23] Similar to this line of thought, Baudelaire argues that each age has its own gestures, smiles and comportment – its own aesthetic. And indeed it is this aspect of beauty which the fashion industry seeks to find in its models as the 'face' of the time.

As I look at one of the models in a Dior advert,[24] I am locked into her gaze. My vision is simultaneously taking in the bold red coat with an elegant collar that folds into the front of the neck, sleeves that end in a large wrap of fabric around the wrist finished off with a large soft fabric button. I am drawn to the mole on the right-hand side of her face, the large black ring on her finger, and the hand that clasps a Dior bag emblazoned with a stiletto. My eyes, though, keep returning to her gaze, which makes me feel like I am getting to know or wanting to know this woman. My eyes dart around the interlocking surfaces to build a picture of this woman and her environment.

She stands in front of a whitewashed brick wall; on the opposite page of this double-page spread the woman is seen in full. I can see a suggestion of the length of her leg through the split of her dress. This is an elegant contemporary home with sculptural lamps, wrought iron curving from the side of the wall. The shape of her silhouette is defined by the coat; it cuts a contour into the image, raw red slicing into the painterly brick. The line of the coat, the shadow, the leg, the lamp – straight defined lines – contrast with the curving wisp of jet-black hair, which mirrors the thin sinewy lines of the lamp as it snakes out of the brick wall it sits upon.

The image takes my breath away. This is an aesthetic narrative, yet what is intriguing and what makes the image work are the imperfections. The image can be read against the grain; the quirks and imperfections, not the 'beauty', make the image so compelling. Repetitive beauty does not prick the senses or sustain the gaze – it is not very interesting at all. The visual pleasure comes from flashes of difference, the 'out of place' that intrigues the eye: a clash of pattern, jarring inconsistency, red fabric slicing white brick. And this is where 'beauty' is differentiated from visual pleasure. Baudelaire similarly argues that beauty comprises two elements:

> Beauty is made up of an eternal invariable element [...] and of a relative, circumstantial element, which will be the age, its fashions, its morals, its emotions. Without this second element, which might be described as the amusing, enticing, appetizing

icing on the divine cake, the first element would be beyond our powers of digestion or appreciation, neither adapted nor suitable to human nature.[25]

Woman adapts and adorns herself by way of her 'femininity' in order to create the aesthetic of the time. It is this element that can be used to bewitch. In fact, Baudelaire states that it is woman's duty to appear magical and bewitching: '[S]he has to astonish and charm us; as an idol, she is obliged to adorn herself in order to be adored.'[26] For Baudelaire, therefore, bewitchment is a role, a duty that a woman must do in order to be worshipped. She has to make the effort to astonish and be adored, to be idolized. And this desire to charm is illustrated in Vogue's 'Charm school',[27] where they offer up '30 tips and tricks' to 'revel in your femininity'. Amongst these tips are: '16. Don't assume trousers have no place in the feminine revival', '21. Enhance the feminine form', and 30, which advises women that autumn blooms are 'darkly seductive' and 'wickedly grown up'. This is all about using one's femininity and sexual attraction to bewitch and be adored.

What does it mean, though, to oblige in one's own idolatry? It is evident in these tips that women can and want to use their womanly figure to beguile, and there are suggestions on how to do this even after the age of 34! (One of these being that we can do it beyond 34 as long as we make more effort to beguile.) We can wear a pencil skirt and cashmere jumper as long as we pull up our sleeves and show some glittering accessory. Intriguingly, visual pleasure is being built up around more artifice. What is implied is that a lack of naturally youthful 'assets' can be compensated for with the art of embellishment. The trickery and smoke and mirrors of glitter, sparkle and secret subterfuge: 'the three-buttons-undone' rule, the 'flirtatious flush', which will 'be mistaken for the real thing', can cast a magical spell that will enchant the world around us.

What is particularly intriguing in the images and tips is the manner in which the artifice that is used to make oneself beautifully seductive blurs quite tantalizingly with the world beyond the body: '15. Smoking-hot red lips are the calling card for the new season. Why not match yours to the paintwork of your purring Bentley and take it to the road.' Or '5. Laugh. It's infectious and spells joy.' Or

'4. Spray and walk in a mist to leave a trail in your wake.' Or '7. Dare the barely there hosiery trend – 10 denier should be all that come between you and the elements.' Language is used here – a 'match', a 'trail', 'between', 'infectious' – to create the idea of a connection with the environment beyond the skin; as if the magnetic spider's web is being spun, dissolving boundaries between bodies by way of lipstick, laughter, perfume and hosiery. For Baudelaire, the artificiality and adornment woman uses to create her alluring image is, he argues, synonymous with the woman: 'What poet, in sitting down to paint the pleasure caused by the sight of a beautiful woman, would venture to separate her from her costume?'[28]

Jessica Feldman's response to Baudelaire's conjectures is useful in moving his line of thought further: 'Is the cushion into which a languorous woman melts distinguishable from her garments and those garments from her skin? For Baudelaire, to question woman's integrity is to question human identity itself.'[29] Woman's culturally assigned gender – femininity – has been used to question her authenticity, her lack of substance and her truth. Femininity has been defined by Freud as 'a dark continent', as 'Other', and as such unfathomable. The feminine lack to the masculine substance, femininity is about creating substance where there is none. And masks, artifice and bewitchment have culturally given shape to this binary identity formation. Identity here is about veiling, therefore hiding lack. It is seen as deception and fabrication and 'made up'.

Clothing and ornamentation are used to give meaning to the female body/self – a meaning that therefore only exists on the surface. The body is conflated with its ornamentation, and thus with the non-self and the 'Other', the object world outside of the female body/self which gives it meaning and allows it to signify. Both Feldman and Baudelaire have discussed the way in which the centralized *moi* of interiority has been attributed to the male and masculinity and the vaporization of *non-moi* has been attributed to the female and the feminine. The 'vaporization' and 'centralization' of the self – the world of the crowd and the world of the self – are very useful terms for my discussion of identity and agency. To expand on this conflation of the body with its ornamentation, Jessica Feldman enquires: 'Who can say where one ends and the other begins?'

Feldman argues through Baudelaire that it is not just female identity but human identity itself which operates in this fashion. We indeed find the self and then lose the self in order to gain a wider expanded understanding of one's sense of being in the world. Where is the boundary, the cut-off point between objects and bodies? Perhaps indeed this is the manner in which identity itself is constructed and imagined in the negotiation between the centralized self (male or female) and the non-self or Other: in the unstable will-o'-the-wisp porosity between the *non-moi* and the *moi*. Maybe the instability of feminine vaporization of *non-moi* – the frivolousness of objects, ornamentation, make-up, aesthetics – surface vacuity, instability and artifice that has been signposted as feminine and female – is indeed applicable to human identity per se, as queried by Nietzsche with his remark: 'Supposing truth to be a woman—?'[30]

Referring back to UK *Vogue* fashioning the 'now', my attention is drawn to the fashion images photographed by Jürgen Teller[31] representing the Fall 2013 collection by Céline. These photographs are imaged like Polaroid instant images, like snapshots. The model appears older than usual, and my eye moves to the large bluish-green veins in her pale hand, which protrude with the same intensity as the loud patterned blue-, green- and mustard-flowered tiles behind her. Her eyes gaze intensely out of the page; they are washed out slightly, the bluish-green blending into the background. The lines of the tiles are slightly askew, out of kilter with the contour and silhouette the model makes in relation to the varying textures of her dress and the furry jumper that she holds close. Her long red false nails and red lipstick stand out starkly, creating a corolla effect which mirrors the tiles. The gaping hole in the sleeve of the blue satin dress flashes skin, like the core of a flower around which the gaunt bones, fingers, elbows, shoulder blades and creased folds of fabric stick out at angles. These flowers look like they have been placed on a wonky shelf, and this eccentricity is exhilarating.

This image is like a painting. It has painterly possibilities. This is certainly eye candy, but it does not sit easily on the eye. There is an awkwardness about it, imperfections that move it away from being purely about conventional 'beauty' (and there is certainly a lot of this in these glossies and in visual culture at large) into other

Jürgen Teller, Céline campaign, Vogue, Fall 2013
© Jürgen Teller and Lehmann Maupin, New York and Hong Kong

Jürgen Teller, Céline campaign, Vogue, Fall 2013
© *Jürgen Teller and Lehmann Maupin, New York and Hong Kong*

intersubjective possibilities. The gaze from this model does not represent vacancy (nor stupidity). There is a sense of visual potency and aliveness in the poetry of 'now' as we crumple and fall into the aesthetics within the gaze of this female body as subject. A sensibility is shared on the surface as exterior, the painterly becomes an aesthetic in which we playfully fuse as objects, as surfaces which overlap with potentiality. And we feel a politics of aesthetics in the imperfections, a shared subjectivity in the visual pleasure within the riot of colour, the crooked tiles, the joyously repetitive loud Mediterranean pattern, the awkward contours.

Unlike art, the fashion spread is promoting a brand in order to sell products within each image; however, the image can still give the reader a shared sense of wonder, connectivity and poetry: of new connections and networks, and new ways to see and configure the world. This is a rebellion of the senses, a riot of colour, texture, pattern and shapes, a bricolage of the imagination, invention and individuality and a new aesthetics of the self as it hums to the rhythm of large sculptural accessories, painted brick, pattern, line.

At the beginning of this section, I referred to Schor's idea of *peinture*. She argues that the sensual of the painterly can create new visual ideas. The painterly as eye candy pulls the eye into the frame in order to draw our attention to other aspects of the image and the paint. She describes the specific aspects she refers to as *terrains vagues*, which are undeveloped areas within the painting that are blurred and undefined. These areas and patches and daubs of paint are 'spaces of waves, the sea of liquidity, where the eye flows idly'.[32] These are areas we are not intentionally drawn to, but areas our eyes flicker over, stare at, as if in a 'self-forgetful' state, or a state of 'boredom'.[33] These are the areas of the image that are not fully integrated, constructed and clear; areas which are perhaps imperfect. This is a visual language of emotion, pleasure, of courage, of being alive, of eventualities, of imperfections: of large protruding veins, talon-like blood-red nails, a visual language which expresses one's being in the world.

A question I would like to pursue here, and which continues to vex me, is one posited by Efrat Tseëlon: 'But if the woman is considered as artifice and fake, is it the case that she hides her real essence, or is she only a series of masks with no essence?'[34] Warwick and Cavallaro pushed me to think more outside the box in a positive, inventive way regarding this question of essence and masks. The body's dressed surface could possibly be understood for these writers as its profound depth. They argue that the sartorial representation of the body becomes a literal metaphor, and posit the intriguing idea of stripping back to the 'core' to reveal a reflection of the exterior.

If we consider the idea of 'vaporization' – the conflation and expansion of the self with and into one's environment – in relation to aesthetics and fashioning the 'now', we can consider the manner in which we feel and extend beyond our self in order to reconstitute ourselves differently. The 'feminine' masks we adopt to make ourselves gorgeous and alluring affect others. Our scent, luscious fabrics and textures that encourage the sense of touch, sight or smell – our 'femininity' – is fabricated not to mask emptiness but to create an intersubjective trace through sensation. One could also say that this becomes an aesthetic expansion of our objecthood. However, rather than again positioning women as objects and therefore stating that subjectivity comes from that position, what is happening here is a challenge to the binary 'either/or' opposition between the *moi* and the *non-moi* in relation to subjectivity. This is a dialectic, not a binary. It dismisses the sense of a solid centralized core whilst being emphatic in stressing the importance of the vaporization process in visualizing poetically the agency of the body–self.

The spectator of a fashion image can communicate the poetics of that body–self through the aesthetics of the object. The body–self manifests itself within these objects and the surrounding environment. This is a visualization of the sensual haptic weight, touch, colour, contours: the substantial sense of that Other's being in the world. This challenges the insignificance of the 'feminine', the insubstantial flimsiness of the *non-moi*, but also challenges the solid encased authorial insistence of the male/masculine centralized core. Ironically, woman's substantiality and 'core' centrality has come from her eternally ageless body, which must remain stable and unchanging, forever young and forever encased in smooth, clear, skinny flesh. Woman's subject position is therefore culturally and historically grounded in an insubstantial lack in terms of her 'feminine' mind whilst simultaneously grounded in her substantial presence as an enforced disciplined 'ideal' never-changing body. A gendered binary policing of body and mind presents us with a narrow limited visualization of woman's self as body–mind.

The pleasure that the fashion photograph gives us is in the visualization, the exteriorization of expansive boundaries between the body and objects. This aesthetic narrative of the self allows for other communication to happen outside of, or against the grain of, the closed system of a solid assured hegemonic capitalist text of white, pretty, very young and very vacant femininity. The hegemonic text is a claustrophobic boundary which enforces and expects a limited exclusive sense of conformity and uniformity. The Other, though, is not so easily knowable or prescribed. In fact, the Other is alien to ourselves. We cannot understand what lies behind those eyes; there is a radical alterity. As Cathryn Vasseleu argues in her discussion of Levinas, the Other is 'unrelatable to the self in any way'.[35]

In my discussion of the fashion image in relation to objects and aesthetics, the feminized vaporization of the *non-moi* expands and defines what lies behind; indeed, what lies in front of those eyes. Subjectivity is a complex unstable changing composition, and can be made visible through our extended objecthood. These material objects become a means of imagining oneself. There is no sense of a division or boundary between the body and the object; there is a poetical sense of breaking down binaries. These are affective material zones. The centralized 'core' manifests itself in many visual shapes, patterns and curves. This 'core' is being played out on the surface and the environment via different sensations, contrasts, patterns and textures, where the self can reveal itself in the way red slashes through a crumbling painted wall, or in the way bluish-green soft protruding veins mirror and blend with repetitive flowered tiles, or in the bold weight of a black smooth chunky ring. This moves us away from the centrality of a 'core' and into an aesthetic exteriority with objects – an Othering with our extended transformative growth and potential.

2

Skin Deep

NAKED GIRLS

There is a new event taking place regularly in secret locations in London and other cities around the world, where naked beauties give themed readings. *Naked Girls Reading* was launched by New Yorker Michelle D'Amour in August 2009 and has spawned in its wake competitions such as *So you wanna be a naked girl?* and the *Naked Girls Reading Literary Prize*. The Naked Girls website refers to this event as 'the world's most salacious and magical literary salon' and as 'the literacy of flesh'.[1] This is an intriguing parallel to draw.

The idea of the literary salon takes us back to its initiation in seventeenth- and eighteenth-century Paris and its movement to England with salon groups such as the Blue Stockings or Holland House. These gatherings were generally hosted by glamorous women such as *salonnière* Catherine de Vivonne, marquise de Rambouillet in France or, in England, the hostesses Mrs Montagu, the Queen of the Blue Stockings in the 1740s, the Duchess of Devonshire in the 1780s or Lady Holland in the 1800s.[2] The salons were attended by a mix of male and female aristocracy, intellectuals, artists and poets who would share ideas, read from their own writings and exchange critical feedback. It acted as a stimulating and creative environment for women who on the whole had no educational or professional outlet for their intelligence or creativity. So what does it mean that women are now doing this naked in secret public locations; what is this all about?

I went to Paradise in West London to see the *Naked Girls Reading Fairy Tales* event. The room was intimate. There were about four

Sophia St. Villier, Naked Girls Reading
© *Tigz Rice Studios, www.tigzrice.com*

small bar tables, behind which were a few rows of chairs. On a stage at the front was a voluptuously decadent red crushed-velvet couch. Candles and incense were burning. There were more men than women – especially right at the front where the view of the stage was clear. But the atmosphere was friendly, comfortable and welcoming. Before the show, audience members were discussing what 'naked' entailed. A friend of one of the performers came to the conclusion that naked would mean strategically covering up the naked 'bits' whilst reclining on a chaise longue. However, when the performers Sophia St. Villier, Lil' Miss Chievous and Crimson Skye finally walked past the audience and on to the stage, they were (apart from accessories) completely and utterly butt naked.

There are evidently questions that this display brings to the fore. It is interesting that at a time when there is such extreme commodification and sexualization of women's bodies there is an event such as this, which openly and gleefully flaunts nakedness. In 2003 the pressure group OBJECT was set up 'to challenge the *sexual objectification of women*' [emphasis in original].[3] On their website OBJECT state that they were concerned by 'the "pornification" of society – a culture saturated by sexualized and one dimensional representations of women and girls, in a way which has little or no parallel for men or boys.' They argue that they are not 'anti-sex, anti-nudity or linked to any religious or moralistic stance'. They are against women being reduced to the status of a sex object, which they argue encourages sexism, inequality, violence and discrimination.

On BBC Radio 4's *Woman's Hour*, a representative from OBJECT and the London Feminist Network (LFN) Dr Julia Long, in discussion with burlesque and cabaret artiste Ophelia Bitz on the subject of burlesque, argued that any representation that sexualizes women and reduces them to sex-object status is doing a disservice to women at large. She criticized burlesque, stating that it continued the sexual commodification of women.[4]

In response to Ophelia Bitz, who argued that burlesque audiences were predominantly female, Long argued that this confirmed her own point – that sexualized display was one of the limited possibilities for women within a male-dominated public arena. This was one of the few public spaces where women were allowed access to success. In our cultural arena, sexual display is sanctioned and validated power.

These are serious and important points. Women should not feel that they have to disrobe or look a certain way in order to earn money, status or attention.

So what is so different about an event where women sit naked in front of an audience in order to read them stories? For North American performance artist Annie Sprinkle, the point of such display is political and commemorative. For example, she dedicated a particular naked reading to sex workers who had been murdered. The murderer had stated that nobody cared or missed a prostitute; they were nobodies. The protest therefore had to happen at the level of the body, in order to demonstrate that these women were embodied subjects – sexual subjects. Sprinkle was bringing the subject back into the body: a naked sexual body that was also a thinking, feeling subject who counted socially, politically and culturally. This is obviously an extreme case. However, it is evident that our hyper-sexualized, slick and commercially airbrushed representational economy has hijacked the sexual body-as-spectacle, which has ultimately estranged the physical, sentient and personal significance of the body from the visuality of the image.

Within our commodity culture everything is sexy. And women's bodies as sexual commodities are used as a sales pitch for just about everything. This is aggressive marketing, a world where sexy blonde bombshells wink at us from gambling website pop-ups and 12-foot-tall women lounge across billboards in their underwear and seduce us from shop windows and bus stops. It is pornographic, as there is no sense of the woman beneath the picture. It is not about sexuality, sensuality or subjectivity; it is about the body's exchange value, the sexualized body as commodity fetish. As Jean Kilbourne argues in *Can't Buy My Love: How Advertising Changes the Way We Think and Feel* (2000): 'We live in a culture that is sex-crazed and sex saturated, but strangely unerotic.'[5] In *Naked Girls Reading* we get to see the naked body, yes, but we also get to see the woman with all her foibles, personality and opinions. We get to hear the character, share her literary tastes and choices and her story, whether that is her undergraduate years studying sculpture or her memories of being read 'Snow White and Rose Red' as a child. We get to meet the whole person.

Two films came out in December 2010 which reveal these different agendas in relation to the sexualized or sexual female body. *On Tour* (or *Tournée*) is a DIY, rough-around-the-edges anti-narrative where the women have fun, have weaknesses and have different body-shapes. The film *Burlesque*, on the other hand, is a razzle-dazzle vehicle for Cher and Christina Aguilera, a slick Hollywood production that uses the genre of burlesque as a backdrop for a musical that ends happily ever after. The body types do not challenge the mainstream representational economy of the young, slim, agile, blonde American who ends up in a heterosexual relationship with the male protagonist (who only wears eyeliner because it is part of the requirements of the burlesque club; there is no challenge to the status quo). There is, though, a cast of strong female characters – it is a feel-good chick flick. But when this is turned into family entertainment, abstracted into pure sex, sexualized bodies and limited stereotypes, what is being promoted? One example of this was the UK's *X Factor* final in 2010 where, inspired by her role in the mainstream blockbuster

Burlesque, Christina Aguilera and a 'failed' contestant performed sexualized routines which outraged many critics and viewers alike. Kira Cochrane commented in the *Guardian* at the time:

> Once again bottoms were aloft, crotches flashing, as if the show's producers were trying to deliver a very special message to the hordes of six-year old girls who were watching. That message was this. 'You too can be one of the richest, most famous, successful women in the world – so long as you're willing to get 'em out and shake 'em.' Excellent.[6]

There is something immensely unsettling about living in a culture that promotes and validates this kind of spectacle. Young women act like this because it is the only way to get noticed as a sexual spectacle – or even as an aspiring subject – in our present cultural arena. Is there any way in which the objectification of women's bodies can be sensually and sexually positive in a culture that operates more on the level of 'sleaze'? In her chapter 'Reinstating corporeality: feminism and body politics',[7] Janet Wolff forwards an example of nakedness that goes awry. She discusses a demonstration that had been organized by a group of women on a male nudist 'beach' (actually an artificial harbour on the seafront at Sandycove, Dublin), who were angry at being excluded. As a protest, this collection of women stripped bare and swam naked amongst the naked men. The protest backfired. The manner in which this was discussed and documented in the press replicated the existing representational economy. The photographs showed one woman fully front-on as she climbed out of the water, with men in the background smiling lasciviously and boys looking on, giggling. With this lechery, she comments, the political intentions were neutralized into a joke. How can women protest using their female body when all that comes out of it is raunchy commercial headlines? She wondered whether the female body could ever be a site for body politics.

This chapter by Wolff was written in 1989, but it is still relevant now. When we are surrounded by a hyper-sexualized exploitative culture, how can the female body speak otherwise? Can the naked female body be a site of protest whilst still being sexy and glamorous, or do 'positive' images just become reabsorbed into the mainstream representational economy as sexualized and saleable? Perhaps a key difference, though, between the 1980s feminist political context and our own in the early twenty-first century, lies in relation to objectification.

In my previous book, *The Happy Stripper*, I argued that burlesque succeeded in subverting and challenging the authority of the normalized image only because this genre of performance and striptease used humour and irony. I argued that without this wink and nudge, subversion falls flat. However there are many areas of burlesque and contemporary art, of and by women, which do not fit this argument. What about those images, for example? The question which remains pertinent is: can we undermine or overwrite existing assumptions without using cynicism, irony or humour? In his essay 'Pin-ups, retro-chic and the consumption of irony', Nathan Scott Epley argues that ironic stances are just empty stances,[8] which in the end lose the posturing subject political power and resistance: 'Rich with understanding, full of appreciation (like camp) for the multiple layers of artifice, cynical irony starts to become "a sort of surrogate for actual resistance and opposition".'[9]

Naked Girls Reading is not cynical. It is not on the whole ironic, but there is of course humour, wit and double entendres. What the event does do, however is link the 'girls' to another counter-history of women's spectacle. We can trace this spectacle back to a history of 'Grrrls' and the history of the 'feminist pin-up'. In her book *Pin-Up Grrrls: Feminism, Sexuality, Popular Culture* (2006), Maria Elena Buszek describes the feminist pin-up as containing an 'aggressive sexuality, imperious attitude, and frightening physique'.[10] Pin-up history is a counter-tradition of glamour, pleasure and fun: of 'showgrrrls' who subvert and challenge stereotypes from within the mainstream. This is important. Control over these images comes from combining a stereotypical sexual 'look' with subversive agency. This is for Nathan Scott Epley the potent recipe for undermining dominant visual codes: 'The secret is in the mix, the pastiche of familiar conventions of female beauty – classic pin-up iconography – combined with elements taboo to dominant ideologies of gender and sexuality.'[11]

An interesting angle to Buszek's feminist argument and historical contexualization comes from her reassessment of feminist attitudes towards this kind of sexy imagery. Buszek discusses a lecture by American feminist art historian Linda Nochlin which she attended. Nochlin, interestingly, is fascinated by the pin-up, a model of feminine sexuality, which she describes as a 'Newd' (as opposed to a 'nude'). The 'nude' frames nakedness within a patriarchal context of passivity, male sexual desire and lack. The 'Newd', on the other hand, has freed itself from this control; it is a nakedness that is more offbeat, as Nochlin states: 'For me, as for the poet-critic, Baudelaire in the 19th century, the classical nude is dead, and deathly. What is alive? The offbeat, the ugly, the other, the excessive.'[12] It is intriguing that Nochlin draws parallels with nineteenth-century France with regard to the death and deathliness of the nude. As with our contemporary era, this was also a time of media excess in relation to sexualized imagery. At that point there was a large-scale increase in the lithograph, and as Abigail Solomon-Godeau states in her essay, 'The other side of Venus', it was at this point when 'modern mass consumer culture would adopt the image of feminine desirability as its most powerful icon.'[13]

In the twenty-first century, advertisements have become more and more risqué and pornographic, but somehow less and less erotic. Advertisers are pushing the boundaries of what is acceptable. An example of this is the banned advert by Tom Ford of the greased-up naked female torso and a fragrance bottle that just covers the shaven pubis. This is perhaps an example at its most pornographic and extreme; however, naked or almost-naked women appear everywhere in our visual economy. We have become accustomed to nudity. It has become mundane. Much of the anger voiced by pressure groups such as OBJECT and new feminists such as Natasha Walter focuses on this sexual commodification of women's bodies. The reason that feminist outrage has surfaced to such a degree in recent years is because of the widespread, almost pornographic, daily normalization of this commodification and objectification.

It is useful again to draw parallels with nineteenth-century France with regard to this seemingly anaesthetized response to the female sexualized image. For example, in his essay 'Art, fashion and the nude: a nineteenth-century realignment', Ed Lilley discusses the status of the nude in relation to Manet's painting *Le Déjeuner sur l'herbe* (1863). What is provocative in this painting is that the fully dressed men ignore the naked woman in their midst, whilst she looks straight out at the viewer. What rings true about Manet's painting is the absurdity of a situation whereby the nakedness that only usually touches and affects us in our personal, intimate and most private lives can be emblazoned so incidentally, so openly and so nonchalantly as the backdrop of our public everyday lives. Lilley argues that even though the nude as an art form is able to 'represent a wide variety of concepts, the discourse of sex has never been far from the surface of its appeal.'[14] However, in relation to this painting, where fully dressed men are standing next to an idealized nude, Lilley argues that the nude 'does not even unequivocally signify sex' but instead 'indicates uncertainty about the status of the nude'.[15]

Naked Girls Reading events similarly challenge the significance and status of the spectacle of the sexualized female body in contemporary culture. It does not signify 'sex'; it is 'sexy', but not in the

Sophia St. Villier, Naked Girls Reading
© *Steve Hart*

pedestrian, limited and frankly uninspiring way in which adverts are. This is not what Lilley would call 'disinterested beauty'. I was overwhelmed by the absolute nakedness of the *Naked Girls*, so much so that I could not concentrate or focus on the first story. This was absurd, surreal and audacious. I had watched the words as they came out from a blood-red mouth and missed many sentences as I gazed at glittering platform shoes, or white alabaster skin and perfectly rounded breasts. I was also five feet away from naked women who were either beginning to slouch, wilt, droop and shake with nerves, or were maintaining a cool smiling demeanour. It was not until the storytelling skills of the second naked girl lulled me involuntarily in that I started to listen carefully to the tales and actually looked down at the table I was sitting at to concentrate on the words and the narration:

MONDAY: This new creature with the long hair is a good deal in the way. It is always hanging around and following me about. I don't like this […]

FRIDAY: […] My life is not as happy as it was.

MONDAY: The new creature says its name is Eve. That is all right, I have no objections […] It says it is not an It, it is a She. This is probably doubtful; yet it is all one to me; what she is were nothing to me if she would but go by herself and not talk.[16]

In this situation, we are absolutely made to experience the nakedness of the spectacle and our emotions. It channels our attention away from a centrifugal focus on the body as spectacle and commodity towards an animated naked sexual female subject who is captivating us as a storyteller. These naked girls perhaps exemplify the wayward 'newd' discussed by Nochlin and developed by Buszek, a nakedness which emanates 'audacity, artifice, and control'.[17] The *Naked Girls* have bodies of various heights, shapes and proportions, accessorized with contemporary signifiers of twenty-first-century femininity: large, perfectly round alabaster breasts, ornate vintage necklaces and bracelets, blood-red lipstick, artificial flowers in their hair, glittering platform shoes, Brazilian 'landing-strip' pubes and various tattoos. This is a sexualized speaking subject who is questioning the settled ideological expectation of what constitutes a twenty-first-century nude. The brazen, unapologetic presence is a powerful assertion of propriety and ownership.

This takes us back to the context of this event, the historical literary salon, whereby the hostess, the *salonnière*, gathered significant guests at her bidding to discuss ideas and listen to readings. In her position as hostess, the *salonnière* was able to wield much power and agency in her curation of the structure, contributors, and therefore potential pool of ideas. The salon was central to cultural and literary life, and an invitation or social snubbing could make or break a writer or philosopher's career. The salon dictated a powerful control over the flavour and direction of social and intellectual discourse.

It is interesting to learn from Steven Kale that 'the decline of the "feminocentric salon"'[18] coincided with the long reign of Louis XIV, whose body politic constituted an 'anti-feminist backlash'[19] against female agency in the kingdom. One of the ways in which this was achieved was through the king's levee or 'getting up' ritual. This system of etiquette involved the naked king being dressed by a strictly hierarchical arrangement of courtiers. Jennifer Craik argues that by way of this ritual, 'the "life" of the body' was 'played out through the technical arrangement of clothes, adornment and gesture'.[20] The body, she argues, is not a given but is actively constructed. The power of the king, his authority as a body politic, was asserted though his naked physical presence and his subjects' obeisance to his body. The power and hierarchy created in this public ritual of the private body enshrined his power through a process of what Craik describes as 'affect-transformation'.[21] The controlled arrangement of gesture and hierarchy at the level of the private body also simultaneously acted as a powerful declaration of authority at the level of body politic. In this ritual the king's body became enshrined with agency and absolute power.

Indeed, therefore, the re-appropriation of desirable femininity by the *Naked Girls* – the sexualization and eroticization of the female body as spectacle – is being similarly asserted through a ritual of gesture, naked flesh and a tightly controlled environment of intellectual intimacy. The naked reading is an assertion of authority over the colonization of the sexual body as image. This literary flesh acts as an antidote to the deathly and death-like contemporary nude, which separates embodied flesh from glossy commodified allure. This could be seen as a contemporary reconfiguration of 'the "feminocentric salon" and salonniere',[22] and a feminist backlash which forces us to reimagine and re-experience the way we think about the female sexual subject…one that is bringing us into her 'private' bedroom to read us a fairy tale.

To Be Looked At[23]

The opening scene of *Tournée* (*On Tour*) presents us with a burlesque troupe unfastening their corsets, applying cream to sore nipples and undressing loudly in close proximity to the camera. It is a flurry of flesh, nipple tassels, tattoos, basques, feather boas and false eyelashes. We watch the troupe's backstage antics. We catch glimpses of their performances from the sidelines, such as Dirty Martini pulling a boa out of her backside. The narrative is visceral. It is rough around the edges. We see laughter, fun and friendship. The women have sexual appetites and initiate sexual encounters. In one scene we see one of the women, Mimi Le Meaux, guiding a man's head down into cunnilingus. This is adult entertainment and aimed, as the performers themselves state in the film, at a female audience.

This is visual pleasure. We enjoy looking at these sexual and sexy women. Our gaze, though, is not lascivious. It is celebratory. These women have fun. They have confidence. They dress extravagantly. They are loud and 'in your face'. Throughout the film the female characters collectively and individually build up a powerful sexual shield. This protective shield is built up to such an extent that when, in an argument, the manager of the troupe rips off one of Mimi Le Meaux's eyelashes, it feels violent and exposing. It makes her vulnerable.

There is a violent edge to the film that makes it strangely compelling. The glamour sits at this fragile edge. It shields and seduces. It is provocative. Elizabeth Wilson argues that 'the daring of fashion speaks dread as well as desire; the shell of chic, the aura of glamour, always hides a wound.'[24] The wound that is hidden behind glamour is illustrated clearly in one scene in *Tournée*, where a woman in the local supermarket tells Mimi Le Meaux that she loved her in the burlesque show and she wants to show her body too. She begins to strip, but in a manner that is inappropriate and out of context, and which seems aggressive. When she gets spurned by the manager, who tries to walk off, she starts to harangue Mimi Le Meaux with insults of *'putain'* (slut, whore, tart). We feel the tension. The woman feels exposed, and we feel her shame. When interviewed during the film, Mimi Le Meaux comments that their shows are for women. Yet there is no sense of shared power or pleasure in this scene. The burlesque show tours small towns in France, which perhaps opens up possibilities for bodily acceptance and sexual expression, but this expression straddles an ambivalent desire.

On the one hand, there is the collective visual pleasure and fun which is gained by the women who look on and clap and whoop – cheering on the female performers in an almost pantomimic way. Ben Walters, in the *Guardian*, describes burlesque as 'adult pantomime': '[A]udiences are willing to celebrate performers simply for having the confidence to put themselves on display. Amateurism – or at least a kind of permeability between performer and audience – is sometimes the point.'[25] At a burlesque show it is mainly female spectators that watch and enjoy the striptease. There is a feel-good atmosphere and a strong sense of collective humour, pleasure and camaraderie. In her book *Stripping, Sex, Popular Culture* (2007), Catherine M. Roach describes burlesque at its best as 'pro-feminist' and 'pro-women-centred'.[26] It is. There is a strong appreciative sense of creating a counter-spectacle which heralds and displays all body types.

This objective is possibly also what attracts audiences to popular entertainment shows such as *How to Look Good Naked*, where participants of all shapes and sizes build up their confidence through clothes in order to then finally strip that clothing off in front of a predominantly female audience who cheer them on. In this particular show, as in burlesque, the gaze is not lascivious. Their sexuality and confidence becomes a shield, which seems to temporarily protect their vulnerability and stem their insecurities. The gaze is affirmative and defiantly accepting. It is self-conscious.

However, does the confidence that we as spectators see in the women who take part dissolve and fall apart when the programme is over, when Gok and the film crew move on, when the cheers and whoops of encouragement stop and the glamorous clothing is put back in the temporary wardrobe?

In his essay 'Cut outs', the preface to Dawn Woolley's book *Visual Pleasure*, which reproduces Woolley's photographic and performance work, Darian Leader asks: 'What does it mean to be looked at?'[27] Pertinent to this discussion is his argument that we become an object of sight, taking on an off-the-peg sexuality as our own because being looked at as 'something' offers us at least an identity: 'transitory, permanent, contested or agreed, it protects us from the anxiety of not knowing what place we occupy for the Other.'[28] The desire for affirmation from the *How to Look Good Naked* crowd is a need to 'fit' into a social and cultural arena where we feel that we only count when we are sexually appealing. Yet in these instances, although we lose ourselves, it seems that being something is better than feeling like nothing. The glamour of the clothing, accessories and posing hides a wound of non-recognition; the gaze sees an image that does not belong to us. It is the property of others.

Related to this point in Dawn Woolley's *The Substitute (Holiday)* (2007–8), we see a heterosexual couple caressing. However, the young woman is literally a cut-out image, cut and pasted into the photograph alongside a three-dimensional man. She is just an image – a fantasy. She no longer exists as a fleshy embodied subject. In the line of his gaze she becomes mortified, animated only by and for his desire. In stills of another piece of work by Woolley, a performance entitled *Cut to the Measure of Desire* (2010), we see a theatrical staging of this fantasy space with woman as an object of sight, and other symbolic signifiers such as a slab of meat, a feathered bird and a plucked chicken. We see stereotypes of female sexuality and 'to-be-looked-at-ness', and conventional signifiers of femininity such as a black corset, red nails and lipstick, a long blonde wig and stilettos. The artist is staging the process by which she is seen as 'an object of sight', an object of another's gaze. Joanne Entwistle argues that these objects, this behaviour and this clothing situate the female body as 'marked': 'marked out as "feminine"' and 'saturated with "sexual" meanings'.[29]

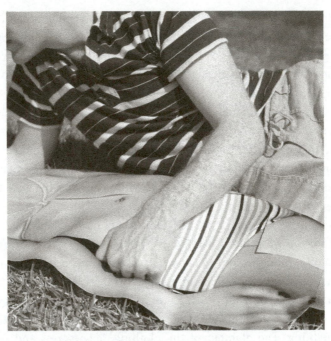

Dawn Woolley, The Substitute (Holiday) *(2007–8),*
1m × 1m, C-type print © the artist

Dawn Woolley, Cut to the Measure of Desire *(Vogelen performance),*
Tableau Vivant (20 minute duration) at City Road Conservative
Club, Cardiff, 2010 © Melissa Jenkins

A key argument with regard to this discussion is that forwarded by Kim Sawchuk in 'A tale of inscription/fashion statements'. In this she argues:

> Whether naked or clothed, the body bears the scatological marks, the historical scars of power. Fashionable behaviour is never simply a question of creativity or self-expression; it is also a mark of colonization, the 'anchoring' of our bodies, particularly the bodies of women, into specific positions, and parts of the body in the line of the gaze.[30]

Conventional signifiers for male fantasy and desire – such as boas which drape over naked breasts and high-heeled stilettos which arch the back, define the buttocks or elongate the legs – 'anchor' women's bodies and parts of these bodies 'in the line of the gaze'. However, objects of desire that flirt on the border crossing between the individual and the Other also have the potential to open up more complex, ambiguous and open-ended meanings which are less predictable. Joanne Entwistle's discussion of clothing as the skin between the social and the natural body is relevant here. In her chapter 'The dressed body' she refers to clothing as a symbiotic marker between the interior and the exterior, where the fleshy body gives life to the clothing whilst the clothing gives a social meaning to the body: 'The body and the dress operate dialectically: dress works on the body, imbuing it with social meaning, while the body is a dynamic field that gives life and fullness to dress.'[31] What is also useful in Entwistle's discussion (with reference to Mary Douglas's ideas) is that these borders have dangerous leaky edges, for it is at this borderline that tension and power reside.

Clothing sits at that intersection between looking and being looked at. It mediates that tussle of power. On the one hand particular motifs of femininity can anchor the female body safely to a fixed sexual identity where the female subject internalizes an image which seems to be organized by normative heterosexual desire. On the other hand, *Cut to the Measure of Desire* reveals other ways of exploring our relationship to the gaze and marks out a more complex relationship between looking and being looked at which does not annihilate the

Dawn Woolley, Cut to the Measure of Desire *(full stage). Tableau Vivant installation at City Road Conservative Club, Cardiff, 2010 © the artist*

subject. In *Cut to the Measure of Desire*, rather than internalizing the image the Other has of us, this image is externalized and as a result becomes strange and unstable. There is an unsettling glut of signifiers, which creates chaos and ambivalence. The image disrupts through its excess. Over-determined objects which are usually immediately readable and meaningful in and of themselves become nonsensical in their overuse and appear grotesque, parodic and meaningless.

With reference to the scene I discussed earlier in *Tournée* where false eyelashes are ripped off the burlesque performer, we again see this disruption of the gaze through the use of baroque extravagance. This is visual pleasure, but visual pleasure that cannot be fully controlled: where thick kohl and excessively long false eyelashes veil, obscure, filter, hide and reinvent. When this shield is ripped off, the subject becomes naked and exposed. The lashes are seen to mediate a relationship with the gaze, which both seduces and shields. These artificial lashes get in the way of the gaze and extend the barrier between the individual and the Other. We cannot see the subject fully. With a flutter, our gaze is dispersed.

In burlesque performance, the erotic objects that are usually used in conventional striptease are given an extravagant theatrical twist.

These objects bear the scars of patriarchal colonization. As Mary Ann Doane comments, the 'gesture of stripping [...] is already the property of patriarchy.'[32] However, what happens in much burlesque performance is that rather than closing down interpretation and the imagination, these erotic objects open up more fantastical possibilities. This different angle on the gaze has been taken up by fashion theorists, who at the turn of the new millennium began to offer up other, more positive alternatives to looking and being looked at, as Jane Gaines argues: 'Wearing high culture blinkers, we are unable to appreciate the strength of the allure, the richness of the fantasy [...] especially if our analysis consists only of finding new ways to describe the predictable mechanisms of patriarchal culture.'[33]

Rather than losing oneself to the gaze, where the subject implodes into objects of femininity, internalizing the images created by the Other, in burlesque the image is externalized within extravagant and fantastic objects. Objects such as excessively long false eyelashes, ruby-red rhinestone platform shoes or powder-pink sequined nipple tassels create a shield, a barrier at a distance from the sexual body. This is a performative visual surface which creates an open dialogue between subject and subject, between object and object, between body and body, between the social and the individual. This visual pleasure intercepts the gaze. It indeed entertains and pleases; but this is also visual pleasure where the gaze empathizes with and is emboldened by the daring audacity of the subject. Carol Dyhouse explores this form of seductive power in her discussion in *Glamour: Women, History, Feminism* (2012). Glamour, she argues, 'spoke of power, sexuality and transgression.'[34] It was also about the sensuousness, reveries and pleasure of fabrics, fur and perfume. Another key point that Dyhouse makes is that 'a desire for glamour represented an audacious refusal to be imprisoned by norms of class and gender, or by expectations of conventional femininity; it was defiance rather than compliance, a boldness which might be seen as unfeminine.'[35]

Glamour, therefore, was a defiant acknowledgement of a shared power and pleasure that came from the spectacle of a subject who was daring to make a spectacle of herself. This extravagant and fantastic display and spectacle of glamour expressed the fleshy embodied sensuality and flamboyance of the subject, but it also spoke of a defiant audacious reconfiguration of erotic objects. In burlesque, extravagant objects such as the aforementioned false eyelashes, platform shoes or nipple tassels (or 'pasties') create another way of seeing and representing which lures the gaze into what Rosemary Jackson would describe as the '"object" world of the fantastic'.[36] The gaze is intercepted by way of conventional symbols of femininity, fetish objects of desire designed firstly to lure in, seduce and intoxicate. The gaze is intercepted by way of its complex and seductive relationship with these objects. Within its glitter, sparkle and flutter the object weaves the social, the cultural and the historical into the sensual, daring audacious narrative of the individual, which operates in excess of the image.

Historically pertinent to this discussion is the argument laid out by Lisa Tickner in her book *The Spectacle of Woman*. Tickner argues that the cultural activism used by the women's suffrage campaign in the UK was an 'agitation by symbol'[37]: an attempt to intervene into the cultural circulation of ideas, messages and images that endorsed a particular way of behaving and had woven their way into the very fabric of women's identities.[38] By appearing en masse on the streets with decorative and eye-catching banners and bright exuberant dress, women were creating a spectacle of themselves and intervening purposefully, reflectively and self-consciously into the process of identifying who they were individually, collectively and politically. They were taking responsibility for how they appeared and reacting to how they were perceived.

The creative flamboyance of the artistic banners, the immediacy of the slogans, the awe-inspiring display of sheer volume, playfulness and fun would have communicated a real panoply of diversity as well as a real sense of infectious solidarity. Most of all, witnessing this display, this spectacle of female agency, would have helped towards de-stigmatizing these women. These campaigners were severely maligned for their activities. Where it hit hardest, though, in terms of propaganda, was in the adverse press, the caricatures of a twisted miscreant unnatural female identity. Convention dictated that women should be fine, delicate, domestic, soft, passive, self-effacing homemakers. Suffrage activists were depicted as their antithesis.

*   *   *

The main point I would like to make in relation to feminist activist history is with regard to the physical immediacy of the public political spectacle of the body. What we can learn from the nineteenth-century suffrage campaigns is that the political use of the body as a site of resistance was relational to its position as a site of oppression. In the mid- to late nineteenth century, seeing the spectacle of the female body as a spectacle of political protest would have appeared unnatural and transgressive. The media's cultural and social construction of the female body had become the springboard to feminist activist cultural intervention. The female campaigners were letting others see that different kinds of identity were realizable. It was therefore participatory; women and men were tempted via entertaining cultural reconstruction to think the unthinkable and imagine the hitherto unimaginable.

The contemporary spectacle of the body as uncensored self-expressed extravagance is therefore a political statement. It is again, like the suffrage activists, an 'agitation by symbol'. As Kim Sawchuk argues, certain cultural practices and signs are overdetermined. For Sawchuk it is by exploring the 'potential richness of objects'[39] that a way forward can be opened up that offers ambiguous rather than entrenched meanings. Objects or signifiers do not automatically have to connote a fixed meaning or ownership. There is no 'master key', and there is no transparent meaning to an object. With, for instance, the ruby-red rhinestone platform shoes which were worn by the host of Hurly Burly[40], Cherry de Ville, classic Wizard of Oz fantasy is fused with a sado-masochistic dominatrix edge. The shoes create a sparkling platform for the woman, who towers/totters over her audience. A borderline compliance-liberation history of the stiletto heel[41] is woven into the humour and wit of tottering, which is taken to the level of the preposterous.

The gaze is bewitched by this visual pleasure, where fantastical objects weave together cinematic fictitious imagery, cultural politics and embodied fantasies, pulling together threads and fragments with no fixed meaning. This 'fiction of female becoming'[42] is at once full of visual pleasure and allure yet seemingly delighting in its intangible fiction, its delicious surface and decorative excess. As Rosemary Jackson states in her book *Fantasy: The Literature of Subversion* (1981), fantastic objects 'are means without ends, signs, tokens, signifiers, which are superficially full, but which lead to a terrible emptiness.'[43] So, looping back again to the beginning of this section to the scene when the burlesque stripper's eyelashes are ripped off: this reveals a reaction to the 'terrible emptiness' of a sign which shields the subject and scuppers, disrupts, bewitches and confounds the gaze. This is a performative object that is edged with violence and whose extravagance seems to create meanings and visual pleasures which are new, yet threatening and dangerous. Ripping off this shield is a reaction to an object – to a sensual subject – who yields everything to the desiring gaze, yet gives away nothing.

PART II

The Pleasure of the Visual
(Being Gorgeous and the 'Low')

3

Crinoline and Cupcakes
Dangerous Identities

Anarchic Femininities

Marie Antoinette (Sofia Coppola, 2006) stands as one of those films that gets under your skin, making your flesh tingle with visceral pleasure. When it first came out it was heavily criticized for its vacancy and its embarrassing and infuriating lack of politics. Continuing the myth, Marie Antoinette does indeed eat cake whilst the country falls. However, the film contains a different kind of politics; what I would call a politics of fun. We remember it all – colours, flavours, textures – with a heightened sense of pleasure: the lines of shoes and the unbelievably tall wigs, the piles of cakes, the dynamic music, the women's friendships, and the exuberant unruliness as young women career dangerously down staircases on pillows. This is a film about liberation and freedom of a different kind to the cut and thrust of world politics. As Nathan Lee argues in his 2006 article 'Pretty vacant: The radical frivolity of Sofia Coppola's *Marie Antoinette*': 'Sensibility is everything in Coppola.'[1]

In this film aesthetics are used to express a shared sense of female experience and burgeoning youthful identities. This is a film about young women finding out who they want to be by way of dressing up, effervescent pleasures and playful encounters. We could say, therefore, that this *is* its substance. The characters push their pleasures to the limit in their quest to express their sense of self and find out what makes them 'tick'. Despite the film being for me a wholly courageous gesture by the director Sofia Coppola, she was punished as a result of her bravery when it was booed at Cannes. In a 2006 interview with Darren Waters, Coppola argued that 'the movie was not a political statement on current times', stressing that it was instead a film about 'young women trying to find their way, their identity.' Lead actress Kirsten Dunst, in the same article, describes the film as being about women who are 'introspective, their troubles and relationships. She speaks to women my age.'[2]

One could say, however, that partying and shopping provides limited experience with regard to personal development and rebellion. And this avenue for excess and identity is perhaps one stereotyped as 'feminine' and endorsed, and therefore excused as female.

It is the excessive behaviour displayed in the film that split the critics. Nathan Lee, for instance, argues that 'the film is most exact when most radically frivolous.'[3] On the other hand, in relation to the character of Marie Antoinette, Alexander Zevin argues in his 2007 article 'Marie Antoinette and the ghosts of the French Revolution' that: 'In making her likeable Coppola also makes her inconsequential.'[4] The hedonistic frivolity of this young, uneducated and uncultured woman, he comments, creates 'a movie totally in thrall to a dunce.'[5] In this section I would therefore like to explore the contentious idea of radical frivolity, and argue for the radical potential of excess as a form of irreverent visual pleasure.

The split strands of reaction to Coppola's film relate to various perceptions of what 'radical' and 'aesthetics' mean. We need to consider in this section how the ideas and ideals of radicalism are framed, expressed and perceived, as well as considering who it is that benefits from this specific framework. Why are some radical strategies – specifically those relating to pleasure, fun and excess –unacceptable, indeed inconsequential? Is the perceived and culturally accepted notion of radicalism perhaps conservative and gendered in its approach to creative political expression? Certain critics are indeed wary of the overt spectacle of pleasure, seeing it as a spectacle which is not taking itself seriously: for seriousness is not considered fun. There is therefore an engrained discomfort with visual extravagance. For feminists such as Laura Mulvey, visual pleasure is seen to benefit a patriarchal male gaze, and radical dissent against this pleasure can be found in its rejection. However, *Marie Antoinette* offers up an anarchic approach to visualizing dissent through a decadent 'feminine' (and perhaps 'feminist') spectacle of visual pleasure.

In his article 'Off with Hollywood's head: Sofia Coppola as feminine auteur', Todd Kennedy argues that, for Coppola: 'The desire to re-formulate ideas about feminine excess is most clearly expressed in what may be her master work, *Marie Antoinette*.'[6] In this debate the film is seen to be full of sensual and visual wonder: a different language of colour, objects, ambient light and sensation. It paints the emotions. Rebecca Arnold argues that it is a 'history of feeling', rather than a 'history of dress'.[7] On the whole, however, the majority of the critics agree that the film is exquisite in its use of painterly cinematography. Nick James, for instance, who is in the main critical in his article in *Sight and Sound*, nevertheless argues that: 'The film's one coup is its exquisite visual beauty, which carefully matches the colour palettes of 18th-century painting.'[8]

As has been stated, however, the reaction to this 'feminine excess' was polarized. The opposing opinion about *Marie Antoinette* is that it is superficial, and as sickly, sweet and bad for us in terms of empty calories as confectionery. For Alexander Zevin, the current interest in the character of Marie Antoinette indicates a conservative undercurrent within our contemporary culture which is anti-radical and anti-revolutionary. The hedonistic excess is, for Zevin, a reflection of Coppola's own privileged lifestyle as celebrity and Hollywood 'royal'. Similarly, Nick James argues that the film 'seems closer to a celebration than a critique of celebrity culture.'[9] The excess is therefore seen to celebrate the aristocratic order, its riches and privileges, rather than its overthrow. The problem critics find with the film is that by concentrating on the 'conspicuous pleasure',[10] the narrative sugar-coats and makes light of important historical unrest. The inconsequential antics of the queen and her 'nauseating fabulousness'[11] are seen to be more important. This is the problem that the French critics had with the film's content (or lack of content). As Zevin argues: 'Because of its subject matter Marie Antoinette crystallizes the not at all innocent tendency of popular culture to suck the past of its ominous potency, its threat to a self-contained present, for purposes of mass consumption.'[12]

The accusation levelled at Marie Antoinette therefore lies in its deliberate desire to concentrate on surface detail at the expense of critical and emotional depth. Ultimately, it is understood to be a self-satisfied celebration of Coppola's own lifestyle and hierarchical privilege, her own 'gilded cage'. The story is seen to promote the tendencies of the Ancien Régime, both historically and also tangentially in relation to our contemporary context of celebrity culture with all its privileged (and at times undeserved) positioning. This is seen therefore to be style, a 'deranged luxury',[13] over content. However, what is more interesting about the figure of Marie Antoinette is that she was historically positioned in the transitory position between the Ancien Régime and the new post-revolutionary order. She was described as an ordinary-looking young woman who enjoyed gossip and fashion, a woman thrown into the tightly controlled rituals of power and etiquette at the court at Versailles. She was a figure who presented, for the public, the potential for 'glitter' to be flexible.

The transition to the Napoleonic era after the downfall of the monarchy signalled the advent of glamour and the possibilities for self-invention. Stephen Gundle argues that what differentiated Napoleon Bonaparte from the former regime was the fact that he was a leader who was the 'fabricator of his own myth', a self-made man 'who had a strong sense of history.'[14] This idea of self-creation paved the way for the character of the dandy, who represented the epitome of style and celebrity (with the English dandy Beau Brummell in the 1890s as the first key figure). Stephen Gundle describes the transition from the court of Louis XVI to the new reconfiguration of power, managed by Napoleon, as a movement from 'magnificence to glamour'.[15]

It was possibly Marie Antoinette's fallibility, however, which brought about her transition to glamour, to its self-conscious image-making. Her human-ness perhaps more than anything else created the first glimpse of celebrity, with all its luxury, sexiness, trash and titbits. Pornographic tales of her debauchery and wild antics were rich pickings for public gossip, literature and ultimately court proceedings. She made herself more accessible and relatable to the outside world, which also meant that she was more open to the judgments of others. Marie Antoinette's anarchic femininities were seen to be far more heinous than the King's political wrongdoing, and were actually seen to pose more of a threat to the body politic. In her essay 'The many bodies of Marie Antoinette: political pornography and the problem of the feminine in the French Revolution', Lynn Hunt discusses how the idea of the 'feminine' in relation to the Queen was seen by the revolutionaries to 'lay at the heart of the counterrevolution'.[16] Transparency – 'the unmediated expression of the heart'[17] – was now the key to the Republic's future.

The 'feminine' therefore was situated in polar opposition to the 'radical', and was seen to represent a lack of sincerity. The 'feminine' was synonymous with the 'aristocratic', and in both cases the danger came from dissimulation. And it was the Queen's use of dissimulation, the 'self-conscious use of the body as mask',[18] which represented such a threat to the new order. The Queen was accused of using her sexually profaned private body – by way of incest, adultery, orgies and lesbianism – to manipulate, control and persuade in matters political within the public realm. Lynn Hunt argues that both Montesquieu and Rousseau stressed the importance of moving women away from public life, for at this point the salon was one public place where society women were gaining strength. For these men, therefore: 'Virtue could only be restored if women returned to the private sphere'[19] and the Queen represented the unwelcome corruption of that threshold between public and private, which was seen to be a very real danger for *La Nation*.

Her criminal pleasure, her *jouissance*, was also symbolic of the growing fear that women were corrupting the male symbolic order of politics and nationhood. For Julia Kristeva the maternal body is described as a means by which women can symbolically bypass the paternal symbolic order by speaking through the female body, through repressed difference. The maternal body is a body that gives birth, a body that lactates, a body that feels and reaches towards *jouissance* rather than pleasure. Lacan's term *jouissance* was a term used by Kristeva to describe a desire to go 'beyond' the Freudian pleasure principle – a more conservative cultural idea of comfortable pleasure – and towards more unattainable, discomforting limits. This aligns with Barthes' concept of 'bliss'. It is the erotic body as a text of bliss that dismantles, or at least lacerates, language itself.[20] Pleasure in this light, therefore, is not just about orgasm; it is also about social, economic and cultural power, about a sense of control over symbolic and representational conventions.

This was a body not subsumed and controlled by 'pleasure' in any traditional sense, but instead was an erotic female body that was engaged with more subversive readings and affects. Marie Antoinette's anarchic excess spilt over boundaries, creating a porous boundary between her affectivity as sensual 'feminine' flesh and her political creativity. This was a pleasure that was not wholly conceived out of sexual objectification and gratification, but also in part from a sense of knowledge and of knowingness. This was its danger. At the time of the monarchy's downfall there was an explosive increase in the production of pornographic images of the Queen. Pornography in this case was used to undermine Marie Antoinette's independent sexual and social authority – an anarchic excess of pleasure that was a threat to the status quo. Stamping male desire onto her public 'feminine' flesh degraded her power. It was an attempt to take away her will and her authority by appropriating and exchanging her body-as-image. The body-as-pornographic-image seemingly makes woman transparent, knowable and containable. By using her body as a site for public male pleasures, patriarchy left its own mark (of desire, money, exchange, property, will and mastery) on her flesh.

The new Republican body politic was to be a body without masks: an 'un-feminine' body. Anti-revolutionary Edmund Burke feared the loss of the seductive splendour of visual magnificence. Its place, he argued, would be taken by something much more dull and plain. Being 'radical', therefore, was not synonymous with being seductive. We can see this synonym in action in current critiques of Coppola's film, with Hannah McGill in her article in *Sight and Sound* arguing that the 'failure to provide true insight into her protagonist's interior life, or to the surrounding society, condemns her latest film to a critical lack of emotional depth.'[21] Ironically, it was Coppola's engendered surface 'masks' which made her film so radically fresh and insightful. This feminized mode of radical address – what I would like to call anarchic femininity – was a way to reconfigure, challenge and question a given spectacle by way of spectacle.

Marie Antoinette is trapped by an imposed image which she is unable to live up to. We see in the film the young Austrian Marie Antoinette arriving at the extravagant omnipotent court and gardens of Versailles. She is made to comply with a heavily ritualized set of rules and a strictly controlled rota of behaviour and routine. Her image as wife, daughter and Queen is unequivocally mapped out. The turning point for her is when she realizes that she cannot be that which she has been told to be: she cannot conform to the given identity that history and culture have created. At this point there is an exhilarating sense of rebellious freedom when she starts her own adventure and personal odyssey with a newly found desire to reinvent her own sense of self.

There are two pivotal linking scenes in the film which clearly visualize the transition from an image that is totally proscribed by pomp and circumstance to one that is more self-consciously controlled. In the first scene, we see Marie Antoinette alone, framed in front of heavily ornate wallpaper as she listens to her mother telling her in a letter that she must conceive for the good of her family and her country; this is her role and duty as wife. Her dress seems to merge with the background as she breaks down in tears. This is followed directly by a contrasting scene which is ignited explosively by the rhythmic beat of Bow Wow Wow's 'I Want Candy'. We see a visual orgy of colour, champagne, cake and crinolines. We then view lines of shoes, and much laughter and lounging around on the part of Marie Antoinette and her friends. This scene ends with Marie Antoinette's coiffeur unveiling her latest wig: a hugely extravagant, towering object complete with various trinkets such as feathers, birds, butterflies and other baubles. The humour of this excess is topped off by Marie Antoinette's final comment for this scene: 'Oh, you're the best! It's not too much, is it?' This scene is deliciously decadent, and contrasts markedly with the preceding scene discussed above, where she is stricken at her own impotency as wife, daughter and as a royal at Versailles.

The radical nature of Marie Antoinette therefore resides in its positive, pleasurable and fun rebellion against spectacle by way of spectacle. This is a creative form of protest that expresses a sense of displeasure and anger, but also acts as celebratory resistance. There is evidently a precedent for this form of protest. For example, 1960s activist Abbie Hoffmann stated that 'one of the worst mistakes any revolution can make is to become boring.'[22] The media, the fine arts and even popular entertainment were seen for Hoffmann as cultural tools of propaganda bound up in the pursuit of maintaining power and concealing real motives. Protest needed to entail penetrating into the circulation of these ideas by way of a 'radical self-expression',[23] alongside a collective vision for a better world. In relation to turn-of-the-millennium global activism, with its parallel fusion of artistic and political intent, Andrew Boyd argues that 'every creative gesture [is] also an interruption of power.'[24] In 2004, in relation to the Reclaim the Streets (RTS) urban protest in New York, Stephen Duncombe argued that 'the form the protest takes needs to embody the politics of its participants. And if we are going to create a world worth living in, then that protest had better be fun.'[25]

However, the accusation of emotional and intellectual nonchalance and destitution hangs over the critique of visual and hedonistic excess. In her chapter 'The politics of excess' in *Bohemians: The Glamorous Outcasts* (2000), Elizabeth Wilson discusses the clash between hedonistic dress and lifestyle choices, and radicalism. She forwards an example of this tension when she discusses the caution, bordering on disdain, that Lenin and his wife felt towards the bohemian activists when they were living in these communities during their exile in Britain. Lenin's wife, Nadezhda Krupskaya, described how one of their comrades lived in a 'nihilist fashion – dressed carelessly, smoked endlessly, and an extraordinary disorder reigned in her room. She never allowed anybody else to tidy it up.'[26] Wilson develops this line of enquiry to question why there is often a belittling focus on lifestyle as indicative of a lack of purpose, seeing this instead more as a radical self-expression: the visual impact that aesthetics can have on the imagination.

The derision shown towards the surface styling of Marie Antoinette is therefore another belittling dismissal of excess, fun and pleasure, and a lack of understanding of its radical potential as a medium for protest. This tension and lack of understanding was what ultimately led to the breakdown of the Situationists in the 1960s, and the point of contention in relation to their protest was pleasure. In 1967 two books were published by the key figures in this movement: Raoul Vaneigem's *The Revolution of Everyday Life* and Guy Debord's *The Society of the Spectacle*. For Vaneigem it was by way of excess and pleasure that one could challenge and reroute spectacle. Debord's approach was rooted in a more theoretical model of 'playful creation'.[27] They both wanted to challenge and obstruct the spectacle of capitalist consumption by way of the *détournement*, which is the 'turn' described by Sadie Plant in her book, *The Most Radical Gesture* (1992), as lying

> somewhere between 'diversion' and 'subversion'. It is a turning around and a reclamation of lost meaning [...] It is plagiaristic, because its materials are those which already appear within the spectacle, and subversive since its tactics are those of the 'reversal of perspective'.[28]

An amusing anecdote – which was possibly the icing on the cake for Debord – was when Vaneigem decided to go on holiday during the 1968 Paris uprising. For Vaneigem, one could only reverse the perspective on spectacle by playing up.

Marie Antoinette could therefore be seen as similarly subversive. Coppola uses the same spectacle of consumption as a 'feminine' form of protest. She is not unquestionably assuming that capitalist consumption is the only avenue for female identity, but by pleasurably plagiarizing this spectacle the image becomes one of reclamation and resistance. It is a gendered perspective on the radical; it gives us a different approach to protest. Alexander Zevin argues that: 'The violence implicit in any radical project is seen, particularly in the aftermath of the Cold War, as an unpaved road to hell.'[29] *Marie Antoinette* perhaps is a different radical project, which does indeed take the paved road, but it does so in order to question that road. The *jouissance* of this counter-spectacle is perhaps not violent or destructive, but this doesn't make it any less radical. And with this in mind, in the final section of this chapter we will be exploring specific examples of this radical politics of fun in relation to a rich repertoire of imagery from high fashion and new burlesque.

CREATIVE SEXPOTS

The September 2013 'International Collections' issue of UK *Vogue* commented that we were presently living through a 'feminine revival'.[30] Evidence of this was aplenty in this edition, which imaged the sensual seduction of fur and silk, the fragrance of alluring scent and the promotion of womanly curves. To a certain degree, femininity as a style is bound up with and supports the status quo, so the question of why this revival and its associated glamour is happening now is perhaps not so important as the question of why so many creative women are staging this excess and embellishment of the feminine in their own acts and creations. For contemporary burlesque performers such as Imogen Kelly and Gwendoline Lamour, and fashion icons such as Vivienne Westwood, an excess of femininity is not only being used as a celebration of the 'feminine' but also to create and perform more dangerous gendered identities and versions of womanhood. In order to explore this question, this section will firstly return to Marie Antoinette.

In her show *Herstory*, burlesque performer Imogen Kelly dresses up as Marie Antoinette and then tantalizingly and cheekily performs a striptease and acrobatic moves before then spreading cake and cream over her body. This performance is excessive, humorous and fun. The clothes are highly flamboyant and the wig fabulously far too tall and pink. She is delighting in her bad behaviour. The unruliness makes this act feel rebellious and fresh. It moves beyond pure titillation. Although her performance could still obviously be critiqued for playing up to the gaze, Kelly does this in such an over-the-top fashion that her act becomes more of an anarchic gesture than a submissive one. She is using all the conventional tools of femininity, and using this gendered play to create a more radical subjectivity and a more intersubjective, politicized connection with the gaze of the spectator. This is a sexual woman who is in charge of her image and her pleasure, but in doing this she is not reneging her power. Indeed, when watching this performance we feel taller: it adds to, rather than subtracts from, our sense of selfhood. In this act, femininity is being used to mischievously step out of line. And as a spectator, this is appreciated with relish.

If we look again at Sofia Coppola's *Marie Antoinette* we see this mischievous and liberating use of the conventional tropes of femininity. As Nathan Lee argues: 'Marie Antoinette copes with spectacle by becoming spectacle.'[31] The spectacle self-consciously created by the character of Marie Antoinette in this film is therefore not a regressive essentialist ideal but a spectacle that speaks back to the audience, refiguring and reinstating the self in the image. Coppola is asking the audience to question the extent to which images impose identity on Marie Antoinette, historically, socially and culturally. The strategy she uses in her cinematography to do this is by drawing parallels with historical paintings. In four different scenes in the narrative the images mirror paintings by Jacques-Louis David, Francisco de Goya and Claude Monet. This is a technique that has also been used in the wider cultural arena of burlesque and fashion, such as John Galliano's Spring/Summer Dior collection in 2010, Dolce & Gabbana's Autumn/Winter 2012 and 2013 collections, or indeed cabaret artist Tricity Vogue's *The Blue Lady Sings* (2010) and *The Blue Lady Sings Back* (2011), which are inspired by Vladimir Tretchikoff's painting *The Chinese Girl* (1952).

Eighteenth-century painting, with its use of sensuous and frivolous rococo fashion and settings, is a specific point of contemporary reference. Fashion designer Vivienne Westwood's Spring/Summer 1996 Courtesan collection contained her well-known Watteau gown, which was inspired by Antoine Watteau's use of *fête galante* paintings, where extravagant dresses and pastoral scenes create a mood rather than a narrative. In 2011 Westwood created her Le Boucher corset, which contained a print of the painting *Daphnis and Chloe* (1743–5). Westwood's garments were also showcased in 2011 at an exhibition entitled 'Le Gout du Jour' ('*A Taste of the Eighteenth Century*') at the Grand Trianon, Versailles. In London's new burlesque scene, Gwendoline Lamour's *The Swing* is a performance of Jean-Honoré Fragonard's painting of the same name.

In this painting from 1767, a young woman swings in a carefree manner in a woodland clearing. She is captured in the image swinging forward, her shoe flying off into the air in frivolous abandonment. This painting is in the Wallace Collection, where they describe the woman as 'delicious in her froth of pink silk, poised mid-air tantalizingly beyond the reach of both her elderly seated admirer and her excited young lover'.[32]

This is tongue-in-cheek and lighthearted. Fragonard was commissioned by 'an unnamed "gentleman of the court"'[33] to paint his mistress. Originally he had asked that a bishop be the one pushing the swing and he, the young lover, be the one who is appreciating the woman's legs. However, Fragonard painted in an unknown, more

Gwendoline Lamour, The Swing, *Belowzero, London, 2008*
© *the artist*

elderly male character in the shadows – possibly the woman's cuck-olded husband. There are many references to the couple's illicit affair, their adulterous unauthorized pleasure and eroticism, with Cupid looking on in disapproval and disbelief. The woman in this scene is painted 'beyond the reach' of both men – she is momentarily carefree and free to do as she pleases. Vivienne Westwood[34] argues that this painting was typical of Fragonard and would have certainly appealed to his eighteenth-century public, who would have understood that the lady was not wearing knickers and that the gentleman standing underneath the swing was looking up her skirt. She states, though, that for the contemporary spectator this Fragonard painting merely looks like a pretty picture.

To examine these eighteenth-century images is to understand how people historically used to think and feel, and also (and more revealingly) to reframe our own contemporary context. It makes us consider our own value system through the lens of history. As we can see with Coppola, Westwood and Gwendoline Lamour, eighteenth-century painting is being imaged in order to more clearly understand the present. They do not achieve this by way of duplication, but by way of travesty's use of pastiche.

In her article on Coppola's *Marie Antoinette*, Pam Cook argues that the past is always viewed through the lens of the present, and therefore 'represents the vested interests of those who reinvent it.'[35] She argues that: 'In the case of historical fictions, travesty collapses boundaries of time and place through pastiche, emphasizing that his-tory is in the eye of the beholder, whether group or individual.'[36] A playful use of pastiche is therefore used with serious intent. Former styles and images are copied in order to reinvent or communicate the flavour of the present time and its relationship to the past. This is a means of questioning the extent to which times have changed, but in doing this we can also further understand how the past is interpreted for the purpose of the present. This evidently links to questions of status and hierarchy, and makes us consider who it is that holds the reins of power and what their intentions are. The way that the past is interpreted, therefore, is never objective, and perhaps says much about the power structures of the day.

*   *   *

So if we consider the contemporary interest in eighteenth-century paintings, what is this 'dialogue with history', to quote Vivienne Westwood?[37] What is being said? What does it mean that subcultural burlesque performers and iconic anarchic female designers are referencing particular Rococo paintings?

It is perhaps useful here to consider another art movement, Art Nouveau, which also drew heavily from the Rococo period. In her fascinating book *Art Nouveau in Fin-de-Siècle France: Politics, Psychology and Style* (1989), Debora L. Silverman argues that: 'By celebrating women as queens and artists of the interior, they developed a powerful antidote to *la femme nouvelle*, who threatened to relinquish her role as decorative object and decorative artist.'[38] By referring back to the sensual frivolity of fabric and pleasure and the organic contours of the feminized interiors, an alternative image was presented as a reaction to the imminent threat of the new woman, *la femme nouvelle*. The art and design of French Art Nouveau was seen to be containing and interiorizing women – drawing them back to their rightful decorative position as object and subject of the domestic and the private sphere.

Art Nouveau was formulated in the 1890s by the official Central Union of the Decorative Arts as part of French cultural reform. Its aim was to create a style and aesthetic particular to France. Silverman argues that one of the key initiatives of this program of reform was to define the 'interior space as distinctively feminine'.[39] Madame Pegard played a significant role in this initiative, for her kind of 'familial feminism'[40] supported the status quo of the bourgeois family structure and value system. For Pegard, women should be seen as equal yet different. Her politics and ideas were encouraged by the Central Union, for at that point a small number of well-to-do women were encroaching on male territory and threatening the division between the public and the private, reproduction and production. As the male publicist for the Central Union stated, 'woman could better win over "the sons of Adam" by remaining her inspirational and enchanting self.'[41] By encouraging 'women's roles as domestic consumers and organizers of the interior world,'[42] the Central Union offered up another alternative to *la femme nouvelle*, where women could work if they needed to, but should focus that work on their own distinct sphere of the interior and the domestic.

In the historical context of Art Nouveau, Rococo styles were being used to contain women as decorative sensuous objects and makers of the interior world. Women were, ironically, at the vanguard of this desire to uphold the logical division of the spheres for them. And if we return to the present, we can see the same thing happening in our contemporary context as female creatives appear again to be focusing on interiorizing and feminizing women. Nathan Lee, in his article on *Marie Antoinette*, describes it as a 'Room' movie, where the film stays within the interior of a domestic setting and the 'private world of the imagination'.[43] However, he adds that 'with each film Coppola's Rooms get better furnished yet more empty. So too their inhabitants.'[44] What does this now tell us? By concentrating on filling the Rooms with an excess of bright seductive 'stuff', Lee argues, the filmic light and fluffy surfaces distract us from more substantial psychological and political insights.

Nevertheless, when we as spectators watch Kirsten Dunst lounging around in her cinematic rooms in *Marie Antoinette*, or Imogen Kelly in her impossibly tall wig riotously stripping in a grotesque gastronomic orgy of food, or Gwendoline Lamour smiling, winking and stripping nonchalantly on her swing, we understand that this visual feast has significance. Like the young woman swinging in Fragonard's painting, in these performances there is a liberating sense of independence and authorship. These are places of play where the women are indebted to nobody and can get on with their own pleasure. This is performative painting which brings feminized space to life, performing historical images to extricate, or at least emphasize, the real from within the mythologized. These contemporary creative sexpots, cheeky and anarchic or indolent and carefree, use feminized performance as assertive rebellion against contained, lost or historical understanding of particular images. These images do not here signify submission. They are given new contemporary meaning by real women actually inserting their own bodies into the frame, bringing to life the indolence and insouciance of the imagery.

In Vivienne Westwood's 'Get a life' art manifesto she argues that creatively understanding historical art, and for her in particular eighteenth-century painting, can offer us an 'antidote to propaganda'.[45] In her manifesto, 'Active resistance to propaganda', she presents us with a dialogue between various 'travellers' on the journey to find art. In one part of the manifesto, The True Poet (the alchemist) states that: 'The originality of life lies in bringing ordinary feelings to our attention [...] The artist's mind is in fact a receptacle for storing up numberless feelings, phrases, images which remain there until a new idea "comes" in.' For Westwood, culture is about constantly trying to understand the present by revisiting historical artworks in order to create empathy for what the painting was saying about the time and subsequently for what it can teach us about now. The other traveller in her manifesto, the Art Appreciator, states: 'So we arrive at perception by imitating. And we can imitate through empathy, using our imagination to get outside ourselves.'[46]

We as spectators feel empathy with the contemporary performers' brand of imitation or pastiche because this is more than just a pretty picture. These are paintings performed to be looked at from a different perspective, and therefore revert the power usually at play in such images. These paintings are being infused with the more anarchic response of real physical bodies. We smile in response to these creative sexpots and in turn feel the sense of freedom experienced by the young woman on the swing who had the audacity and sexual insouciance to wear no knickers. We empathize with the playful sense of liberation and escape that it must feel like to swing nonchalantly, out of the grasp of any suitors. In being looked at, yet frivolously indifferent, the performers infuse the painting with a different perspective, which is fun, playful and positive. By way of the affective and emotional elements of colour, light, texture and touch they paint the cheekiness, the excess and the pure indulgence of the creative sexual subject.

We smile at the cheekiness of these performances, which subverts the very spectacle of 'to-be-looked-at-ness' conventionally used to attract the scopophilic erotic attention of the spectator. In cinema, women were (and indeed still are on the whole) the 'natural' focus of the 'male gaze', but as Susan Haywood points out regarding the spectacle of woman, 'in relation to the erotic, she is simultaneously positioned as subject (she contains, she is the holder of the erotic) and as object (she marks, she is the site of the erotic, the "to be looked-at-ness")'.[47] Indeed, when heightened colour was brought in this 'double positioning (subject and object)' became even more ambiguous, for women were already the site of the erotic gaze, the 'real', yet colour emphasized the artificiality of this site, putting emphasis on the idea of fantasy, and also who the author of that fantasy was.

A heightened use of colour, visual excess and extravagance appeared at first in cinema in order to differentiate 'reality' from 'fantasy', such as the technicoloured world of Oz and Dorothy's glittering red slippers. Edward Buscombe in 'Sound and colour' comments that the visual pleasure of Technicolor was used in musicals, costume dramas and fantasy pictures because the narrative was 'not held down by reality, past or present' and it created imagery where 'our imaginations can soar.'[48] What was particularly exciting about colour, though, was the possibility for subversion in relation to the female body and the gaze. Neale argues by way of Julia Kristeva that colour has the capacity to 'pulverise' meaning.[49] He uses Kristeva's ideas about colour from her book, *Desire in Language* (1980), where she argues that colour is expressed through a 'triple register' which operates objectively, subjectively and via 'the impact of censorship as a sign in a system of representation.'[50] Intriguingly, though, she argues that because colour affects us so profoundly internally – in terms of our psyche and unconscious – it is capable of subverting and shattering the meanings that it has been symbolically ascribed.

Colour, Kristeva argues, 'achieves the momentary dialectic of law – the laying down of One Meaning so that it might at once be pulverized, multiplied into plural meanings. Color is the shattering of unity.'[51] This understanding of colour is significant regarding the female body and representation. Colour in eighteenth-century paintings such as those by Fragonard is used to mark out and contain pleasure as a site for the gaze. Stealing from these images, contemporary performers use excessive and flamboyant colour counter-strategically. The spectacle of pleasurable looking is being marked as a site for the gaze by way of the conventions of femininity, with colour directing the gaze and attention onto this conventional site of desire. However, in contemporary performance this visual pleasure articulates a twenty-first-century sensibility which subverts and disrupts by upturning the deadening yet safe expectations of submissive female codes of being pretty and being looked at.

I would describe the contemporary use of eighteenth-century painting in Coppola and underground cabaret as scopophilic pastiche, and Todd Kennedy poetically and succinctly forwards an excellent example of this in the following passage, which describes a scene of excess and decadence in *Marie Antoinette* where the character of Marie Antoinette is pointedly indifferent to the gaze:

> She is surrounded by pink pastry. As she seductively leans back, dips her fingers in icing, and licks them, she would seem the perfect embodiment of the object of the gaze. At this very moment, however, she sits up, turns her head toward the camera and stares directly back at the audience, cocking her head and eyes for a second as if to say, 'What are you looking at?' She then lies back as if the audience is not worth the bother.[52]

Like Kirsten Dunst as Marie Antoinette, Gwendoline Lamour and Imogen Kelly cast a carefree look at the audience as if they are not worth the bother. These women are stepping into their historical Rooms in order to have fun – smearing themselves in gastronomic pleasure, lounging around as part of a visual orgy of colour, texture and object, and generally playing up.

Yet still we have the idea of these creative sexpots being trapped or trapping themselves within Rooms. For they can walk out of these pleasure domes, can they not? What can be argued is that by stepping into these cultural spaces of 'vested interest', the performers are using pastiche to create questions for the audience. Is the light and fluffiness of crinoline and cupcakes the only cultural identity available to women? Is this a limited visual vocabulary for sexual expression and fantasy?

However, by gatecrashing these historically patriarchal, fictionalized and mythologized Rooms, these contemporary performers offer us a direct assault on both history and the present. Rather than being consumed as a pretty picture, by performing these images so indulgently these women are pleasurably consuming their own images. As spectators we too can take great pleasure in enjoying this unauthorized consumption.

4

Powder Puffs and Beauty Spots
Spectacular Objecthood

BEING AN OBJECT[1]

In June 2011, the popular UK women's magazine *Psychologies* published a 'Positive Beauty Manifesto', which was endorsed by celebrities such as actresses Gillian Anderson and Susan Sarandon, comedienne Miranda Hart, Kids Company founder Camila Batmanghelidjh and black model and Lancôme ambassadress Arlenis Sosa Peña. In this manifesto were '10 things we believe about beauty', which included: 'Beauty is the celebration of what is unique about each one of us'; 'Beauty should celebrate intelligent, individual and confident role models'; and one that is particularly relevant to my discussion: 'A woman can play with her image, make-up and clothes without being superficial.'[2] The fear that women put more store by powder-puff than world affairs is therefore still an ongoing concern. Some women feel that their desire to play with their appearance is still judged as flighty and frivolous, with the worry being that women spend more energy on what they look like than on what they do. In the London-based cabaret group Blue Stocking Society's 'Manifesto', Tricity Vogue writes:

> Nowadays, even though times have changed, it seems to me there is still an assumption that a woman who makes herself sexually attractive will also be stupid, or has to make herself appear stupid in order to be found sexually attractive. We're loving the chance to challenge those assumptions.[3]

She stresses that she has 'two MAs' and 'half a PhD'.[4]

One could question, however, what the desire to challenge these assumptions achieves when young women have such a lack of role models beyond the world of being pretty. A report carried out in 2012 by Girlguiding UK, 'Girls' attitudes explored... role models'[5], highlighted the narrow range of role models which are available for girls and young women aged 7–21. This report is disconcerting, if evidently conservative in its approach. But why do intelligent, vivacious women want to make it their life's work to prove to us that they are sexy too? And what do these same women do when they are rejected socially because of being old and 'washed up'? One example amongst many is UK newsreader Anna Ford, who protested in 2007 against the inherent ageism in the BBC when she was demoted and sidelined into a less visual role. Nobody wanted to be reminded of their own mortality. Yet as we all know, Bruce Forsyth was happily accepted by the public as a presenter on *Strictly Come Dancing* in the UK when he was in his 80s, even though his female co-presenter, Tess Daly, was youthful, blonde... and could not dance. She was there to look pretty. He was there to be the comic, the 'brains'.

Women's appearance is still important, and a fashionably beautiful veneer is highly prized and sought after – and in some cases bought (if we consider plastic surgery and make-up) – even though looking good is seen to be in opposition to being good, or at least being competent. As a related point, it is interesting that Bette Davis is quoted as having said, with reference to her co-star Joan Crawford in *Whatever Happened to Baby Jane?*, that: 'Miss Crawford wanted to look as nice as she could; I wanted to look as terrible as I could. Miss Crawford was a glamour puss. I was the actress.'[6] Feminists have therefore underplayed the importance of 'looks' as the 'be-all-and-end-all' of success. Why are femininity and glamour seen to be (or why do they have to be seen to be) in opposition to seriousness and capability? Why is it not possible, as the two manifestos illustrate at the beginning of this chapter, to play with your image and femininity *and* be taken seriously?

Academics have tried to reframe the feminine and the feminist. Indeed, Elizabeth Wilson's *Adorned in Dreams* (1985) took to task feminism's castigation of fashion as flighty and unpicked the logic behind fashion's lowly status. In doing this Wilson created academic prestige for fashion history and theory as a discipline (or perhaps interdiscipline) worthy of study. Since this work, other prominent academic contributions followed suit, including writing by Stella Bruzzi, Valerie Steele, Caroline Evans, Joanne Entwistle and edited collections by Malcolm Barnard. Fashion academics have forwarded clothing as a language which is expressive of the embodied situated subject in relation to their sociocultural and historical context. However, feminists have had a problem with fashion because it has been seen to trap women within their image and consequently exclude and distract them from a political context. The superficiality of surface appeal has pointed women towards a political dead end.

A useful analysis of this impasse is forwarded by Efrat Tseëlon in *The Masque of Femininity* (1995), in which she argues that: 'When vanity, artificiality, and extravagance in fashion are condemned, they are not seen as external behaviours, but are given metaphysical meanings. They are seen as indicators of female (in) essence.'[7] Feminists have therefore not necessarily been wary of fashion and beauty per se, but have been critical of how negative gendered meaning has been given to appearance and surface appeal, because for women 'appearance and essence are intertwined'.[8] This is to say that women's extravagance has been taken to reflect their lack of a solid centre, their emptiness. Fashion has traditionally been equated with femininity, and femininity is in this view culturally and socially reflective of a frivolous, flimsy vacuous lack, where the sense of self is determined by the approval of others. The clothing emphasizes the outside, the exterior – 'prettiness' – as women's social currency and means to success.

The desire to find a 'real essence' is why feminists moved away from the 'artificial' to a more 'natural' look. As Linda M. Scott argues in her book, *Fresh Lipstick: Redressing Fashion and Feminism* (2005), the key sticking point polarizing feminism and 'fashion' relates to artificiality: '[F]eminists have criticized whatever the prevailing fashion found attractive, advocating instead a more "natural" look.'[9] However, if we were to all be 'natural', she argues, then we would not clean our teeth, wash our bodies or brush our hair. She stresses that: 'What is natural for human beings is artifice.'[10] Pamela Church

Gibson also explores this by quoting from Janet Radcliffe Richards' *The Sceptical Feminist* (1982), stating that this desire for the natural stems from 'a misunderstanding about the "natural" person being "the real thing"'.[11]

It is not necessarily the case that feminists have mistaken the 'natural' for the authentic. What has been the problem is that culturally, 'femininity' has been marked as lack. Underneath the performance and artifice of femininity, woman are seen to veil a lack of substance. In other words, the mask *is* the woman. Socioculturally this is the polar opposite to the seriousness of the 'suit', which is seen to encase a solid substance: an assured, reliable sense of competence and ability. This represents a credible authentic 'self' because the body is covered from neck to toes. When the body is revealed there is a sense of revelation at the expense of mind. Likewise the embellishment, extravagance and colour of 'feminine' fashions add to the sense of the outer shell, the surface, being an indicator of self and personality under which there is nothing. The suit is whole and complete, emphasizing its solidity not as a body, but as a mind. The clothing is not a distraction. But if the masculine silhouette connotes 'mind', 'strength', 'competence' and social and political 'power', what is the politics inherent in powder puff and beauty spots?

These issues will be explored by way of the act that I referred to in the introduction to this book: the Blue Stocking Society's Audacity Chutzpah's *A Complete History of Women's Liberation in the 20th Century in Six and a Half Minutes*. This cabaret performance (which I first saw live at Bethnal Green Working Men's Club, London), Chutzpah's signature act, sees Chutzpah stripping off a variety of stereotypical time-specific costumes to music signposting specific periods of feminist unrest. The final layer is stripped off to reveal nipple tassels and knickers, with Chutzpah holding a banner across her chest that reads 'Liberated'. The fashions of the eras link into 'empowering' points for women: the suffragettes in their Edwardian dresses holding up placards, the war effort with women working and driving trucks, the 1960s/70s free love and political songs, the 1980s 'material girl' through to the 'Girl Power' of the Spice Girls and the more raunchy all-womanly cultural icons of the new millennium such

Audacity Chutzpah
© *Photograph by kind permission of Terry Mendoza*
www.retrophotostudio.co.uk

as Beyoncé. Femininity and fashion in all these instances point to specific social and cultural liberating activity on the part of women.

At key moments of feminist protest, however, there has been a rejection of glamour. As has already been stated, the 'natural' was seen to be a desire to frame women more clearly as political. Glamour and artifice were not compatible with politics or serious debate. Yet at these key points the spectacle of protest has indeed been glamorous, or at least has displayed a playful 'femininity'. This still feels like a strange configuration. I remember chatting over a drink at a burlesque event to a young female master's student of law, who was imagining the irreconcilable image of these glamorous burlesque stars, all powder puff, feather boas and nipple tassels, walking into The Hague Institute for Global Justice. Thinking about this flourish of excess and extravagance as these women flounced in and sat down in a cloud of powder, perfume and feathers made us laugh. The image of these glamorous women jarred humorously with the serious business of human rights and justice. It seemed preposterous. Yet we were both attracted to and in awe of these glamorous performers. What was that power?

If we relate this question of women's 'liberation' to Audacity Chutzpah's performance, there was again humour and irony in reading 'liberation' in terms of the frivolousness of fashion and femininity. The audience was enjoying the play on 'liberation': here powder puff and human rights were on an equal footing. Sensual affairs were being given the same significance as world affairs, political emancipation and democracy. In this performance intelligent women were therefore able to be sensual and sexy without threatening or undermining their political emancipation. This was a powerful image, and perhaps an image that some feminists have been (and perhaps still are) uncomfortable with. In *Living Dolls: The Return of Sexism* (2010), Natasha Walter comments that:

> In the past, feminists have often seen only the negative aspects of beauty and fashion industries. I still believe that there is great enjoyment in these pursuits [...] If we were seeing a growth of individualistic, pleasurable engagement in fashion and beauty, then the culture for young girls would not feel so punishing.[12]

Pamela Church Gibson speaks about this strand of feminist antagonism towards fashion and beauty in her essay 'Redressing the balance:
patriarchy, postmodernism and feminism' (2000) when she refers
to the second-wave feminist Germaine Greer's polemic against the
fashion images in glossies such as *Vogue*. In *The Female Eunuch*
(1971) Greer argues that the alluring images of models limit the
possibilities for what women can be in the social and cultural arena:
'She is the Sexual Object sought by all men and all women [...] There
are stringent limits to the variations on the stereotype, for nothing
must interfere with her function as sex object.'[13] However, by way of
a humorous play on 'liberation' in terms of powder puff, Chutzpah is
turning upside down the assumption that a woman who is concerned
with her appearance cannot possibly be intelligent. This is witty
because it is quite a different approach to young women's perception of traditional feminism. Drawing together the feminine and the
fashionable with the feminist is still politically audacious.

It still induces 'a politics of discomfort'[14] that you can indeed
swirl and spin nipple tassels whilst not being reduced to being seen
purely as a sex object. The pleasure that comes from this image
derives from its anti-hierarchical challenge. It questions what is seen
as consequential and inconsequential, substantial and insubstantial,
intelligent and stupid, serious and frivolous. This is an assertion of
the flamboyance of the 'feminine' by way of fashion. This is perhaps
inverting Joan Riviere's original notion of masquerade, established
in her 1928 essay 'Womanliness as masquerade'.[15] This concept was
used to describe the way in which one of Riviere's female clients
(Riviere was a psychoanalyst) used femininity to veil the reality of
her actual power/intelligence and make her less of a threat in the
male professional world. 'Womanliness' – feigning neediness, weakness and fragility – was being used to temper her threat, which thus
allowed her to play in a male field as competent; and 'womanliness'
was used secondarily to maintain sexual and gendered attractiveness
to the opposite sex.

What is particularly compelling and challenging in relation to
Audacity Chutzpah's performance is that 'womanliness' is not being
expressed as the negative imprint to masculinity, but is instead being
imagined otherwise. In Chutzpah's survey of liberation we see her

smoking a joint, singing an activist song, flexing her muscles like on the Rosie the Riveter 'We Can Do It!' poster, or displaying a more voluptuous 'womanliness' much like Beyoncé's hyper-feminine performance and indeed the burlesque cabaret show that I was watching being performed by Chutzpah herself. The power created by the image of an intelligent sexy performer comes from the fact that 'femininity' is not being used to represent a compromise. It instead creates a different silhouette for competence, political dissent and proactivity.

It is useful to think about this use of femininity as a kind of 'drag' in the same sense as when Julie Hanson speaks about her experience of drag kinging. She argues that in her performance as a drag king, she uses 'available sociocultural scripts' to re-inscribe an already 'marked' embodied 'norm' as 'otherness'. By dressing up as a man and enacting a female masculinity within her female body, she argues that drag kings can 'imag(in)e, convert and recognize themselves as radically "other", even though ostensibly through the "same" body/self.'[16] The female body is never denied; it is not performed as 'lack'. What is happening instead is that there is a process of 'moving beyond'[17] where one can perform 'in excess of'[18] the constraints that are socially enacted on the female body. This is a process of becoming, where different ways of conceptualizing, performing and experiencing the body 'come to matter'[19] and are corpor/realized.

Femininity can similarly be performed beyond and in excess of habitual thinking, whilst not devaluing or deactivating the political subject. Femininity or 'womanliness' embodies 'otherness' rather than 'lack'. What is happening here is that the femininity which is normalized as the essence or 'inessence' of being 'female' is being used to destabilize binaries whilst playing within the rules. Chutzpah's performance celebrates female dissent, yet this spectacle of femininity is still quite fresh and radical as it seems to play into and embody stereotypes: how can something the 'same' be different? However, performing femininity is actually more of a radical gesture than performing masculinity as a woman, because it is so much more engrained and naturalized within our sociocultural binary system. This is what is incredibly challenging for feminism, or for how we perceive feminism.

* * *

To conclude this section, I will return to the statements in the manifestos that began this chapter, which create a politicized subtext to the imagery we see in glossies and popular culture of 'sex objects'. They act as a supplement to representation, creating a collective space where women with a will for change can feel part of a wider collective of individuals. This sense of belonging can be related to Lauren Berlant's notion of an 'intimate public', where non-dominant groups can claim space through affective bonds. Berlant describes this collective space as 'a porous, affective scene of identification among strangers that promises consolation, confirmation, discipline, and discussion about how to live as an x.'[20] This connective space allows for resistance and enjoyment where life as an 'x' can be debated, questioned or enjoyed.

Clearly some women are still finding a politicized need for beauty manifestos in popular culture. And this collective unease and protest is being voiced at a grass-roots level. Although feminism is now adamantly rejected as old-hat and unnecessary, young or young(ish) women are still looking for like minds to express new ideas about the pleasures of dressing up and for other positive debates about play and image that do not discredit their intelligence. Feminism needs to take stock and think through this unease with 'femininity'. As a movement it has been affected by and taken the shape of its heterogeneous feminist subjects. And it can only move into the future and be healthy and buoyant if it maintains this openness towards the world outside of itself and its different possibilities. I think that it is continuing to move forward. It is in the process of embodying that change.

Subcultural Models

I walked into The Old Queen's Head in Islington, London, apprehensive. What had I let myself in for? It was quarter to two on a Saturday afternoon and I had booked myself in for an afternoon at a *Dr. Sketchy's Anti-Art Class*.[21] I had been in a nude-drawing class before; that was not the issue. But in this class I was not going to be able to fade into the background; I was not going to be able to be just an observer. That was the problem.

Dusty Limits, Dr. Sketchy's London
© *James Millar*

Dusty Limits, Dr. Sketchy's London
© *James Millar*

The event was up a small flight of winding stairs. I went in (comfortably), got some paper and sat down. In front of me was a stage. Quite a few people (mainly women, but of all ages) were already seated. There was a friendly atmosphere. All of a sudden there was a flurry of activity as a large hen party flocked in – and then the event kicked off. The compère, cabaret singer/comedienne Claire Benjamin, dressed as Frida Kahlo, got us all to 'loosen up' with a scribble before introducing us to our model for the afternoon, Tempest Rose. I could not help but take a sneaky peak at this glamorous woman standing on the sidelines. This marked the start of our afternoon of sketching.

In her essay, 'Border crossings: womanliness, body, representation' (1995), Hilary Robinson argues that: 'The body is not a *tabula rasa* upon which gender is projected, but rather gender is one of the aspects through which the body is produced and thus represented, through which it represents itself, produces and is given meaning.'[22] In this section I would like to consider the way Dr. Sketchy's makes us rethink the manner in which the body is given meaning in representation, and how this 'Anti-Art' drawing class helps to scupper and reimagine the process in which the female body is drawn (or withdrawn). As has been described in the last section, gender is engrained and encoded into the body. As Grosz argues, gendered constructions have been 'deeply etched into and lived as part of the body image.'[23] And our understanding of what the body means (its depth and truth) comes from how the body is represented as image.

Warwick and Cavallaro, in their book *Fashioning the Frame* (1998), argue that the body's

> hypothetical depths may turn out to be fictitious, indeed [...] the body may only exist in and through representation. Such representations are always, to some degree, sartorial, since even the nude figure immortalized by high art is an artfully tailored construct, designed to frame the body's potential seamlessness.[24]

Thinking about the nude figure as sartorial representation is a useful idea, for it allows us to think about nakedness as 'tailored' and put together in the same way that we might put together various items of clothing, or cloth to make an item of clothing. This way of thinking allows us to understand that the subject matter of the nude is not objective but something that is constructed by the artist and therefore not necessarily representative of the subject, the female nude.

To think about the body as constructed fiction is to consider the possibility that our perceptions, ideas, values and ideals are being enacted on the disorderly body to make it appear orderly to our way of thinking. Culture is being used to order the disorder of nature, to control the chaos of what lies under the flesh. As Lynda Nead has stated, the female nude idealizes and aestheticizes the female body.[25] The metaphor of tailoring and seams, therefore, allows us to start to think about representation more as the weaving together of swatches of fictions or texts. The seventeenth-century Latin meaning of *text* is 'woven', and of course we can expand that metaphor into the idea of intertextuality and contextuality. For David Joselit, new configurations, new subjectivities, come about by way of a 'play of surfaces'.[26] No individual identity, he argues, can exist singly, but each individual is made up of 'co-existing subject positions'.[27] In other words, one could say that our 'depth' is made up of enticing mergers.

The nude therefore represents the body as potentially seamless, a bodysuit constructed to hide its constructedness and to create a sense of perfection: a form without orifices, without messiness. Aesthetics and beauty are sewn into the subject and then dissolve the stitches. This suffocating image is therefore a fabrication which paints the woman's subjectivity and sexuality out of the picture. These images in art history inscribe particular knowledge, disciplines and rules about that sexed body, reiterating a particular way of behaving and being. In relation to this point, Catriona Mackenzie, in her 2010 essay 'Imagining oneself otherwise' (2000), argues that women's desire to physically please is closely bound to and by the dominant cultural imaginary that dictates to some extent how women act, behave and see themselves:

> Even if these representations are oppressive, in the sense
> that they present agents with severely curtailed avenues for

achieving social recognition, the fact that these avenues afford the main means of achieving social recognition nevertheless provides agents with a strong incentive for identifying with them. It may also provide them with a strong incentive for resisting innovative cultural imagery.[28]

This desire to conform to a particular amenable image is theorized by Deleuze and Guattari in their chapter 'Year zero: faciality'. Certain values, truths and ideas – which they describe as: 'the organization of power'[29] and 'the computation of normalities'[30] – inscribe the contours and characteristics of a 'face'. This performative process of faciality, where 'our selves are flattened into types'[31] is, David Joselit argues, 'the price we pay – in unequal measure according to our race, gender and sexuality – in having to exist as images for others and in having to adjust to the images others have of us.'[32] The impact and genealogical inscription of these sexual, racial or gender stereotypes makes it very difficult to break the acceptance and 'knowability' of these moulds. It makes it very difficult to make fresh inscriptions, and much easier to slip back or remain within the same established striations of conformity. As Deleuze and Guattari state: 'How tempting it is to let yourself get caught, to lull yourself into it, to latch back onto a face.'[33] However, as they stress: 'Dismantling the face is no mean affair.'[34]

Art, they argue, can be used to deterritorialize the face. If you know your face, then through art you can undermine its signifying, subjective position and begin to make it faceless. However, they warn that one should not then go on to reterritorialize art. Art should be the beginning of the process, not the end product. Fresh lines need to be drawn, active lines of flight. In his essay 'Aesthetics: a place I've never seen', Stephen Zagala explores the ideas of Deleuze and Guattari in relation to art. In this essay Zagala argues for art's role as a catalytic stimulus for political change. Art can create new forms of ethical activity out of 'blocks of sensation'.[35] In relation to this point, Zagala intriguingly states that: 'Philosophers create concepts of sensation, just as artists create pure sensation of concepts.'[36]

However, Dr. Sketchy's is anti-art (as its title proclaims), anti-artist, anti-academic, anti-skill and therefore dismissive of art's hierarchical authority as a catalyst for political change. It has no faith in art's capacity to deterritorialize the 'face', and questions the ethics of art's territorial control over 'sensation' and representing the female subject. Dr. Sketchy's reconfigures the notion of the artist and the activist through the disorderly 'powder puff and beauty spots' extravagance of the 'artiste'. This anti-art class turns 'art' upside down. It is a parody of a life class, where there are no rules apart from not taking oneself too seriously. This is about collectivity and fun, and a controlled unruliness. What is it therefore a class in? It is certainly anti-academic, and definitely flouting conventional hierarchies of power. These are artistes, entertainers, who are hijacking art as entertainment and mocking its seriousness – dragging 'art' into the 'low' arena of stripping and pub culture – in order to turn the tables on the 'high' and have a ball.

The traditional idea of a life-drawing class is that the model and his or her embodied phenomenological experience are almost irrelevant. 'Objectivity' is the key – the artist has the power to frame the model through the eye, or 'I'. This 'Anti-Art Class' dashes objectivity and encourages participation: the space between the 'art', the model and the spectator is dissolved.[37] Drawing on this subcultural model, I was attempting to define the image by way of the costume changes and feminine accoutrements. I was enjoying the visual pleasure of the fascinator, the tall, feathered headdresses and bejewelled turbans, nipple tassels and long false eyelashes. We, as a room full of participants, were taking pleasure from these objects as 'blocks of sensation': the bold colour, the sensual textures and the flamboyant agency.

The music playing in the background was Nina Simone's 'I Put a Spell on You'; I had pencilled this on the top of one of my drawings and am considering this again as I take another glance at it. Who was being represented in this image? 'I put a spell on you': Who were the 'I' and the 'you' in this drawing? Where do we locate agency, the sensation of feeling the impact of another behind (or in front of) our eyes?

Pertinent to this is a paper given at a recent conference by a young female artist[38] who was presenting her fascinating artwork in process. She had found a collection of images of showgirls, which she then recreated by photographing herself performing likewise.

Bettsie Bon Bon, Dr. Sketchy's London
© James Millar

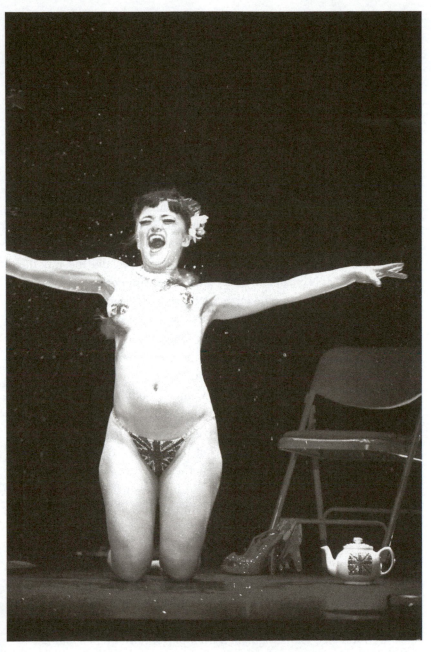

Bettsie Bon Bon, Dr. Sketchy's London
© *James Millar*

In the process she was trying to find the point at which the images had agency. What did it take to perform agency through an image? How does one represent the agency of a subject? These showgirls had agency in their images, yet somehow this young woman felt that she could not always relocate this. She was, she said, a failed showgirl.

The desire to locate this agency on the part of not only this young artist, but also on the part of our present culture, which is now utterly embracing the 'low' of showgirls, music hall, burlesque queens, retro pin-ups and other starlets, is perhaps recognizing the need to re-channel desire into a pleasure and control that is more resistant and affirmative. The artiste is an important historical spectacle in relation to the agency lost in 'art'. This desire to 'rebrand' the trace left by these historical images which at some point ideologically lost their power is also the desire to rebrand and reclaim the way the female subject is imaged in the present. Rosi Braidotti discusses this in relation to pornographic imagery. By way of Susan Kappeler's *The Pornography of Representation* (1987) she argues that pornography creates a sense of dependency, but 'without taking responsibility for it'.[39] The power that the individual accrues comes from 'negative passions' such as envy and frustration.[40] The agency of the subject is lost in the repetitive inscription of women's bodies as consumables. This is an object dislocated from subjectivity.

We see in relation to the aforementioned example that agency was somehow lost in the attempts at reiteration. By mimicking the performance there was a desire for authenticity, yet by recreating an image faithfully we are perhaps lulled into a sense of security, and 'latch on' to a particular face (to revisit Deleuze from earlier): being graceful, posing confidently, donning the relevant accessories, styling the relevant 'look'. Yet by doing this there is a repetition of 'norms' which simply repeat the same performative rhetoric. Judith Butler's differentiation between 'performance' and performativity is perhaps useful to this discussion. Butler's argument is that

> performance is distinguished from performativity in so far as the latter consists in a reiteration of norms which precede, constrain and exceed the performer and in that sense cannot be taken as the fabrication of the performer's 'will' or 'choice'.[41]

*(l-r) Tricity Vogue, Dusty Limits, Bettsie Bon Bon
and Clare-Marie Willmer, Dr. Sketchy's London
© James Millar*

There is a clear split therefore between performance and performativity, with 'performance' consciously performing gender; where there is a knowing intentional sense of distance from the 'set of norms'. One is self-conscious that one is playing the part. The norms are, as Geraldine Harris argues, in 'citation marks'. With performativity, on the other hand, these 'norms' are a daily performance where there is no distance or control – something we perhaps see as 'natural' and take for granted. This is not a kind of 'drag' because women experience 'femininity' as 'lived' and situated in their female body. It is culturally engrained: they cannot simply take off the mask. It is much more problematic. Women are, though, perhaps knowingly living this, taking it as read whilst knowing that it is a text for reading.

To locate agency would be to see the fabrication of woman as culturally and historically gendered yet also to understand this fabrication as embodied, situated and collaborative. Agency is therefore not something that can be performed seamlessly but is something interwoven, and perhaps can even be located as the stitching which sews together and winds its way through various surfaces. Agency perhaps is apparent when we are made conscious of the seams. But how does this happen?

Thinking about this question of agency in representation, I return to Dr. Sketchy's. Where was agency located here? The model and compère were insistent that we did not take ourselves too seriously, and undermined any serious attempts to draw this model 'properly'. In the first drawing, which we had to do without looking at the paper (this quick two-minute drawing was, 'Frida Kahlo' said, to 'loosen us up'), I tried to image the model by way of cleavage, nipped-in waist and dots from a bandana. From thereon in, though, every attempt at 'serious' drawing was scuppered by way of instructions to draw bananas, oranges, a duck-billed platypus or my dreadful attempt at drawing Freud hugging Tempest Rose. The instructions prevented us from creating a pretty picture. At every attempt at imaging the subject, the 'I' evaded me. However, amongst these absurd and ordinary images there was clearly an affirmative trace of something else.

I would like to consider the way that the subject is represented as image in relation to Warwick and Cavallaro's idea of clothes as 'intoxication' and as 'a surface prism'. These ideas capture a positive, creative sense of the subject as diffused through a splintered and fractured display of colour, flamboyancy, texture and shapes and movement. This also helps to understand this as an intersubjective and inter-corporeal space, where objects and bodies create a physical and psychological sense of excess and pleasure. I would argue also that this analogy of intoxication makes us think of a dizzying sense of life out of kilter, where the ordinary can make us laugh, where we can lose control or make a spectacle of ourselves, or say things we really shouldn't: where we could possibly lose a clear sense of propriety and self-consciousness – where indeed pleasure and excess can create a nauseating sense of disorder. Trying to make a representation of the subject is therefore surely a tricky enterprise.

All these strange images keep floating and flouting, erasing and drawing on top of my sense of order. This is a clouding, dreamlike stream of consciousness: a disorderly arrangement. The seams of the nude have been revealed. The surface is not comprehensible or knowable; it is not pristinely ordered and uncomplicated. The stitches are coming apart and imagery is coming through as ghostly imprints. Freud's analogy of a child's mystic writing-pad is a useful reference point for this chaotic and fractured desire to frame the subject and capture an image on paper.

Freud used this analogy in order to understand the seemingly inexhaustible 'receptive capacity'[42] of our memory. The 'receptive surface' of a child's mystic writing-pad seemed to him to be a closer analogy than writing on paper that gets thrown away or chalk on a board that gets rubbed out. With every fresh mark, the inscriptions on a mystic writing-pad build up, never fully going away. On the thin opaque surface there is the simplicity of the fresh inscription, but in the wax underneath there is a complex interplay and archaeology of marks and grooves. The fresh impression that is inscribed on the top layer simultaneously becomes part of that complex history. This analogy is useful because of this palimpsestic idea of a surface which is full of heavily engrained inscriptions outlining cultural ideals, values and images. This is a surface full of ghostly suggestions, faint pictures, fragments of memories and images that evade comprehension. And then there are the newer inscriptions, which layer themselves on top as part of this rich chaos.

I would argue therefore that the plain surface waiting for our fresh inscription is already alarmingly alive. Drawing into this surface, we are drawn into the intoxication of jarring inconsistencies. These are images that also connect the 'I' with the 'you'. The trace of graphite is the resonance of this difference, the chasm that lies between, yet connects what is over there to what is over here. It is the attempt to make connections, to tune in, to understand, to translate, to articulate. Drawing the subject could also be aligned to the 'psychic imprint' discussed by Derrida, for it is the unfathomable difference between the world as it stands and our lived experience of that world that creates an impression on the senses, or a 'psychic imprint'.[43]

Framing the subject is not seamless. It is collaborative, and we feel the surface pulsating, breathing, smiling. It has a life that also includes monstrosities, strangeness, silliness and absurdities that we don't fully understand. The fantastical, as we know, is not always princes kissing princesses. On to the surface we draw our own ideas, our engrained notions of how things are. The opaque sheet has been pulled back to reveal the palimpsest of images obscured by control, an ordering of the chaos, which makes the orderly out of the disorderly, the incomprehensible seem comprehensible. Our expectations are befuddled. What is revealed is what has been concealed by this ordering. When we mark the surface, we inscribe into established deep striations of preconceived ideas and ways of seeing which we keep re-inscribing, reiterating and scarring. Yet surrounding this established 'face' of heavily engrained repetitive marking, other marks are exposed as alive.

Sara Ahmed would describe this shared understanding as 'feminist wonder'. This is knowledge that

> allows us to see the surfaces of the world *as made*, and as such wonder opens up rather than suspends historicity. Historicity is what is concealed by the transformation of the world into 'the ordinary', into something that is already familiar, or recognisable.[44]

This visual unruliness scuppers expectations. What is revealed within the 'ordinary', what is made visible by the hobgoblins as the emperor's new clothing is at once both familiar and obstructively unfamiliar. What is left behind in this anti-art class is a completely different kind of trace.

PART III

Bitter/Sweet Poetry
(Being Gorgeous and the 'High')

5

The Paradoxical Body

FASHION AND ART

In 1998, Vanessa Beecroft's *Show* (*vb35*) was performed at the Guggenheim in New York. This was sponsored by Gucci and photographed by fashion photographer Mario Sorrenti. Twenty models – fifteen wearing Tom Ford-designed Gucci bikinis and high heels, and five naked – posed for two-and-a-half hours looking blankly out into space. This intriguing marriage of fashion and art, with its overt product placement, plays out the spectacle of Rebecca Schneider's 'commodity dreamgirls,'[1] (which we see again in subsequent performances such as *vb56* in 2005, where topless knicker-clad models in stilettos laced up to their thighs lounge about amongst Louis Vuitton handbags).

'Commodity dreamgirls', Rebecca Schneider argues in *The Explicit Body in Performance* (1997), 'sing a paradox', for 'they cannot be that which they are given to be.'[2] The images that we see of young, thin, white females that surround us every day on billboards, bus stops, the internet and in glossy magazines advertising different products induce a desire for more, but unlike the product, the young nubile models can never give us that which we desire. We cannot possess them. They stoke a desire that can never be fully quenched. These young women stare vacantly out at us with, Schneider argues, 'recessive vision'.[3] This is teasing disembodied vision that recedes infinitely into an empty performance of commodified insatiability. These dreamgirls can be 'acquired through exchange', posits Schneider, 'but when they are bought and possessed, what is discovered?'[4] Using images of young desirable women who are always out of our reach to sell objects feeds the desire for more. Even when bought, the object never fully satisfies our desire. The 'real' is never fully attainable. The fantasy is never fully satisfied.

In drawing fashion and art together in her performance work, Beecroft allows us to ponder this desire – the gap between fantasy and reality. Caroline Evans has argued that this gap is effaced in the fashion catwalk show by the theatrical experience – the 'enchanted spectacle'[5] – where the fantasy and bewitchment of the visual extravaganza hides the commercial intentions of the show. As Evans argues: 'Guy Debord described the society of the spectacle as one in which image effaces reality; and this could be a paradigm of how the fashion show has operated in the past to disguise its commercial origins and goals.'[6] Evans is stating, therefore, that art and entertainment are being used to sugarcoat the commerce. One could argue, however, that they are not necessarily confusing the commerce but simply enhancing and glamorizing the intention of the show: the allure of the commodity.

In Beecroft's long 'live' two-and-a-half-hour installation performances, the models certainly wilt, twitch and become fatigued. This is a collision between glamorous fantasy and real time. We are implicated as voyeur; we feel awkward staring; we consume these images and take pleasure from looking. The spectacle flickers madly between sign and flesh, between the pleasures enjoyed in consuming these objects and the more awkward self-conscious pleasure of gazing at these women as fleshy thinking and feeling subjects. Beecroft's work makes transparent what Abigail Solomon-Godeau refers to in her essay 'The other side of Venus: the visual economy of female display' as the historical 'coupling of eros and commodity',[7] where the display of 'ideal' femininity enacts the allure of the commodity, which is in Beecroft's case the fashion brand of Gucci. As Solomon-Godeau argues: 'In becoming not only the commodity's emblem but its lure, the feminine image operates as a conduit and mirror of desire, reciprocally intensifying and reflecting the commodity's allure.'[8] She forwards Alphonse Mucha's nineteenth-century femme fatale image for Job cigarette papers as a specific example of this, for this image both lures us in in terms of sexual attraction and pleasure, and simultaneously seduces us into wanting the product by way of this misplaced desire.

A perfect contemporary example of this coupling of eros and commodity is the Dita von Teese hologram that was first showcased at the launch of the Louboutin retrospective at the Design Museum in London in 2012. In this hologram the stripping Dita von Teese literally morphs into a Louboutin shoe and then back into Dita. The erotic hologram performs the illusion of the commodity as allure, the image as surface, as illusionary magical glitter and dust. The striptease demonstrates the seamless interweaving of woman and shoe as fetish.

Relevant here is a discussion in Laura Mulvey's *Fetishism and Curiosity*, which succinctly summarizes how commodity fetishism works to bridge sexual allure with the lure of the commodity in order to conceal the reality of its production and seduce a buyer whilst disavowing that intention: '[T]he commodity presents the market with a seductive sheen, as it competes to be desired.'[9] She takes Hollywood cinema as her example to demonstrate how both structures of meaning flow into each other:

> The popular cinema, itself a commodity, can form a bridge between the commodity as spectacle and the figure of woman as spectacle on the screen. This, in turn, leads on to the bridging function of woman as consumer, rather than producer, of commodities.[10]

This bridging technique, she argues, allows for things to seem connected even though they may not be.

As we can see with the Dita von Teese hologram, this bridging technique is perfectly illustrated. There is a self-contained circuit of desire. The sparkling life-sized shoes are sexualized and made all the more seductive by transforming into the stripping burlesque icon who herself is wearing these items. This not only gives the items their sex appeal but also links the items to the female consumer, as the shoes are linked inextricably to the female sexual body and its feminine allure. This circuitry of desire is made the more fantastical by the glittering illusion of the three-dimensional hologram, which is out of reach and untouchable. Stripping off the accoutrements of femininity such as long black gloves and tossing them teasingly to the side, we are drawn into the absolute magic of the illusion. The layers are peeled away to reveal nothing but intangible self-contained pleasure. Baudrillard argues that 'what fascinates us' about this self-contained circuitry of pleasure is

> that which radically excludes us in the name of its internal logic or perfection: a mathematical formula, a paranoic system, a concrete jungle, a useless object, or, again, a smooth body, without orifices, doubled and redoubled by a mirror, devoted to perverse autosatisfaction.[11]

Another example of this 'internal logic or perfection' which is 'devoted to perverse autosatisfaction' in the bridging of the object, the female image as allure and the female consumer, was the concept store collaboration between Louis Vuitton and Japanese performance and conceptual artist Yayoi Kusama for Selfridges in London from August to October 2012. Kusama, who has used the infamous 'spots' in her installation pieces since the 1960s, created for Vuitton a breathtaking visual spectacle. As I approached the entrance to Selfridges, a giant model of Kusama loomed over me. Then as I moved through the rotating doors, the obsessive, repetitive red and white spots became the motif which drew me hypnotically around the department store. The models of Kusama were eerily lifelike – uncanny, even – and I met these duplicate models in glass cabinets, in both miniature and giant proportions. I was mesmerized. I watched others who were equally captivated by these gorgeous window displays. What was drawing me in, though, was not the pristine surface of the iconic burlesque stripper (or in the case of Beecroft's performance piece a skinny pubescent model), but Kusama, an 83-year-old Japanese conceptual performance artist.

On entering the store we were immersed in the world of luxury shopping. It was wondrous to see. All of these high-end objects were perfectly presented; even tea seemed quite out of this world. Fashion labels such as Mary Katrantzou, Stella McCartney, Miu Miu and Jimmy Choo dazzled us. But what did it mean that the fantasy and allure of the object was based on the aged figure of Kusama, as opposed to Beecroft's naked models or the surgically enhanced Dita? What was dazzling us? This spectacle beckoned us in. We were intrigued again by the marriage of fashion and art. For the first time, all of Selfridges' twenty-four windows were dedicated to one brand.

Part of the seductive appeal of Kusama's spectacle was its obsessive identity, which bordered on madness. What firstly lured us in was the eye-catching contrast between the red and the white (signifiers for 'sale') as well as the simple composition and repetition of a singular motif – the polka dot. We are well aware of our malleability to the image and commodity. We want to be seduced. Yet we also feel suffocated by this honey, whose only intention is to entrap. The excess of luxury induces an almost nauseous sense of panic in its sensory overload. Beguiling. Intoxicating. Making me lose my head.

In Daniel Miller's book *The Dialectics of Shopping* (2001), he discusses the 'madness' that shopping was seen to induce in well-to-do female shoppers at the turn of the century. The term 'kleptomania' was coined by doctors and psychiatrists and championed by Sir Arthur Conan Doyle to try to understand and 'resolve the contradiction'[12] of middle-class women stealing. By ascribing a medical, unconscious reason to this action, the illogical activity was made more palatable. Shopping made these women lose their minds. Let us hasten to add here that the same understanding was not given to poor women who stole bread to feed their family – they were sent to gaol. The condition of kleptomania therefore resolved the contradiction between the 'real', or ideal, and the lived female experience – the 'real' ideal of how respectable women should behave, and the lived problem that many of them were stealing.

In her book *Temptations: Sex, Selling and the Department Store* (1993), Gail Reekie also writes about the diagnosis of kleptomania. She states that in the late nineteenth century this mental sickness was seen as feminine, further strengthening gendered stereotypes of women's psychological and biological weakness, irrationality and vulnerability to temptation. Women were seen to have a natural proclivity towards impulsive acts of self-indulgence, and could not resist finery – they were weak-willed. Although on the one hand this was seen to make women ideal customers and more easily seduced by mass marketing (if they desired something, they had to have it), on the other hand women were also 'frustratingly difficult to manage'.[13]

Other intriguing examples of this stubborn agency are forwarded by Bill Lancaster. During the 1880s, 'jays', or 'tabbies', were seen as a menace to economic prosperity. These women would spend time inspecting goods, using the shop's facilities, trying on clothes and even making the most of the free delivery service before sending back goods without payment. Lancaster also discusses examples of working-class women, some of whom were fastidious and awkward as customers and others who took pleasure from just walking around nineteenth-century shopping malls without buying anything: 'Just aboot ivvorythin' ye cud think on! Naw! A didn't buy nowt. Couldn't see owt A needed!' Lancaster argues that these examples show 'women's ability to peel off the veneer of unreality that often surrounds the shopping experience.'[14]

Indeed, after having been seduced into the Selfridges store by the Kusama/Vuitton window display and having followed the strangely eerie cabinets and multiple Kusama models bedecked in Vuitton accessories and polka dots galore, the commercial product left me somewhat disappointed. In this instance the illusion of the object was revealed; the artistic spectacle usurped the prize. This installation recreated the internal logic of desire and madness, yet what lay at the centre of this splendid madness was rather disappointingly just an overpriced, quite ordinary-looking handbag and scarf.

Laura Mulvey discusses the illusion of the spectacle in relation to a scene from *The Wizard of Oz* where Dorothy's dog Toto pulls down the curtain to reveal the 'Great Wizard'. This glamorous sheen hides the reality of the process, which she argues maintains the illusion of the spectacle. However, even though the Great Wizard and the reality of his deception are revealed, Dorothy's belief in the magical abilities of the shoes still persists. For even when Toto pulls the curtain down and exposes the Wizard as a fraudster without any special magical abilities – the 'magic' of Oz only being created by way of cogs and wheels and buttons – Dorothy still believes in the power of her shoes. This is the ability to make something happen by way of self-belief, even though it seems to loudly contradict reality. The ruby-red slippers, the electric-blue dress, the yellow-brick road, the flamboyant colour of the Emerald City also become symbolic of the pleasure that can be experienced from the imaginary and the phantasmagorical. The sparkling shoes become symbolic of Dorothy's belief in transformation: that they could take her home.

The meaning of the sentence 'I know, but…' creates a resolution in the contradiction between the bare reality and the fantasy, between subjective conceptualization and objective reality. Magic is produced in full knowledge of its illusion. We are enchanted even though we know we have been deceived. Enchantment and deception are codependent. Seduction happens in full knowledge of the mirrors and smoke. The fleeting illusion of a rainbow is still breathtaking, even though we cannot touch it; it is not 'real'. Similarly, we know a new pair of shoes will not change our life; however, we want to *believe* that a new pair of shoes will mark a fresh exciting new beginning – *every* pair. The magic comes through the 'make-believe'. We want to believe.

Window shopping promotes this magic of make-believe. During the nineteenth century, shop window displays and browsing were popular forms of entertainment, and entrepreneurs Harry Selfridge and L. Frank Baum both saw themselves as enhancing women's lives in some way through the art of window display – which encourages the pleasures that come from 'just looking'.[15] Harry Selfridge himself created an environment that was welcoming and accommodating to women, including ladies' public toilets and a reading room, restaurant and crèche. Lindy Woodhead includes a quote from Selfridge in her book: 'I came along just at the time when women wanted to step out on their own. They came to the store and realized some of their dreams.'[16] L. Frank Baum in particular was an ardent feminist and supporter of women's suffrage 'who saw his work as an enhancement of women's lives, not as a form of systematic deception.'[17]

The dialectical opposition between deception and enhancement, which is condensed in the experience of shopping, is very intriguing and better explored by drawing on Baudrillard's discussion on the commodity fetish. Baudrillard speaks about its two-pronged significance. He relays firstly the original seventeenth-century meaning of the term 'fetish' – when it pertained to 'fabrication' or 'faking' – and secondly the more contemporary meaning of the term, which links to ideas of enchantment. In the second meaning, the object contains magical properties which give the subject similar magical possibilities for transformation. This second meaning, he suggests, is more akin to 'magical thinking'.[18]

This magical thinking can be seen in the fetish of the ruby slippers, which comes to represent a magical belief that seems to bypass objective disillusionment. There is an inherent contradiction in Dorothy's belief in the power of these shoes even after the deception has been revealed. There is a desire to believe in the face of fabrication; and there is therefore an unresolved contradiction between fantasy and reality, between subjective agency and objective circumstances.

Women's contradictory relationship with the commodity fetish and commodity capitalism is complex and contradictory. At the turn of the twentieth century, when middle- and upper-class women were buying clothes from department stores and then parading them in the public domain, they were also colluding in their own commodification as object and image. Being consumers created the opportunity to enhance and express women's sense of self, but it also simultaneously transformed them into a spectacle and advertisement for commodity capitalism. Caroline Evans forwards the intriguing perspective in 'The enchanted spectacle' that women were party to this complicated positioning as object, subject and image, arguing that middle and upper class women could be understood as 'subjects of the society of the spectacle' because they were 'active consumers of luxury goods', adding that 'when they turned themselves into a vision by donning their purchases they became, simultaneously, its object and image too.'[19]

This therefore can be seen as pleasurable collusion. However, in this complicated positioning, subjective conceptualization inadvertently becomes a promotional tool for profit-making and is constructed on the back of capitalist gain. Self-conception – body image, style, trends, beauty, pleasure and enjoyment – is formed in many instances as a direct response to imagery and adverts. There is therefore a fakery and dishonesty in the seduction, which feeds on insecurities. The subject–object–image position does not sit smoothly and is not without problems. There is a violence inherent in the pleasure; a violence which is not evident in the example forwarded of the Von Teese/Louboutin collaboration.

The Dita hologram enacts the process of commodity fetishism and replicates the system perfectly. This is smooth and seamless pleasure, where the subject, object and image are one and the same. This is a seemingly self-congratulatory system. There is no critique. It is marvellous mimicry – a perfect symbiotic relationship. We cannot touch the body of this performer; we are not looking at a 'real' body. But it is an image of collusion and collaboration between the real and the fantasy body. The commodity creates a vehicle for the real body. The 'real' Dita von Teese moulds and surgically enhances her own body to embody 'perfection'. The glamour of the shoes enacts the fantasy of the female sexual subject. The glitter and sparkle of the seduction, the devastatingly dominant heel, the smooth perfectly formed orifice into which one can slip a perfectly seamed stocking. Embodied in that shoe is a commodified dream body and sexual feminine allure which completely and utterly transfixes and dominates vision. This is a pleasure that comes from being perfectly pleasurable.

For Beecroft and Kusama, the models and mannequins mimic the madness of commodity capitalism – its pleasures, suffocation and subjectivity. It does not step outside of the regime of consumption or commodity fetishism. As Jennifer Doyle argues in her book *Sex Objects: Art and the Dialectics of Desire* (2006), Beecroft's performance art is both a 'gorgeous spectacle' and a 'sexual compromise'.[20] We are seduced yet feel the heat of shame at looking at these young naked female bodies as they flicker between 'flesh' and 'sign', between object–image and subject, between animate and inanimate, ideal and real, passive and active, control and out of control. Indeed, in the case of Kusama, creating an artistic panoramic collaboration for a luxury brand and department store could also perhaps be interpreted as an artistic and intellectual compromise. And the anticlimax of the very ordinary handbag at the centre of this creative display brings us down to earth sharply.

This is therefore a paradoxical pleasure that is caught in a compromise. Is Beecroft's work a critique, or institutionalized titillation? Was the Kusama/Vuitton installation a cynical deployment of an 83-year-old Japanese woman to play up to a new growing luxury Asian target market, or was this a critique of representation by using a more mature model–artist? Was it promotion, or a new model of conceptualizing women's subjectivity and their complex relationship to commodities and shopping? The work, of course, represents all of these positions; this is what is so intriguing. The artists highlight this compromise and these contradictions.

In their article 'Pleasure and political subjectivity', Amy Swiffen and Catherine Kellogg argue that the fetish can give one a 'place of play': 'It is a means of reconciliation with the contradictory authority of law.'[21] This is useful because with Beecroft and Kusama the branded object, the commodity fetish does indeed become a place of play, which highlights a compromise for the artists where the positions of subject, object and image cannot be collapsed into one another, and yet cannot be easily disentangled. As Swiffen and Kellogg state, this is not transgression; it does not challenge the system. In this 'place of play' pleasure is problematic and contradictory; 'pleasure' indeed becomes transparent.

The pleasures of the object therefore come as a compromise to the subject; however, this compromise simultaneously makes transparent the deceptions of the process. And the interception of 'shame' or 'disappointment' with 'seduction' is the key to tying this section together. Elspeth Probyn argues that 'in shame one feels viscerally the conditional sense of "as if": a tense that highlights the implications of one's present actions.'[22] It is '[i]n shame', she argues, that 'the feeling and minding and thinking and social body comes alive. It's in this sense that shame is positive and productive, even or especially when it feels bad.'[23] Visual pleasure, which is at once seductive and shameful, fantastical and disappointing, makes collusion transparent and as such makes us reflect on the implications of that very collusion. Fantasy and pleasure are tied up with commodification: the commodification of our own bodies as image and the prostitution of our own pleasure to the profit of commodity capitalism.

And yet when that bubble is popped and the smooth, seamless, seemingly natural is disrupted, the subject is still able to retain agency within the process of pleasure. Fantasy and play persists in spite of and despite the bare reality of the object's motives. Swiffen and Kellogg argue that this 'place of play' ascribed to the fetish object actually allows one to both 'deny and asseverate the law'.[24] We are implicated in the commodification process, yes, but we are also aware of our role and the pleasure we gain in this process. Fantasy and collusion are interwoven into an object that acts as both honeytrap and as conduit for agency. Play – which induces both pleasure and shame as well as excitement and disappointment – gives us knowledge about how the fantasy space of the object operates and in turn what this can tells us about our contradictory self. 'Just looking' pierces the illusion of the fantasy object and peels off the 'veneer of unreality',[25] but by separating out the illusion from the reality we are also presented with a much more complex understanding of the paradoxical female subject and her place of play and display within commodity capitalism.

GLITTER AND MEAT

In this section I would like to return to a piece of work that I mentioned briefly in the introduction – Helmut Newton's *Sie Kommen* (*Here They Come*, 1981). I came across this photograph in Berlin in 2006 as I was walking up a staircase on the way to a quite different exhibition. I was shocked yet strangely enthralled by this astonishing photograph of women standing monumentally tall, naked except for emblematic 'feminine' accoutrements of sexuality such as high heels, lipstick and shaved pubic hair. This image is at once appalling and magnificent in its corporeal objectification. Seeing Newton's originals is unsettling. They loom over us, Amazonian. I was left disturbed by my ambivalent feelings towards them. Each pore, downy hair on their arms, crease and fold is lovingly captured with absolute clarity. The objectification is monumental. We fall under their spell. They affect us, yet they also disturb. They are art objects. They are also desirable sexual, female subjects. My gaze was felt.

Jemima Stehli's *After Helmut Newton's 'Here They Come'* (1999) is a replication of Newton's photograph. Stehli mimics the photograph by placing herself in the frame as the naked object and subject. In her reproduction, the other three women are absent. Flanking the left-hand side of the frame, Stehli fills the place of the fourth model. The camera's shutter release cable and button is in her hand.

Stehli's artwork ponders objectification. From the mid-nineties to the turn of the millennium she produced what appeared to be seamless reproductions of 'objectifying' art practice such as Allen Jones' *Table* (1969), a sculpture of a woman in 'fetish' clothing bent down on all fours holding up a glass tabletop, which is attached to her shoulder blades and buttocks. She wears a black corset exposing her naked breasts, which hang down pendulously towards a soft white fur rug. Her accessories include long black leather boots, gloves and false eyelashes, and she gazes at herself in a handheld mirror, which lies underneath her.

Stehli places herself within a history of objectification to see what it means to be a woman in this traditionally patriarchal context. She reintroduced her contemporary body-as-artist into the frame in order to test out and highlight the gaze as potentially reciprocal and pleasurable yet also questionable and paradoxical. We are left uncertain as to her motives and the stubborn and effective power and evident pleasures of these dominant traditions. Stehli's cool neutral reconstructions of erotic photography and the female nude are unsettling in their verisimilitude. The close semblance to patriarchal traditions leaves the spectator unsure as to Stehli's politics. These pieces reveal and acknowledge both an uneasy entrapment and a pleasurable containment within traditional representational social and cultural forms. Although this performance work contains and grapples towards expressing new models of subjectivity, it has not yet found new modes to express this paradox. This imagery, however astute, still 'grates' (to rephrase Mary Kelly); it still brims over with health, youth and white prettiness. It feels too contained, too respectful of traditional forms, and slightly too accepting of the status quo.

In Stehli's reconstruction we are also disturbed by the fact that the original photograph was staged and taken by Helmut Newton, a male photographer, and that *Sie Kommen* may well have been Newton's own dominatrix fantasy. By inserting herself as the female artist into the image, does Stehli change anything? What does this image now mean? There is no simplistic response. By replacing one of the models with a female artist as object and subject, we still question her motives. Is she complicitous 'meat'? Does she want us to look and enjoy her as an object? How is this subversive? Does she give up her claim to 'being' by casting herself in this way? If so, why is that the case? Casting a spell on us with her sexual being, she is and is not an object. By being the art object, Stehl makes us aware, makes us conscious of the subject in the image, but in consuming it we nevertheless negate her. This piece powerfully enacts the feminine body as a paradoxical 'thing' that is both vulnerable and affirmative. As an image she is still 'meat', yet it seems that 'being on the brink of enslavement'[26] is an extremely pleasurable place to be.

The original Newton image sits within a context of 1980s feminism and power dressing. The 1999 reproduction sits in a moment of performance art history that earmarks a period of transition in terms of sexual 'power' and the politics of representation. Dita von Teese comments in her book *Burlesque and the Art of the Teese* that feminists have never had a problem with the idea of the dominatrix, yet have had considerable problems with the idea of the submissive damsel in distress.[27] This point is worth our consideration: the Newton image may well speak to our time differently because of our current cultural shift with regard to the female body and its objecthood.

Feminists have had – and indeed still do have – problems with submissive representation and objectification because of the continual problem in relation to mind–body dualism. In the mind–body dualist split women have historically only been the flesh. This dualistic approach, where mind is seen as separate from fleshy sensuous matter, is embedded in Western philosophical and social traditions.[28] In this tradition the body is an obstacle to spiritual transcendence; the rational thinking subject must be abstracted from the (male) body in order to attain periods of pure thought and self-knowledge. The female cannot however transcend material matter because her reproductive capabilities firmly anchor her mind to her body, binding her inexorably to the life–death cycle. Elizabeth Grosz argues that this mind/body opposition is frequently linked to the distinctions between

> reason and passion, sense and sensibility, outside and inside, self and other, depth and surface, reality and appearance, mechanism and vitalism, transcendence and immanence, temporality and spatiality, psychology and physiology, form and matter.[29]

These dichotomies were implicitly married to the underlying distinctions between masculine and feminine and male and female. One side of the pairing is therefore deemed less significant, a negative imprint of the stronger, more dominant side. Femaleness is inextricably linked with this subservient, unreflective 'feminine' side of the pairing and therefore paired with the instinct, the quotidian, and the corporeal.

In the 1960s performance artists were challenging this reductive legacy of dualist philosophy, which conflated 'femaleness' with corporeality and the alignment of masculinity and 'maleness' to disembodied 'mind', by introducing new ways of exploring objecthood. Carolee Schneemann's *Meat Joy* (1964) is an attempt to anchor the sensual (female) body in subjectivity so as to challenge these engrained binary pairings where female difference can only be understood in terms of inferiority and lack. Her performance celebrates flesh that is at once grotesque, gory, smelly, erotic and playful. Bodies writhe under plastic, which gives the viewer a sense of wrapped corpses; bodies are pressed against paper like packaged meat in a supermarket, and drenched in blood and raw meat, hinting at slaughterhouses and carcasses. Ultimately this is bringing the subject back into the flesh: this is a performance about an embodied fleshy, sensual female subject.

At a similar period in avant-garde performance history, the Viennese Actionists were also creating challenging theatrical assertions of the body that were sometimes violent, and consistently taboo and shocking. Their work, however, was markedly different from Schneemann's oeuvre, being more of an assault on than a celebration of the flesh. The Viennese Actionists were creating performance pieces where the male subject had also been violently disconnected from his fleshy sensual experience. They were acting out their male body as fully visceral as a direct challenge to the myth of the male existential subject as wholly transcendental. Schneemann's practice was not therefore isolated. Activist performance art was acknowledging the violence incurred by culturally splitting the subject (the disembodied 'I') from the object (body).

In such pieces as Otto Muehl's *Material Action 3: Bread-crumbing a Woman's Backside,* Hermann Nitsch's *Action 8: (Penis Rinsings),* Günter Brus' film action *Self-Mutilation* or Rudolf Schwarzkogler's

Action 1: Wedding (1965) the body is self-consciously used as a pleasure-tool, a plaything, an art object, an 'objectified' thing. As Otto Muehl claims, 'a person is not treated in the material action as a person but as a body, the body, things, are not viewed as objects for our purposes, but have all purpose radically removed from them.'[30] The performances act as a humorous, grotesque, disturbing and damning reflection on the violence incurred by attempting to extricate the body from its personal, political or social nexus, the subject from its objecthood.

In one performance/film, Brus turns a naked woman-as-object upside down with her breasts on display to a mainly male, white audience and 'shags' her like an inanimate hole. He then violently rips off a chicken's head, and finally finishes off by defecating on a sign that reads 'The End'. These actions were and still are extremely challenging and obviously overstep ethical boundaries of acceptability. Nitsch argued that the performances were about 'waking people up'.[31] The publicly enacted, emotionless affair of physically/metaphorically/parodically 'shagging' a woman-as-rag doll provoked laughter and titters of anxiety from the predominantly male audience. The laughter and embarrassment point to incredulity at his audacity, but also to a knowing embarrassed recognition. It is pointedly shocking and taboo, yet by publicly staging this action Brus demonstrates not just physical violence but also bodies that are marked by more complex social, historical and cultural encoding and signification.

Schneemann and the Vienna Actionists' objectification of women's bodies is evidently differentiated because engendered sociocultural messages or scripts impact upon male and female consciousness in distinctly different ways. In our visual culture, women are habitually represented as submissive. This in its wake creates aversion on the part of women to this kind of reductive imagery where the female body becomes just a passive object which is acted upon. However, moving this argument into the debate provoked by Dita von Teese when she questioned why feminists still have a problem with submission, what happens if the female subject wants to become a willing object – willingly and defiantly submissive? What happens when she sacrifices her subjecthood to the voluptuous gaze of another? And what does it mean when we ourselves, as the viewers, feel submissive to the cruel mercy of this terrifying self-destruction?

In the Newton fashion photograph, *Sie Kommen*, the flesh sizzles like sausages. Each hair follicle extends its skin and fine down out towards the spectator, whose skin similarly has goose pimples. There is a surface etching where subjecthood stands proud.

It would be useful to discuss this surface expression of the subject in relation to Elizabeth Grosz's discussion of embodiment, which reconfigures notions of interiority – of agency, reflection and consciousness – as an open corporeal 'surface' inscription as opposed to a profound psychical depth.[32] A useful analogy used by Grosz is that of the etching process. This model, she argues, takes into account the tension between the surface and the marker, 'the specificities of the materials being thus inscribed and their concrete effects in the kind of text produced.'[33] The surface has a 'texture' and therefore its own 'resistance'. Describing this exchange primarily as an 'etching' process provides us with a more positive reading. It brings into play questions of reciprocity, negotiation and exchange – of 'give' and 'take', and 'pleasure' and 'pain' – but also highlights questions of power, control and sexual ethics. As Grosz suggests, this 'sexual ethics' needs to take account of this continual negotiation where differences remain intact but where 'some kind of an exchange is possible'.[34]

In Newton's piece there is an erotic sensuous exchange. We fall under these women's spell (being spellbound is the original meaning of glamour, the Scottish 'glamer', or glamorous) but we are also jolted into an awareness of their hold over us, and our hold over them: we are aware of this dialectic of control. This succinctly performs Merleau-Ponty's concept of 'flesh' as 'thinkable by itself', described by Elizabeth Grosz as 'the condition of seeing and being seen, of touching and being touched, and of their intermingling and possible integration, a commonness in which both subject and object participate, a single "thing" folded back on itself.'[35] The experience we feel when looking at *Sie Kommen* certainly relates to this idea of a single 'thing'. Grosz argues, though, that to conflate subject and object positions is to run the risk of losing all traces of ambivalence and paradox. There needs to be a join; the interaction between these two surfaces is not always harmonious and they should not be collapsed onto each other.[36]

What we experience when looking at Newton's image is indeed a collapse, a momentary collapse of subjecthood onto objecthood, a terrifying collapse of the subject onto their flesh. This is a sadomasochistic dialectic of power where monumental objectification both elevates and annihilates the subject. Bataille's poetical essays in *Visions of Excess* perhaps help us to articulate this deadly and alluring state. In 'Rotten Sun', Bataille uses the sun as a metaphorical symbol that is at once perfectly beautiful yet horribly ugly. The sun is at once two suns: when not looked at directly it becomes 'the most *elevated* conception', 'perfectly beautiful', but when 'scrutinized can be considered horribly ugly'. The sun inspires awe yet facilitates violence. In relation to this, Bataille also discusses the Mithraic cult of the sun where people would strip naked in a pit whilst a priest would slit the throat of a bull. The blood from the thrashing bull would douse the naked skin.

Horrified and pleasured at the warm blood from freshly slaughtered dying flesh, what is expressed here is the sacrificial blood of the subject as soma and psyche, self and other collapse onto one another. Fittingly, this is poetically expressed by Bataille in relation to the cock, 'whose horrible and particularly solar cry always approximates the screams of a slaughter',[37] where 'the summit of elevation is in practice confused with a sudden fall of unheard-of violence'. The experience is paradoxical and decadent where death and eroticism co-mingle. And it perhaps gives us a new understanding of the relationship between the skin of the subject and the flesh of the object – a different understanding of our contradictory self, where our erotic sensibility, awakening and consciousness as subjects violently emerges out of the powerful affective force of our visceral bodies as objects.

In her book *Contract with the Skin: Masochism, Performance Art and the 1970s* (1998),[38] Kathy O'Dell makes a very useful connection between the masochism used by performance artists such as Gina Pane, Marina Abramović and Chris Burden, and the tense era which saw America move out of the Vietnam war. These were performance artists who used pain and violence in their performance work either through slicing the body (Pane's *Action Psyche*, 1974), giving the audience licence to violate the body of the artist (Abramović's *Rhythm 0*, 1974) or being shot (Burden's *Shoot*, 1971). Their way of treating the body was time-specific. The artists, O'Dell argues, were etching onto the surface of their bodies a contractual agreement with their audience. The cutting, splicing and violation of the body became a renegotiation of boundaries and power. Masochism and wounding was a metaphor for their questioning of institutionalized control over bodies. O'Dell's observations are useful as these artists were operating quite clearly in relation to their historical and cultural situation and needs. As Moira Gatens also argues, 'it is clear that *how* we conceptualize the body forms and limits the meaning of the body in culture in various ways.'[39]

In relation to this, then, how is our conceptualization of female identity and representation limiting the meaning of the female body in our current culture? Jemima Stehli's reconstruction of Newton's *Sie Kommen* is important in relation to this question. How does the image work now, and why did this image move me? For me, the experience of looking at the Newton image became another contract through the skin: a contractual surrender to an erotic violent dissolution and renegotiation of knowledge and power. Stehli reconstructs this for a more contemporary audience in order to reflect on objectification in our visual culture. In the 1960s the Vienna Actionists and Carolee Schneemann were using their bodies in the context of their time to expose the violence that is incurred by splitting the subject from the body-as-object.

Today this violence is still apparent in imagery where women's bodies are pictured as commodities, as 'things' with all agency removed. However, what Stehli's work makes us question and reflect on is how the imagery we see around us limits the way in which our bodies are made meaningful. It prevents us from understanding our bearings in the world through our objecthood, and acts as an impediment to the erotic potential of our bodies as objects. Our visual sense of ourselves as objects is severely curtailed, not as objects where agency has been removed but where we surrender to our bodies as sensorially rich objects that can challenge and open up a wider experience of the world. On top of this, the limitation of our bodies as objects is twofold. Feminists have been pushed by untenable sexualized imagery to a point where it has become very difficult to see *any* positivity at all in objectification – and this makes me feel cautious, too, in my dealings with this subject.

There should rightly be caution and trepidation regarding any discussion of women's submission or surrender to objectification. The popularity in 2014 of the mainstream US singer (formerly children's TV star) Miley Cyrus, for instance, came from her submission to the media's need for her to bare everything, an inevitable car crash emblematic of a culture which expects and insists on constant sexual visual availability being women's only provocative contribution to the adult world. Not wanting to be seen as dull or a killjoy, sex becomes the way that women can image themselves as exciting, daring and popular, and thus commercial. This process makes women submissive to the capitalist desire for images of sexy, sex-crazed women, whilst simultaneously making them feel like there is a choice in the matter. This sort of imagery has become ineffective and ineffectual: it is dull – even deadly – submission.

In her book *Theorizing Desire* (2008) Kristyn Gorton argues through Emmanuel Ghent's work 'Masochism, submission and surrender: masochism as a perversion of surrender' (1990) that submission is different from the idea of surrender. 'Surrender', she argues, does not have to be negative. It can also be a positive means of attaining agency where women can feel 'met' or 'known' 'without having given expression themselves'.[40] This differentiation, I think, is important to my discussion and our contemporary context. Looking at 'surrender' as being actively passive, which I realize seems like an oxymoron, is however a useful way to describe the voluntary/involuntary desire to be led somewhere unknown. Related to this point, Laura U. Marks[41] refers to Leo Bersani's discussion of gay men's passivity in anal sex with his point that breaking boundaries of the body does not necessarily result in the destruction of the self.[42] Marks relates this to the haptic experience, and states that it 'may be transformative but need not be shattering'.[43] Marks' ideas, where one 'gently or "cruelly"' has the boundaries of the self broken down in order to surrender to 'new experiences',[44] are therefore highly relevant to my discussion.

*   *   *

The hyper-sexualized and pornified imagery that surrounds us does not (on the whole) affect us; we are not transformed or excited and we are not opened up to new experiences. This kind of imagery makes a spectacle out of a predictable sexual 'freedom'. This habitual 'explicit' sexualized imagery ironically performs something much more pedestrian and moves us away from extreme and explicit moments of affect, moments which have the potential to change, challenge and shake up the predictable. We need moments when we lose the self in order to reconfigure new ideas and feelings; erotic imagery should leave its trace. Helmut Newton's imagery in a contemporary context offers up something else. We yearn for imagery which takes us out of our comfort zone, and there is a need for this kind of exposure. We are crying out for affective images of our objecthood that make us tremble rather than wince: the kind of imagery that transforms the way we think, rather than telling us how we should feel.

6

The Sexual Body

SEX

The promotional video for Louis Vuitton's Autumn/Winter 2013 collection by Marc Jacobs entitled *Love*, directed by James Lima, sees models with slick bobs, silky undergarments and fur coats slinking up and down half-lit backstreets and talking furtively through rolled-down car windows. In one scene a model is seen inside a car, touching herself and exposing her desirable breasts. Cinematically this video is gorgeous. It is seductive and lush. The models are breathtakingly beautiful, their movements lithe, balletic and sexy; the lighting is subdued and ethereal, evocative of that liminal bewitching hour of intoxication and immorality before sunrise. This is 'prostitution chic', and has been heavily criticized for making prostitution sexy. But if fashion is a reflection of the moment in which it is situated, what does this say about sex, women and representation today? Rather than just discounting *Love* as misogynist and downgrading, could we look at it beyond that reading as an indicator of a different approach to sexual politics and the female body?

Life as a whore has historically been positioned at the opposite end of the political spectrum to life as a feminist. However, in the 1990s there was much political activism in terms of prostitutes' rights and the assertion and insertion of female pleasure and agency within the sexual and within the pornographic. High-profile popular 'postfeminists' such as Camille Paglia argued that they were pro-prostitution and pro-pornography.[1] A cultural overview of this historical point will therefore make an interesting starting point to this discussion on sex, the 'whore' and representation, and will help to deepen our understanding of what is happening now.

The 1990s was a decade that saw the 'low' moving into both the mainstream and high fashion and art. This was an era when pornography and sexual excess was to some degree commercialized, mainstreamed and trendy with the rise of pole dancing, a proliferation of strip clubs and magazines such as *Loaded, Maxim* and *FHM*. Pornography was more easily available at home, online and in newsagents at children's eye level alongside other, more mainstream newspapers. In the early 1990s Madonna's quite explicit coffee-table book *Sex* was published, and Jeff Koons' series of images *Made in Heaven* (1990–1) of himself and his soon-to-be wife, porn star/ politician La Cicciolina (Hungarian-born Ilona Staller) were produced, graphically showing both of them having sex and revealing their genitals for the camera.

Culturally, women were seen to be embracing the 'low' and their 'whore' status as sexual, trashy, lewd, loud, perverse, sassy, cheap and sexually more assertive. Embracing the world of 'porn' and sex work was to eschew any classification or hierarchy – women were questioning (and indeed pushing the boundaries of) acceptability in relation to the sexual. And this also affected the political sphere, with porn star La Cicciolina's campaigns for her Radical Party (1987–91) including striptease and memorably parading down an Italian street on the back of a float showing her breasts and pulling her buttocks apart whilst blowing kisses to the spectators. By the late 1990s artist Natasha Merritt's *Video Diaries* were expressive of this desire for self-validation and self-revelation by utilizing this porno-aesthetic to try to insert the sexual female subject into a market that was drowning in the two-dimensional pornographic.

Porn star/whore/artist/activist Annie Sprinkle's performance work in the 1990s was also reflective of the changes to feminist activism that were taking place at that time. Sprinkle made so much of a spectacle of herself that her performance moved beyond pure eroticism. In her act she openly invited the audience to manhandle her ('All forms of exploitation welcome') and let the audience know that they could bring their own camera. She inserted a speculum up her vagina and washed publicly in a douche. In her essay 'A provoking agent'

(1993) Linda Williams argued that Sprinkle's sexual performances were rooted within the conventions of pornography and the persona of the 'whore', and that she drew 'upon the performative traditions of the sexually saturated "woman", without simply duplicating them'.[2] As Williams argued, all the classifications – whore, feminist, artist, woman – pointed to crippling unwieldy systems of signification: '[I]f there is no subjectivity prior to discourse, if subjects are constructed in and by an already existing cultural field [...] what hope is there for that woman's ability to "act otherwise"'.[3]

However, Williams also argued that Sprinkle's 'sex-positive... spectacular orgasms'[4] gave the female body its resistant position within the already saturated realm of the sexual. We could perhaps argue, though, as Johannes Birringer does, that 'The Overexposed Body' (1991) had 'lost its privileged position' [...] 'its "resistance" to the repetitious Spectacle'.[5] Does the ability to make a spectacle of oneself still give women the space to resist and subvert this repetition? Sprinkle's determination to reveal female sexuality and corporeality beyond the two-dimensional image somehow gave her act more credence and more of an angry edge. As she stated: 'In a way I wanna say, "Fuck you guys – you wanna see pussy? I'll show you pussy!"'[6]

The ladette culture of the 1990s in a sense represented this momentum in sexual politics, where women dressed like women but behaved like men, giving the slick pornified culture a dressing-down. Thinking therefore about the 1990s, where porn was trendy and the political was expressed through the active sexual body, what has changed? How does today's loud, drunken, unruly sexuality of girls 'out on the town' differ from the ladette culture, for instance? Is there subversion and agency within this 'performance'? Are they sticking the finger up, or simply conforming to expectations? This was in the back of my mind when I went to give a paper at a conference, *Dressed Bodies*, in July 2013.[7]

After I had given my paper, a question was raised about the use of excessive femininity by burlesque performers: was it a form of drag? If so, did that same use of drag apply equally to the UK's Geordie girls 'out on the piss'? (This was the content of the paper that preceded mine, where the presenter had spoken about the brash inappropriate behaviour of groups of young women in Newcastle when out drinking together.)[8] I said in return that the loud and 'lairy' sorority of the Geordie girls was similar to burlesque performance because this bawdy hyper-sexualized femininity was also a form of 'drag'. However, I also replied that this behaviour was not in my opinion a critique of representation. It was not self-reflexive. Unlike the better forms of burlesque, it was not political. This seemed to cause a stir.

The term that I applied, lairy, is perhaps a useful adjective to propel this argument forward. The *Oxford Dictionary of English* defines it as an informal adjective meaning 'ostentatiously attractive and flashy'. This definition is helpful to this discussion as the girls are making a spectacle out of their inappropriate and excessive dress and behaviour, a spectacle which pertains to questions of performance, femininity and class. This is a display of loud and inappropriate 'sluttiness', which takes us back to the questions raised regarding Annie Sprinkle yet also makes me question who this show is for. If the 'ladette' was challenging gender expectations for her sex by being laddish yet feminine, how is the Geordie girl resisting through her hyper-feminized sexual display? Or is her lairiness just a need for validation?

There is a picture by the artist Alex McQuilkin entitled *Untitled (Will Fuck for Validation)* (2004). In this photograph the artist is looking out imploringly at the viewer with a tear-streaked face and dressed in a long blonde bobbed wig and a clingy low-cut white vest (one writer called it a 'wife-beater'[9]) with the words 'will fuck for validation' emblazoned in green glitter where the top stretches taut across her breasts. The manner in which she dresses creates stereotypes of femininity, a femininity which is enslaved by the men it seeks to win over. This is a femininity which entraps the female body within the visual. Her sexual persona has been created to please – woman as pathetically feminine, subservient, accessibly 'fuckable' and in need of substantiation through sex. As a woman, she is using her sexual body to gain attention, to get a drink, a man, a 'shag'. She is using her pornographic body and its rate of exchange, and is therefore at the mercy of what value (or lack of value) others ascribe to it. In this instance we see a woman who is whoring her body correctly at the behest of commodity capitalism and social, cultural and sexual mores. This is performativity as complicity.

However, this 'drag' is also a theatre of a commodified fantasy enacted on and through the female body. A woman's body is always a marked body. Perpetual media images which stress that women's social worth comes through their sexual power create harmful stereotypes. Caroline Lucas, Green MP for Brighton, stood up to speak in Parliament in June 2013 about her desire to combat media sexism, before taking off her jacket to reveal a T-shirt with the slogan 'NO MORE PAGE THREE' whilst holding a copy of *The Sun* with its image of a topless Page Three girl fully in view. When she was asked to put her jacket on, her comments were as follows:

> It strikes me as an irony that this T-shirt is regarded as an inappropriate thing to be wearing in this House, whereas, apparently, it is appropriate for this kind of newspaper to be available to buy in eight different outlets on the Palace of Westminster estate.[10]

In response Jim Hood, the Labour MP who was chairing the debate, stated: 'I am not commenting on what the member may wish to say in the debate. I am only addressing the appropriate means of dress.'[11]

It was not what she was saying, necessarily, but how she was resisting by way of dress, that was inappropriate. The visual spectacle, enacted through dress, would leave a resistant trace as theatre. The nakedness of the Page Three girls and their objectification was perhaps irrelevant here; what was interesting was how politics was being enacted through the theatre of the body. Disrobing inappropriately in such a formal, political context left a mark, a residual resistance which could not be easily forgotten – the message emblazoned across the female chest of a politicized female subject left an indelible mark as spectacle in excess of the political message. Much like the work *Untitled (Will Fuck for Validation)*, this theatre of excess was showing the show – in fact exceeding the show. And this was hard to forget. Stripping off had its place (which was the irony here: this paper was on sale at eight points throughout Westminster), and this was not one of them.

Comments in blogs following this episode described Caroline Lucas as 'immature' and a 'total twit' who had 'clearly lost the plot'.

The plot that had been lost was a dull debate. She was creating a memorable spectacle, using performance to conflate the spectacle of the body with the spectacle of the political subject. In doing this she was showing the trace of the subject in the commodified 'show'. She was clearly successful in demonstrating the power of imagery, with this form of dissent having a rich history which can be tracked back to the early demonstrations by women's suffrage activists. In the early women's rights parades, the politics of the subject was being played out through the creative flamboyance of the artistic banners, the immediacy of the slogans, playfulness and fun. This fusion of art, theatre, spectacle, dress, feminized modes of address and body politics allowed women to be both political and social agents as part of a self-constructed cultural spectacle.

Women who were active within the first wave of feminism quickly realized the important connection between representation and politics. By controlling their public image, positively performing their identity as female agents, they could challenge misrepresentations and stereotypes that had been perpetuated by institutions and had deeply scarred the cultural, social, economic and political arena. By appearing en masse on the streets with decorative and eye-catching banners and bright exuberant dress, women were creating a spectacle of themselves and intervening purposefully, reflectively and self-consciously in the process of identifying who they were individually, collectively and politically. Most of all, witnessing this display – this spectacle of female agency – would have helped towards de-stigmatizing these women.

Similar to the spectacle of activism performed by the early suffrage campaigners or the MP Caroline Lucas, there is another interesting conflation of the political subject onto the spectacle of the pornographic body in the short film 'Impaled'. This is directed by Larry Clark and is one of the films from *Destricted* (2006), a compilation of short films on the subject of the erotic. 'Impaled' is a humorous critique and exposé that brings the awkwardness and imperfections of the human into the pornographic. It operates in excess of 'the show' and shows the trace of the subjects. In this film, a young man comes to a casting for a porno film thinking that his luck is in. He is able to try out several women to see which one he would like to make the film with. He selects the 40-year-old as he has never experienced sex with an experienced older woman and wants to seize this opportunity. When the 'filming' begins, the lighting is unflattering, the setting and atmosphere stark and public; it is awkward, uncomfortable, unedited and gauche. The young man is asked questions by the director, which robs the moment of any titillation. As the title has it, the young man is really 'impaled' on his own penis.

This is different, though, to the imperfections and awkwardness in the soft-porn images by the doyen of high fashion, photographer Terry Richardson. When I recently flicked through an issue of cutting-edge fashion magazine *Purple*,[12] I noted that Richardson's images take more of an unedited 'Readers' Wives' approach to soft porn. The photographs in this edition are of models and actresses shown 'before they were famous'. The images act like a 'natural', albeit naked, exposé. The 'pussy' being shown here is indeed more 'low', an unabashedly 'natural' interpretation or revelation of the nude, yet the 'natural' feels intrusive, revelatory, exposing, and as such exploitative. This is voyeuristic imagery – perhaps, as Rick Poyner states, a critique on the 'slickly marketed and spiritually inert world of mass market pseudo-porn.'[13] Like Page Three, however, this imagery seems to have lost its context.[14] Much like the other pornified images in the mainstream – such as Jennifer Lopez, her legs spread-eagled with her barely covered vulva shoved into the camera during the family show *Britain's Got Talent* in 2013 – this imagery has outgrown its use. It is politically and visually out-of-date and defunct.

In terms of activism, the desire to theorize resistance through the body has moved from an assertion of the essential sacredness of the body in the 1970s, to the AIDS-driven and feminist politics of the body as battlefield in the 1980s through to the sexualized excesses, perversions and pleasures of the body in the 1990s. In this current decade – the 2010s – there seems now to be a play on the politics of resistance through the spectacle of the feminized object, finding agency by way of dress, fantasy and play. In the Vuitton fashion video, *Love*, we see that the complicit commodified image of the feminized object is interrupted by the fantastical, the playful and the haptic imaginings and sensations of the female models. The film flickers between the prostitute fantasy and 'real' life behind the scenes of the fashion show, which is in black and white before the models come out of doors, set along the catwalk, followed finally by Marc Jacobs in his pyjamas. Modelling in this instance is seen as a form of prostitution: prostituting the use of one's body to sell clothing.

There is therefore an ongoing fascination with the dialectical image of the 'whore'. Rebecca Schneider comments that the prostitute has held this fascination because of her capacity to be 'commodity and seller' in one. Her reference to Susan Buck-Morss' interpretations of the whore as metaphor in line with Marx is useful to quote:

> The image of the whore reveals the secret of their own social product [...] Whereas every trace of the wage labourer who produced the commodity is extinguished when it is torn out of context by its exhibition on display, in the prostitute, both moments remain visible.[15]

Woman's commodified body as image is used to sell almost everything. Her sex appeal becomes the rate of exchange and thus her inferred value. By stealing into representation by way of the whore metaphor, women can infer another meaning, a trace of an exchange, which is usually secreted out of the glib, stereotypical and quite damaging economic and cultural transactions. In these transactions, where goods are bought on the inferred suggestion of a sexual promise, the trace of the subject is extinguished out of the process.

Love makes visible the trace of woman, her creativity, pleasure, play and desire: her sensual relationship with the object. The sexual client in *Love* is the clothes; paying for the sexual service which comes with one's relationship with the fabrics, the cut, the sensual field; whoring oneself to the objects in order to feel and look drop-dead gorgeous. In this film the women are falling in love with their own pleasures and their own desirability. The image of the whore as feminized object represents woman's need for both validation and agency. This undoubtedly shows complicity with the process of com-modification and the media's spectacle. Yet in this gorgeous visual pleasure the cinematic goosebumps leave a trace which resonates in excess of this drama of submission[16], a residual trace which cannot be fully appropriated and therefore acts as a form of resistance.

MASTURBATION

The front cover of the catalogue for Tracey Emin's first major retrospective pictures her backside as she runs naked down a street holding a Union Jack flag. Indeed, this audacious nakedness meets us as we arrive at the Haywood Gallery, with the image printed large-scale on fabric, flapping carelessly and daringly in the wind. This huge, in-your-face image brought a smile to my face as I arrived to see this exhibition one rainy grey day in May 2011. What made me smile was the exhilarating freedom I felt vicariously at witnessing Emin running down the street stark bollock-naked.

Inside the exhibition are various images of Emin naked, alone and masturbating.

In her review in the *Observer*, Laura Cumming discusses Emin's 'dainty-dirty'[17] approach to sex and self-representation. In *Sometimes I Feel Beautiful*, a C–type photograph, we see a life-size image of Emin lying naked in the bath, her head reclined, reminding us of the Degas images of sinuous women bathing. In these images we catch a glimpse of these naked women as they luxuriate in warm water, their hair floating loosely in the water as it laps at them gently. These images are of course paintings of women undertaken by a male painter: private moments painted for a public forum. Yet the images created by Emin are purposefully and self-consciously controlled in their intention to 'go public' with activities that usually go on behind locked doors.

Why indeed, though, would you want to go public with activities which are meant to be private and personal? The out-of-place awkwardness in sharing this solitary act, where pleasure becomes 'dirty' when made public, is best illustrated by the British sitcom *Gavin and Stacey* when a brash female character strides through a busy kitchen, saying 'Excuse me', and then proceeds to wash her middle finger under the tap. This taboo is filled with humour, yet still feels shocking. Rather than using humour, however, Emin's pleasure is tinged with negative feeling and angst where sexual pleasure is fused with guilt and wrongdoing. Masturbation is something that is undertaken as a kind of punishment – masturbating to make the pain and self-hatred go away. It seems, as Sally O'Reilly argued, that Emin's 'melodramatic pitch'[18] risks 'perpetuating the damaging stereotype of the hysterical woman.'[19] Her large-scale quilts on which she has scribbled about the early beginnings of this masturbatory self-pleasure/self-hatred aged eight add to the overarching sense of obsessive guilt, anger and misdirected desire.

However, like the painter Marlene Dumas, who also deals with the taboos of female sexuality, Emin's 'dainty-dirty' work opens up much room for discussion regarding pleasure, creativity and desire beyond 'the phallocentric gaze'. Dumas has said: 'I paint because I'm a dirty woman.'[20] She has a reluctance to focus on intercourse itself and instead explores female exhibitionism, nudity and masturbation. The work is about her own 'perversions', as woman as a self-pleasuring agent is still publicly taboo, still 'slutty', still 'dirty'. She keeps her work 'dirty' in the sense that painting is messy and to clean it up would be to remove the physical, the bodily, the messy, from the process. To clean it up and make it more clinical would be to separate the doing (the process of goo and visceral mess) from the doer. In her painting, the agency inherent in gesture is embodied.

In his article on Dumas in *Flash Art* (2009), entitled 'Yes we can', Rainald Schumacher discusses Dumas's paintings in relation to the frightening and incessant amount of pornographic imagery that surrounds us. 'Shouldn't somebody try to make something positive out of it?'[21] He argues that Dumas's paintings do indeed make something positive out of this plethora of negative imagery:

> Her paintings leave the pornographic dead-end street behind, which only leads from one perversion – which becomes mainstream – to the next one, and, instead of depicting everything in the deadness of painstaking precision the paintings reinvest sexually explicit imagery with an element of secrecy and promise. They return to the field of eroticism and desire.[22]

In works such as *Exposure* (1999), *Fingers* (1999) and *High Heel Shoes* (2000) there is another way of representing the meaning and pleasure of the female sexual body beyond phallocentric control and mastery. As Adrian Searle comments: 'The women in her paintings, for all their pouts and bedroom glances (some of which are very fierce), are painted with a kind of intimacy, which, paradoxically, reclaims their independence and their dignity.'[23]

In Emin's collection *One Thousand Drawings*, made up of pictures drawn from the late 1980s to the late noughties, we see many images of the female sexual body – its pleasures as well as its pain – created in Emin's scrawling free style. Yet I feel that her animated drawing of naked masturbation with its jerky movement and scratchiness and stiletto shoes moves us perhaps in a less 'hysterical' direction than her other angst-ridden self-hating imagery and text. This animated drawing of a woman in stilettoes masturbating fervently expresses, like Dumas's work, something more positive. In the act of drawing and animation, and indeed masturbation, we have the idea of gesture. This is gesture which is expressing the subject through the language of drawing, but also gesture which is an expression of the erotic and gendered subject through the language of the moving body. Like Dumas, Emin is making us aware of the fact that seeing does not take place through the eyes; it also happens, as Laura U. Marks argues, through the skin: it is haptic.

The senses are interlinked with vision, with how we perceive the world and how we feel that we are perceived. Susanna Paasonen, in her book *Carnal Resonance* (2011), discusses the way in which sensation and perception are profoundly fused together. When we are affected by what we see – when we feel shame, or pleasure, or anger, or excitement – the body seems to go 'its own way' and flush, tingle, burn, tense up or shiver: this is the internal body mixing with images of external bodies. She argues that this is because we have an internal bank of images and sensations, of memories and imprints which she calls 'somatic archives or reservoirs'.[24] When we experience something we are moved in a particular way because of how our reservoir is formed, which also determines how we react to the world and how it impacts on us. The way we react to experience therefore is always changing as our 'reservoir' is always recalibrating.

Nonetheless, how men and women 'bank' these images, sensations and memories is culturally differentiated, for our subjective positions

differ in the way we perceive ourselves as gendered. Emin's jerky
masturbating animation is in a sense therefore performing and defin-
ing the territory of these culturally defined limits of the sexual and
gendered female body. This could be why heels figure in so many of
Emin's naked erotic drawings, photographs, films and paintings. They
are a cultural 'given' in terms of 'femininity' and 'sexuality'. Is she
mediating her subjectivity in relation to this to define and imagine her
own territory? There is an evident need to retain the heels to somehow
eroticize the female body and to assist and procure self-pleasuring.
Do the heels act as wilful perversion? Do they give us the 'dirty' in
the 'dainty'? What does this image say about female sexuality, femininity and female subjectivity or intersubjectivity beyond any easy
interpretation regarding pleasure and the male gaze?

In her seminal essay 'Objectifying gender', Lee Wright argues
that the stiletto heel is an object which is 'seen as being exclusively
female'.[25] In fact she contends that this exclusivity has been in place
since the nineteenth century, when it was discontinued as part of
men's dress code. But it was the role of stiletto heels for women in
the 1950s that is the most pertinent element of Wright's argument.
She refers to their liberating role at a time when women were looking for a means of expression outside of the domestic. As opposed
to the retrospective feminist interpretation inferred on the stiletto
as an object of entrapment and subordination, it in fact acted as a
symbol of glamour, independence and collective defiance against
traditional roles. This was therefore a 'defiant gesture'[26] expressed
through style. It was undertaken by a younger generation of women
intent on expressing their newfound economic freedoms through a
more 'liberated femininity'.[27]

The key to this defiance was therefore to express a rejection of the
roles inhabited by their mothers through style. Wright discusses the
'winkle-picker' shoe as an example of this rebellion against convention, and this chimes with my own experiences of teenage rebellion
in the 1980s. Wearing the 'winkle-picker' was similarly a 'defiant
gesture' interlinked with the first sexual adventures of puberty and
adolescence and worn defiantly in spite of all the images shown in
biology lessons of 'winkle-picker'-deformed feet that seemed to echo
the deformity of Chinese foot-binding. As Wright succinctly argues,

the stiletto represented a desire to embody a new modern female image which enveloped the vibrancy and desires of the 'now'. In relation to my 1980s example, for teenage girls this style represented a rejection of authority, conservatism and being sensible, and flirted with danger, with the irresponsible and the 'bad'.

As Wright argues, stilettoes were firmly established by the 1950s as part of 'woman's culture'.[28] This was a means by which younger women could mediate their individual and collective identities in relation to both their predecessors and one another. Even though stilettoes were seen for instance as 'shackling' – both in terms of stereotypes and in terms of ill-health – they were still appropriated as liberating objects. In fact it was by virtue of their very 'badness' that they represented such an exquisite symbol for rebellion. Bearing this in mind, though, what does it then mean to image oneself masturbating in heels?

I began my last book, *The Happy Stripper*, narrating my experience of watching the artist Ursula Martinez strip. This performance clearly left its mark on me. But what I did not question at that point is why, even when completely naked, she kept her stilettoes on. She was never fully naked, and I would argue that if she had slipped off the stilettoes on stage she would have felt much more vulnerable. Stilettos likewise adorn Tracey Emin's feet in drawings of her masturbating frantically, or photographs of her luxuriating in baths. In the photograph I mentioned earlier, *Sometimes I Feel Beautiful*, where Emin is lying naked in the bath with her eyes closed, we feel the hot steaming water sending a shiver up our spine as she reclines, relaxes and daydreams. In this image, her feet dangle outside of the bath to display her stilettoes, erotic stimulants for sexual pleasure as one imagines and feels oneself as beautiful.

If heels act as emblems of erotic femininity, as Valerie Steele asserts in her essay in *High Heels* (2011), then it would be useful to contrast these with emblems of erotic masculinity displayed in Sam Taylor-Wood's short film of a young man masturbating in the open against an epic 'Wild West' backdrop. It is interesting to see how pleasurable subjective positions are formed in relation to these gendered objects. In *Death Valley* (2006) the 'cowboy' drives his truck into the open expanse in order to drop his jeans around his ankles and masturbate hard until he climaxes. This is an epic masculinity projected quite literally onto a wild arid landscape, displaced onto the wild untamed expanse of American wilderness and other signifiers of 'manliness' such as a cowboy hat, jeans and a truck. This is a gesture which is confident and assured – he is literally 'cock sure', without shame, which is part of the daring appeal of this film.

In contrast to this lack of containment, Emin's masturbation animation utilizes the intimate private language of the bedroom. It is a contained, scaled-down gesture: on a bed, in a house, within enclosed walls. It is also drawn and animated, so therefore removed once again from the actual act. The male masturbation scene is of course acted out, but it is reproduced in glorious technicoloured detail. It is an exhilarating, audacious performance of the physical male body and the visual taboo of an erect ejaculating penis. In this gesture, an erotic masculinity is played out against and through surrounding motifs. This relates to the gestural painting of the Abstract Expressionists in terms of a masculine 'mastery' of the object, a mastery which combines gesture with trace. Hilary Robinson argues that the paintings created by such 'masters' were seen to represent 'a metonymic trace of the artist'.[29] Their subjective trace, the 'I am' was displaced onto the object, the painting, through gesture.

According to Luce Irigaray, boys and girls differ in the way that they map out and express their subjective territory through gesture: 'Girls describe a space around themselves rather than displacing a substitute object from one place to another or into various places. They enter language by producing a path, a river, a dance and rhythm, a song'.[30] Irigaray describes the manner in which young girls dance, spinning and whirling around and around in a circle as an example of how girls define their own territory, their own subjectivity away from their mother. The performance allows the girl to express an 'I', an 'I am' as a girl, and define a territory of her own to both protect, describe and differentiate her sense of self from that of her mother.

Like the little girl who comes into language by swirling and spinning to create her boundaries and understand her limits, the drawing of frantic self-pleasuring is the negotiation through the body of a more liberated femininity. This is a process of performativity, of becoming, of mediating a subjective and collective positioning/territory in relation to gendered objects and through the sexual pleasures of the body. Differing from my example of the male sexual body in *Death Valley*, where 'erotic masculinity' is displaced onto objects through distance and through mastery, in the animated drawing erotic femininity is described and re-inscribed by a process of incorporation and reinvention through the sexual female body. This is a process that is enfleshed and opens up possibilities for intersubjectivity.

An interesting point made by Irigaray is that the territory created by young girls is 'defensive' but 'can then become creative'.[31] The animated drawing of masturbation leaves a different sort of trace on the viewer. This represents a collective trace of erotic femininity and the sexual female body as socially and culturally inscribed. Yet the drawing creates and reimagines more positive configurations for pleasure and creativity which are liberating, audacious and defiant. A drawn woman, in a drawn room, on a drawn bed...any woman's bed, any woman's room, any woman's imagination. This acts as a trigger for my memory of a young woman in London one day:

> Her shoes were glittering, staggeringly high. The sheer exuberance of those shoes made me notice her. I tried to catch a glimpse of her in the crowd as she disappeared eventually out of view. A positive encounter. Drawing boundaries and borders – imagining what female identity might constitute now. Imagining one's own identity. Marking the body and adding positive experiences of the body to the archive. Shifts our perception of our bodies...bodies relating to other bodies... territory...

In the translator's foreword to Deleuze and Guattari's *A Thousand Plateaus*, Brian Massumi discusses his use of the term 'to draw'.[32] He states that the English term is an insufficient translation of the French verb 'tracer', which means both 'to draw' in the graphic sense and also 'to blaze a trail' or 'open a road'. This embellishment of 'drawing' in light of the French verb can help to explain the process of marking, of opening up new territories and new possibilities for subjectivity: a collaborative sense of drawing the unknown, of drawing new ways of seeing, thinking and representing.

When I went to see Ursula Martinez stripping right down to her stilettoes, the physical immediacy of a slim, stripping, smiling spectacle destabilized clichés, and this feeling of destabilization continued to resonate long after the striptease had finished. Likewise in Emin's drawings a line is being drawn between the explicit and the audacious, which again destabilizes clichés and stereotypes. The Emin animation fuses self-pleasuring gesture and creativity with clichéd symbols of 'erotic femininity'. The wilful, shameless celebration of masturbation as art, in an art gallery, made me smile, as did the audacity of perverting a clichéd symbol of 'oppression' into something pleasurable and creative. The trace that is left behind for the viewer becomes an unofficial confrontation with mainstream 'perversions', replacing the incessantly pornographic with unofficial 'perversions', 'dirtiness', imagination and orgasms. This is a revision and revitalization of woman's culture and experience, taking ownership of the body; it is a collective, variant 'I am'.

Like the Dumas image of exhibitionism, masturbation and high heels, Emin's drawings are erotic images that leave a different trace on the viewer and register on our bodies as positive. We enjoy looking at these images. The animation is uplifting...it makes us smile. It is shocking because it is different to other images that we usually see. This experience shifts and reconstitutes our somatic archive; it reconfigures 'femininity'. This is not self-wounding or passive. The stilettoes in this piece speak the 'now' to other women who perhaps think similarly and can empathize through the body with that liberating spirit. This is a defiant gesture that leaves an intersubjective trace. Rosi Braidotti would describe this as a process of affirmative becoming. It is the force of positive enfleshed memory, of repeating 'beyond negativity'.[33] It is a yearning for a better future that changes the flow of negativity and the possibility of openness, promise and reinvention.

Remembering the daring audacity and exuberance of a young woman in London one day...

Part IV

A Rebellion of the Senses

7

Pleasure, Violence
and the Sensual Spectacle

CRUMBLING BATH BOMBS AND FLAKING NAIL VARNISH

Karla Black's artwork for the 2011 UK Turner Prize, which was held in the Baltic Centre for Contemporary Art in Gateshead, was made from a distinctly 'girly' palette of eyeshadow, lip gloss, nail varnish and powder-pink pigment. Black creates sculpture with painterly attention to colour, form and perspective: her work is all about materiality and aesthetics. On entering her installation, we are met by the sickly sweet smell of bath bombs and see foundation creams or lipsticks smeared on surfaces. This is about smell, touch and visual delights. We are encouraged to go under the cellophane-like fabric, which is cast about our heads and hangs down over us, den-like. Small children, unaware or unconscious of art gallery protocol, rush behind and between the installation materials, pulling on adult hands. The adults hang back, unsure and awkward at first as to whether they should (or can) immerse themselves in this cocoon.

It is this idea of 'physical engulfment'[1] that Black herself discusses in the video that I watch in the café as I mull over my own experience of her artwork. It is the materiality of the work which is important – the desire to make you, the spectator, feel the physicality of the work and its sensual properties – and your relationship with this material world. This multisensory experience reflects an interest over the last few years in the sensual and the interactive in art, as illustrated by other blockbuster exhibitions that followed in its wake, including Yayoi Kusama's *Obliteration Room* (2012)[2] at the Tate Modern, *Rain*

Room[3] at the Barbican (2012–13), and *Light Show*[4] at the Hayward Gallery (2013), which was described by the *Observer* as: 'A pleasure trip for all'.[5] The 'live' experience of being part of these installations is what this kind of art is all about. The experience and the trace that is left behind on the participant *is* the artwork, whether that be the physical experience of being part of the material world, the playful experience of affixing stickers to bare walls or the surreal experience of being in a rainstorm but not getting wet.

This is a different experience of aesthetics – aesthetics which is finished off by the spectator/participant. It is about feeling a bodily connection with other people in these rooms that makes us feel inquisitive, excited, playful, exhilarated, awestruck, anxious or simply frustrated. The final sentence of Katharine Welsh's essay in the Turner Prize 2011 catalogue is that Karla Black's work 'is "almost" beautiful.'[6] It is this idea of the work being '"almost" beautiful' which is so endearing and fascinating. This is a work that is uncomfortably unfinished, and we as spectators do indeed feel an element of frustration when looking at Black's exhibition, where paint does not cling completely to the surface and breaks up, when we feel unsure as to whether to enter or to observe, or when we see bits and bobs scattered on surfaces in a seemingly haphazard higgledy-piggledy fashion. It is this unpredictable and unstable factor in Black's work that is compelling.

In the cultural arena at large, we are accustomed to seeing artwork and imagery that is finished off, Photoshop picture-perfect, beautiful. Why, though, has aesthetics just become about beauty and the sublime? Ben Highmore asks this pointed question in his writing on affect and aesthetics, where he argues that aesthetics is about a synaesthetic experience when our senses interlink and correlate; it is about their 'utter entanglements'.[7] Aesthetics deals with how we are affected as sensual beings by the material world around us, 'how the world strikes the body on its sensory surfaces, of that which takes root in the gaze and the guts and all that arises from our most banal, biological insertion in the world.'[8] Traditionally art has fixated on aestheticizing beauty and has bypassed all the other elements which make up most of our everyday lives. Most affects such as boredom, irritation, hope, weariness, contentment and trepidation are not included. Aesthetics has in the main, therefore, failed to register the holistic intensity of our sensual life. It has ignored what it believes is insignificant and un-noteworthy, the not-quite-beautiful, the unfinished.

Our quotidian dealings with the world therefore go un-narrated. And it is this kind of aesthetics – the narration of our more unstable relationship to the world – that Karla Black's work represents. Once we enter her installation we smell sweet sickly fragrances, we see the textures and goo which evoke the sensual everyday of our visual experience, the out of place, even awkward, private relationship with the materiality of our everyday. What is particular to Karla Black's installation is that it narrates familiar snippets of narrative, the aesthetics of what is seen as a very female or 'feminine' experience, which makes us think of foundation cream smeared on a mirror or a bathroom cabinet doorknob, or the leftover slimy residue of soap on the edge of the bath or soap dish. The questions that arise from Black's work, that differentiate it from the other multisensory block-busters that I referred to earlier, stem from its more acutely gendered evocation of materiality.

The installation engages us by way of materials that are situated in many women's physical everyday experience, such as bath time 'smellies', foundation creams, make-up, baby oils and petroleum jelly. And it is impossible to isolate these 'objects' from their female-orientated position in the ordinary everyday world of many (although of course not all) women. The materials that we encounter in Black's work are the residue and traces of conventional daily paraphernalia which link femaleness to beauty. Her sculptures are evocative of a 'feminized' aesthetic entanglement with the material world and its cultural ideas of beautifying and cleanliness. They capture the visual idea of bath bombs disintegrating and dissolving on the edge of the bathtub, the dusting of powder footprints on bathroom tiles, or the residue of deodorant in the air. What we have in this installation is the visceral trace left behind in the intermingling of body and material.

Ben Highmore argues that: 'Much of what constitutes the day-to-day is irresolvable and desperately incomplete, yet, for all that, also most vital.'[9] What this means in effect is that the imagery we see around us becomes unsatisfying, for it avoids and finishes off sentences which hold more potential when unfinished. Fragments leave an element of open possibility. They give us a partial glimpse of physical interaction and are suggestive of transition and transformation. The finished 'look', the perfected image, the made-up beauty does not deal with the broader spectrum of feelings and sensations which fold into this finished body. It offers up a very limited, narrowly edited aesthetics of beauty. It is the 'ugliness' of the body as process – with all of its sensations, perceptions, feelings and physical awareness – that tells us much about its material being in the world.

Black states that part of the process in her work is that she damages the objects and then allows this to become part of the installation's character when she works them back into the materials. The fragility of the materials, their transitory and decaying qualities, the crumbling bath bombs or flaking nail varnish, all become part of the aesthetic and painterly quality of the sculpture. These are restless, dissatisfied, crumbling, dissolving 'almost objects'.[10] They are visual snubs and residues of ephemerality, temporality and the unfinished. These 'almost objects' are in a state of unresolved messy anti-form between states. The gels that never set, the paint that does not fully stick but sits in broken up striations, and the bath bombs that form in-between shapes are all in a 'suspended state of being'.[11] They all hold the potential for transformation as they are in an indefinable state that is unresolved. Beauty that is finished, complete and stable is an aesthetics cut off from our broader aesthetic dimension of being – the banal, the routine, the boring, the biological: the durational experience of the body as it continually responds to its physical environment.

Karla Black speaks about sculpture as 'real and really here',[12] as opposed to painting, which historically is a form that represents something else within its frame. Sculpture is about its own material form. It speaks of itself. Painting is a form that traces another form in order to aestheticize it into something pleasing. For Black, therefore, the materiality of the sculpture is its aesthetics. For me, her sculptures take their form in the transitory point linking materiality and representation. They are both painting *and* sculpture. They are suggestive of both presence and absence: of dropping a bath bomb into warm water and then fishing it out again as a fizzing shape left to sizzle on the edge until it finds another shapeless form. The crumbling bath bomb therefore becomes that encounter as trace and residue, and is suggestive of the interlocking sensations and perceptions that make up that interaction. In that process it contains the entanglement of affects and sensations and thoughts: of feeling restful and content, of feeling warm scented bubbles and water on naked flesh, of relaxation, of perhaps sadness, insufficiency and worries; the quirks and complications of human emotion.

The sensations suggested in Black's sculpture are therefore situated between 'fabric and feeling', between the literal and the metaphysical: when, for instance, feeling battered and bruised, we are soothed by a bath into which we melt and dissolve. Ben Highmore argues that: 'The words designating affective experience sit awkwardly on the borders of the material and the immaterial, the physical and the metaphysical: we are moved by a sentiment; our feelings are hurt; I am touched by your presence.'[13] Similarly Katherine Welsh argues that to write about Black's work is to keenly evoke 'tensions and apparent contradictions between form and anti-form, materiality and immateriality, mass and weightlessness.'[14] This in-between-ness and tension can therefore be better understood in relation to Highmore's discussion on aesthetics and affect and the awkward borders between the body and the experience.

Many feelings that we have are described metaphorically: feelings of warmth, being cut deeply, bruising your ego, making your heart flutter. Yet these metaphors illustrate a very real material physical actuality, and a dialogue that cuts across various affective registers. The feelings and sensations that we experience in our interactions with the material world are perhaps invisible or barely perceptible yet are registered intuitively in the body as real: skin crawling, a shiver of pleasure, shame which makes us cringe, or disgust which makes our bodies recoil. In this experience the metaphorical skims the surface of the real. This is sensation felt in the body as a process of being which aesthetics attempts to capture as trace. Aesthetics therefore is an attempt to represent that poetical erosion between the literal and the metaphorical.

A relevant aside to these ideas relates to the film *Smoke* (1995), directed by Wayne Wang and written by Paul Auster, where the metaphor of smoke is used to evoke narrative from a different perspective.

In this film the protagonist, played by Harvey Keitel, is a Brooklyn tobacconist. His shop is the hub of the smoking community, a place where customers gather to have a smoke and pass comment. At the same time every day Keitel, the proprietor, comes out of the store with his tripod and camera. When he sets up his equipment in exactly the same spot, at exactly the same time every day, and takes a photograph, there is a different flow of narrative taking place. This I found (and still find) compelling. After he takes his daily photograph he returns to his shop to smoke and 'shoot the breeze' with his customers.

This is what C. Nadia Seremetakis would describe as a moment of '*stillness*': a moment when we stop, when time metaphorically slows down for us and we step out of the customary quotidian flow of the present into a different passage of time. She describes this in relation to a coffee break that she used to witness an old Greek man taking every day, when he would break from his normal duties and chores to sip his coffee and chat. Condensed in that coffee cup was the momentary freedom for his mind to roam. For Seremetakis, the smell, taste and ritual of coffee acts as a spur to the 'now' of one's unregulated ruminations. This kind of moment, she argues, is a 'meta-narrative' or an 'alternative perceptual landscape'. It is, she states, 'a moment of poetry'.[15]

This is the potency, poetry and politics of films such as *Smoke*: the heralding of the ordinary, the un-noteworthy, the un-narrated. C. Nadia Seremetakis discusses this sense of the unmarked and unattended, the buried and the discarded, as '*dust*'. To move from *dust* to *stillness* is to momentarily reflect on what has been annulled, whitewashed or made to seem irrelevant. In the cut and thrust of work, money, rushing around and formal structure, moments like these are paramount. In these unstructured, informal, un-narrated moments behind closed doors, in askance glances, loosened tongues, quiet autumn parks, 'chewing the cud', there is a quiet subversion happening. Senses are awakened by colour, smell, humour, alcohol, caffeine or intimacy. It is an unmonitored erosion of authority. Intriguingly she describes this as 'a politics of the senses'.[16]

Karla Black also creates this 'moment of poetry,' the trace of the 'now' in her work, which operates in a similar way to the metaphor of smoke. 'Smoke', though, is a metaphor for male companionship, the pleasure of laughter, friendship, community, sharing, intimacy, finding commonality and contentedness. Smoke represents that moment when we inhale and suffuse our body with emotions and thoughts. And in the activity of inhalation and exhalation the smoke disappears and reappears. It captures and represents the emotions, sensations and perception of the memory of a moment as it impacts on the body. Black's work is more about the not quite beautiful, the unfinished, the sensual affective messy matter of a being-in-process: the biological, the banal and the boring; the rituals, the routine of concealer, of lipstick, of powder, of moisturizer, of shampoo, of soap. This is the residue of the repetitive, the routine and the banal as materiality. It is transformation as unfinished process.

Representation in Black's work is not mimetic. How do we make tangible as aesthetics something we feel and remember through the skin? Representation is different. In *Matter and Memory*, Henri Bergson discusses two kinds of memory that could be summarized as repetition and representation. Repetition is more formulaic in that one acts out the past in the form of a learned habit or 'lesson', like reading or reciting a poem:

> At each repetition there is progress; the words are more and more linked together, and at last makes a continuous whole. When that moment comes, it is said that I know my lesson by heart, that it is imprinted on my memory.[17]

With representation we create a picture which is a composite of thoughts, emotions, experiences and fragments. However, as Bergson comments: 'To *picture* is not to *remember*'.[18] Both *Smoke* and Black's work *picture* through a material sensation of an elusive trace.

Black's sculptures, however, represent the gendered trace of picturing women's bodies, for bodies are culturally affected. We struggle or play with cultural expectations. Our affective experience relates to how we see and feel in relation to these expectations, which are the learned repetition of beauty, appearance, presentation and image. How we feel, or look, or think, perhaps counters how we should feel, or should look, or should think. A meta-narrative therefore similarly builds up, or crumbles away around 'beauty' objects, which represent an intimate fragile relationship with our material world and how it impacts on us. Seremetakis argues in *The Senses Still* that: 'Re-perception is the creation of meaning through the interplay, witnessing, and cross-metaphorization of co-implicated sensory spheres.'[19] And indeed Black's installation of objects evokes a layered response to beauty and objects.

The various affective sensations that cross over and co-implicate bodies with objects are configured by way of metaphors of dissolving, crumbling, suffusing, breaking up, diffusion, evaporation and dissipation. These nearly- (or anti-) objects – these no longer perfect, changed, damaged, creased or crumpled objects – represent perhaps the durational rather than static and still experience of bodies. This is a politics of the senses, an aesthetic of the not quite beautiful of almost objects. In this gendering of trace there is a meta-narrative which runs counter to a regulated sense of 'beauty', of wholeness, of perfection, which is condensed in these almost objects. Instead we experience creases of activity, dirt, grime and pink scum circling the inside of the bath, left to wash away the day... the heavy sigh of feeling content, or feeling less than perfect. These are sensations of our private unregulated life, or perhaps the residue of a life and body that is claustrophobically regulated.

Karla Black's painterly sculptures work at the level of the body and the emotions. It is how we feel in relation to how we should feel that is represented by way of crumbling bath bombs, smears of lipstick, smudges of concealer or powdered messy footprints. These objects are seemingly large and loom over our heads, fragile, screwed up and barely painted, or lie beneath our feet, crumpled and creased, far from noteworthy, strangely banal. The narrative that we feel as we walk through Black's installation comes from an aesthetic which creates a tension between the surface and the senses: a large hanging of cellophane which gives a rustle of significance, a just perceptible dusting of a surface, a scribble that barely holds, a cloud of smoke that blows away. What this opens up is our complex subtle relationship with gendered objects. This is ephemera, which in transition gives way to a metaphorical poetical narrative of the body as it connects and collides with its material world.

TOXIC FLOWERS AND BARBED FLESH

I was first captivated by Sigalit Landau's *Barbed Hula* (2000) at an exhibition about performance and body art in Berlin. In this video we see a lithe, naked female torso being pierced with barbed wire as a hula hoop is rotated rhythmically around the young woman's waist. The woman stands on a beach. There is a calm idyllic seascape in the background; the waves lap at the shore. This fusion of visual pleasure and violence is similar in tone to Helen Chadwick's *Effluvia* (1996), where deadly liquids violate the senses by way of visual intoxication. We also have this violent succulence in Pipilotti Rist's *Sip My Ocean* (1996). This video presents us with a close-up image of a gorgeous bikini-clad 'ideal' female body swimming and treading water: 'a perfectly packaged wet dream'.[20] We are given permission to take pleasure, to 'sip up' her glamorous and erotic imagery. However, as we visually devour this imagery, our pleasure is disrupted when Rist's seductive sickly-sweet pillow-talk singing becomes more of a Yoko Ono shriek. It is both amusing and irritating. And this is perhaps what is exciting and significant about this kind of practice.

Violence is being used here to irritate pleasure; it is not being used to distract from the glut of the visual. A work by Chadwick, Rist and Landau is indeed gorgeous to look at: a veritable visual feast. Yet captured within this pleasure is also a violence, which Chadwick's enticing photographs of various liquids demonstrate. They combine colours which are aesthetically beautiful, but there is violence inherent in this beauty. This is not easy pleasure; after taking gratification from the visual composition we then learn of their deadly form. Yet acquiring knowledge of the violence makes this work more engaging. This is a sensual aesthetic, a beauty which is not passively innocuous. It hums aesthetically with painterly pleasure whilst sensually acknowledging its displeasure. Works by Chadwick, Rist and Landau create a trajectory of women's art practice which explores a visual pleasure that takes rebellious delight from its own violence. The vitality in their work comes from creating opposition from within the pleasurable frame of reference. It does not deny, denounce or renounce visual pleasure but instead concedes that in the act of looking and being looked at some form of wounding is implicit in the pleasure.

Sigalit Landau, Barbed Hula, *2000, Video, 1:52*
© *the artist*

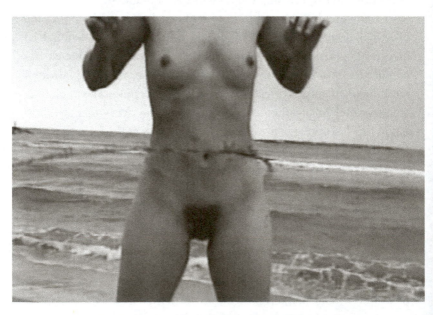

Sigalit Landau, Barbed Hula, *2000, Video, 1:52*
© *the artist*

In order to understand this practice further it would be helpful to explore some of this work in more depth, and I will begin with Pipilotti Rist's *Ever is Over All* (1997), for this set a precedent for the kind of art practice that fuses glamour and violence. After discussion of this video, and as a link to my final concluding remarks about Sigalit Landau's *Barbed Hula* (2000), I would like to then sidestep to a piece of work by artist Gillian Wearing entitled *Dancing in Peckham* (1994). The freedom expressed in Wearing's work helps to develop the discussion of Rist's imagery, for it also violently transgresses engrained, suffocating clichés and images. Wearing and Rist's images reveal the violence felt in and through the body as a result of festering cultural clichés about how bodies should act or be imaged. These are bodies that transgress mental boundaries and make the impact of the violence accrued by those slumbering festering images visible.

So firstly to Rist's *Ever is Over All*. This is a short video of Pipilotti Rist as the protagonist skipping down a quiet orderly street in Zurich where she lives. Gleefully smiling, she begins smashing car windows with what has the look of a fragile flower but the solidity of a club. There is a gorgeous, vibrant use of colour and texture. This is a riot of the senses: a sensual, gorgeous, carefree heroine, flamboyant gestures, a joyful animated grin, a delicious combination of electric-blue fabric dress and ruby-red slippers. A policewoman passes by and gives her an affirmative smile and salute. This imagery is juxtaposed by an adjacent screen, which displays a field of the same flowers as the one she is holding moving monumentally in the wind. Both videos are in slow motion, exaggerating and relishing this fantastical display. It is seductive and tantalizing, and makes us smile. Rebecca Lane describes this as a technicoloured *Wizard of Oz* with its fairy tale-like rebellion of the imagination. This anarchic vandalism is, she argues, not strictly social transgression, but 'mental transgression', 'transgression of mental norms'.[21]

I first saw this video in Berlin in 2006 in an exhibition of video art. The spaces were a maze of tunnels and cave-like dens, which gave the exhibition an underground countercultural sensibility. The curatorial aesthetic was that of anarchy and subterfuge. In one cave-like niche was Rist's dazzlingly hypnotic spectacle. This image of a liberated female body hits us via the senses and we are compelled to watch, spellbound. Peggy Phelan cites this as a feminist 'revenge' text: '[T]he daring exuberance of thinking outside the law, imagining a different relationship to property, to movement, to the criminal power of beauty itself.'[22] Similarly, Michael Rush describes this video as 'life-affirming' and 'a breezy feminist tract'. The heroine is, he argues, 'tremendously appealing, even as she loudly subverts social constraints.'[23] Rebecca Lane, on the other hand, disagrees with this synopsis, and I am inclined to agree. This is, as Lane has argued, not purely about social transgression; there is something else lurking behind the rebellion.

Rist argues that her slow-motion, narcotic and alarmingly innocent imagery is a fight 'against clichés by exaggerating the person and giving her an unusual presence on screen.'[24] *Ever is Over All* is celebratory in tone, but it has an underlying resistance. Her video work has been criticized for its shallow 'MTV' commercial/commodity pop-cultural identity, but equally it has been applauded for using this very contemporary identity as a mode for meaningful expression. For Rist, this imagery can instigate penetrating social change. She argues: 'The holy-unholy subject of gender has taken hold of the unconscious in a particularly powerful way.' It is, Rist continues, in the unconscious 'where prejudices slumber'.[25] And it is only by way of 'different' images that change can be directly affected at a deeper psychological level. Rist therefore uses the exact media that communicates and inculcates these 'festering' images to reach out and coin new fantastical figurations that shake up clichés and prejudices and embed other possibilities.

In his article 'Plastic surgery', Barry Schwabsky comments that Rist is not a formalist as such but uses the medium of video to express her own subjectivity with all its images, feelings and sensations. He argues that 'subjectivity itself is the medium'.[26] The split in the debate over Rist's work as such is because subjectivity is threaded through a medium that has already been colonized. As Schwabsky comments, 'commercial space is struggling to become subjective space, to colonize the mind, the body, and above all that strange unnameable somatic membrane where they fuse.'[27]

The idea of colonization is a very important point. The commercial world – advertising on billboards, magazines, online images, television, art, fashion and films – impacts on the way we visualize ourselves and imagine our own bodies. The anarchic unruly pleasure we feel when looking at Rist's violent images is provoked by the fact that gorgeous bodies do not usually act this way. The images we habitually see, and that have colonized subjectivity, are those which make those bodies – whether sexualized, obedient, submissive, still or posed – not disruptive, wilfully destructive or insubordinate. This Disney princess is running amok, ruining the narrative, disrupting the plot and wreaking havoc on the smooth structure of innocence versus evil. As such, her 'look' has been perverted; it is pleasurably out of place. The vivid lush colours, fabric, silhouette and glittering shoes are delicious to the eye, yet feel anarchic and out of place within our habitual commercial space.

What is interesting with Rist's *Ever is Over All*, therefore, is the idea of shaking up the unconscious and smashing up what has become inculcated psychologically as 'normal' or 'natural'. This jars. And it has to. For the prettiness taken as read as docile is now violently smashing out of its mould. We feel and see these images through the somatic membrane between the body and the mind, on the level of sensual surfaces – the skin, the screen, the image, or the dressed body – so it is highly appropriate that the violation of these expectations, clichés, prejudices and 'festering' images affect us through the same delicious surface. In doing this, they dramatically pierce this surface and wake us up. Rist's work presents us with a female body which goes against the grain and in doing this creates counter-images which flicker profoundly in our imagination. This is a body that is misbehaving freakishly and dangerously, and thus creates a spectacle which pricks our senses and brings a smile to our face. This is sensual spectacle as audacious rebellion, where the pleasures of fabric are revolting against convention.

We also see this audacious protest expressed in Gillian Wearing's work, where a carefree, female body nonchalantly transgresses expectations. The violence in Wearing's work is not as literal as in Rist's video, but is still felt in the shocking inconsistency between how Wearing is behaving and how we feel she should behave. And this is what is provocative and intriguing about Wearing's work. It acknowledges the suppressed violence which perpetually encases normalized actions and imagery: an oppression that weighs down upon and simmers just below the surface of the image. In Wearing's work, this oppression is made apparent, for we see a jarring inconsistency between her liberated body – a body that is not behaving as it should do – and the uncompromising prejudice that is triggered as a response to her uncompromising rebellion. And watching this kind of work affects us at the level of the senses, as shame or pride floods through our body.

Which brings me to the video *Dancing in Peckham* (1994). This is a 25-minute video by Gillian Wearing of the artist dancing in a Peckham shopping mall to the internal soundtrack of Gloria Gaynor's 'I Will Survive' and Nirvana's 'Smells Like Teen Spirit' that she is imagining in her head. The image of Wearing dancing wildly and unselfconsciously is compelling to watch; it makes us both cringe and smile at Wearing's nerve.

This kind of self-expression sits beyond the realm of our conventional and comfortable expectations. The spectacle of the female body here is therefore out of place and as such would most probably provoke laughter, anxiety and aggressive taunts and jeers. This is a shockingly transgressive body that aggrieves our expectations. We expect bodies to behave in certain ways. As Gordon Burn states, 'images accumulate sensation'.[28]

There is a jarring note struck between the shopping mall as non-place (which Marc Augé argues 'creates neither singular identity nor relations; only solitude, and similitude')[29] and this expressive body. This is an 'out of control' hysterical body that shows a total disregard for boundaries and conventions. Loud explosive private sensual gestures emanate from this 'low' mute public body. The public and the private blur in an awkward and unwieldy fashion. The shopping mall, disco dancing and this wilful explicit female body as spectacle clash and morph together in uncomfortable ways. Burn comments: 'To give vent to unembarrassed self-expression and self-display in such a non-place […] becomes an act of willful and (this is the implication) punishable transgression.'[30] There is therefore a sense of disbelief at her wilful rebellion.

Yet we quietly admire her audacity in breaking mental barriers. This is a fresh challenging image. The imagery speaks to us; all of these actions resonate in the imagination long after the 'performance' has ended. The knowing smile between the policewoman and the artist in *Ever is Over All* allows us to share the 'joke', but it is still internal to the circuitry of the moment, to the framework of the art. Likewise with Gillian Wearing's piece: her dancing is insular. She closes her eyes. We can feel her sense of exhilaration. We can be a party to the politics of the senses as a form of resistance, but there is no direct address, so we remain aloof, gazing spectators. She becomes more like a 'freak'. With Rist, we are spectators to an intimate communication that we can sympathize with, but we are not party to that intimacy, to that fairy tale that breaks into reality. We watch it play out on the screen.

The rebellion stays within the artwork, it is framed – in a bubble, even – and there is no connection to the spectator outside of the art narrative. There is perhaps a kindred yearning and a vicarious camaraderie. The moment as such lives on in our memories, but it doesn't mark us personally. We are not a party to it. We are not involved. And yet we are deeply affected by this behaviour. It fills us with hope and ignites our rebellious approval. What exactly is happening here? These women are still trapped within the image. What is taking place that makes it feel new and exciting?

What this in fact offers us is a different kind of politics of representation: a politics that embraces the sensual spectacle of being gorgeous, but not without acknowledging the violence of imposing a restrictive ideal.

And this moves me on to this chapter's concluding discussion, where my comments will relate to Sigalit Landau's *Barbed Hula* (2000). In this video, the body and violence are again framed, this time within a seascape. This video takes the form of a painting. The frame does not change, but this is a moving painting. The undulating body of the young woman mirrors the rhythmic undulation of the waves behind her as she slowly rotates the barbed wire that pierces her flesh. We are accustomed to seeing young, nearly naked bodies, but we are not accustomed to seeing these bodies self-mutilating in such a brutal yet playful manner. The image is shocking, but we are still utterly transfixed. This is a pretty picture which is wounding itself, and as such lures us in. We are spellbound as we blink and stare harder in disbelief at its brutal mix of beauty and self-torture.

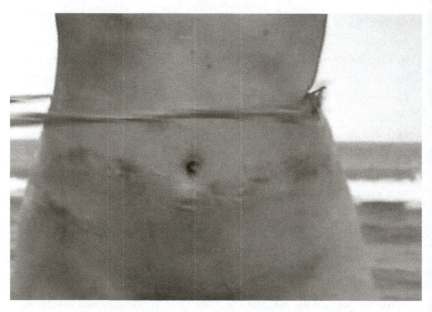

Sigalit Landau, Barbed Hula, *2000, Video, 1:52*
© *the artist*

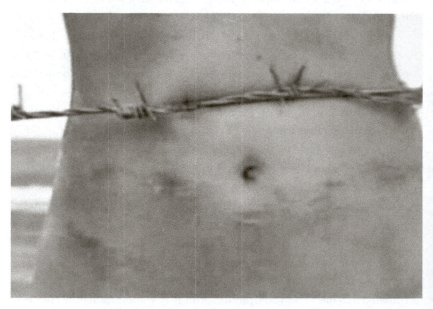

Sigalit Landau, Barbed Hula, *2000, Video, 1:52*
© *the artist*

Hula hoops and beach life are linked to innocent play. They go hand in hand with slender prepubescent bodies, and therefore the rhythmic self-harming seems all the more horrific. Seascapes link into ideas of natural beauty and Romantic discussion of the sublime. By placing the female body as the centre point of this picturesque panorama, Landau is making us aware, with each rotation of the hoop, of the psychological process that marks, tears and rips the body. The pain that we see with this body beautiful is self-inflicted; the desire to be perfectly feminine and conform to ideals of beauty comes at a price. This is a body suffused with pain and violence. The harmony of its 'ideal' aesthetic is broken up by its psychological damage and discontent. Creating this 'natural' beauty entails brushing knots out of our hair, exercising through pain barriers, dieting and self-regulation, even extreme forms of surgery. This is a body that hurts, and feels pain not just because of the punishing rituals of beauty but also the punishing need to live up to ideals and expectations which are engrained as 'perfect' in our cultural psyche, the 'fascism of beauty.'[31]

Yet women are, dangerously, not just passive spectators to this 'fascism' but are also party to it, as young women jump through hoops to achieve the impossible, always conscious of their less than satisfying selves in relation to these idealized bodies. Beauty is commercially blemish-free. It does not show pain. *Barbed Hula* makes us see the pain in the process of looking and being looked at. Painting oneself into the pretty picture forces the spectacle to implode and effectively destroy itself, demonstrating its powers of self-annihilation (anorexia being an extreme example) but also one's subject-power to control and obliterate what has been imposed. However, this reveals a more healthy representation of the toxicity of beauty, which also unabashedly takes into account the upbeat, the playful and the exhilarating pleasures of one's body as sensual and as aesthetic.

Pipilotti Rist, Gillian Wearing and Sigalit Landau reveal to us a lineage of women's art practice which performs visual pleasure that does not exclude the affective dimension of pain, self-harm, violence or toxicity. The gashing fresh wounds which cut deeply into beautiful, firm flesh act not only as a sign of anger, self-admonishment, guilt and self-hatred but also of a rebelling unfinished creative body. This is not, to quote Shohat and Stam, 'an abstract rage against figuration', but perhaps more what they would call 'rebellious beauty'.[32] For this rebellious beauty is not about revealing a distorted *body* as such but a distorted *psychology* that mismatches the moral 'purity' of the female feminine ideal. There is a moral aspect to beauty; beauty is linked to righteousness, purity and innocence. The performance art that I have discussed, however, represents an image that bites back and reacts. It is angry, hurt, polluted even. This image becomes a more rounded aesthetic dimension to the nude, to beauty and to the body.

In this practice, where images of lithe female 'ideal' bodies wreak havoc from within the frame, we are seeing a profound rebellion of the senses. This is a sensual spectacle of pleasure and violence, both forcefully assertive in its desire to image the body–self differently by breaking boundaries of behaviour and also in its need to strike out against convention from within its grasp. What is important to make clear is that this havoc is being wreaked from within the frame, and thus becomes a much more effective means of sabotage and insurgency. This is playful and energetic, taking control of pleasure in order to critique, undermine and take back the reins of power. In doing this it makes the process and mechanics of visual pleasure transparent. An anarchic sense of pleasure and displeasure is made apparent.

This is a riot of destructive pleasure and a celebration of disorderly desire. It is also a regenerative, refreshing expression of more 'ugly' emotions and affects. These are images of 'ideal' bodies which are breaking taboos, misbehaving, being violent, self-destructive, bleeding, wounding, and out of control – and as such this trajectory of performance work leaves us with a profound counter to the continuing proliferation of imagery where no hair is out of place.

8

Creative Spectatorship and the Political Imagination

Masquerade Balls and the 'Green Fairy'

On a frosty November evening in Sheffield I found my way to the Queens Social Club for an evening at Burly Q. I was warmly welcomed and led to my table by an elegantly dressed young woman in a moustache. Scattered on the table in front of me was a series of sepia-tinted cigarette cards, upon which were the images of the acts which were to follow. Around me the audience was thickening: an elderly gentleman in a 1920s white suit and a fez wandered past, a woman in a glittering turban sat nearby and I noticed a woman in a Pierrot costume standing at the bar. This was lively and fun, and intertwined with an exhilarating sense of the extravagant. The dressing up made the event special; it gave it an element of drunkenness and magic. The spectators at this event were also the performers, and stepping through the door was like stepping through a mirror into a masquerade ball, or indeed slipping into the cinematic pages of an absinthe-fuelled *fin-de-siècle* novel.

The compère, Penny Dreadful, a woman dressed as a man, came on to the stage, and the evening of cabaret, magic and circus acts commenced. I turned over the cigarette card bearing her cross-dressed image, which read: 'Penny Dreadful hopes that tonight's audience is not playing the role of the "straight man"'.[1] And indeed all of the audience members were playing roles which 'queered up' gender and sexuality in some demonstrative manner. They were delighting in dressing up and being part of the event. We see this also in many

Penny Dreadful
© *Dave Glossop*

other cabaret events, such as Bête Noire, La Rêve and Café de Paris in London, where we can experience a variety of wondrous acts similar to those at Burly Q (which in one evening comprised a heady concoction of puppetry, singing, cross-dressing, glamour, striptease, physical comedy, juggling, fire-eating, magic and a tongue-in-cheek Rapunzel). The performers included Leggy Pee and her puppet partner Charles M. Montgomery, Mamzelle Dotty moving and manipulating objects such as crystal balls, and Honey Wilde with her cheeky, glamorous humour. These performers engage us by way of dazzling skilful artistry, charismatic personalities, gentle humour and an innocent bygone feeling of charm.

The back of Mamzelle Dotty's cigarette card reads: 'Through her performances she wishes to inspire and bring magic into the mundane.'[2] Indeed, this is serious play: bringing 'magic into the mundane' is absolutely what the event is about. The audience can watch this display with absolute delight and wonder as Mamzelle Dotty appears to defy danger and perform seemingly impossible acts. We watch as she plays with objects such as fire and crystal balls, creating feats of magical visual pleasure. And it is this magical performance which enables the audience to feel that life is being expanded beyond the conventional parameters and boundaries. The performance injects life with the curious, the unexpected and a sensation of the fantastical and dreamlike. The audience at Burly Q also embraced this sense of the extraordinary, the eccentric, the bizarre and the quirky in their dress.

But what sort of a space was this? In *Rings of Desire* (2000), Helen Stoddart argues that this 'capacity of the human body to perform beyond its normal or even imagined limitations in forms which are entertaining, astonishing and beautiful' lays at 'the very core of circus'.[3] This would therefore mark Burly Q out as a circus space. It does indeed present us with a most wonderful mixture of the magical and the curious. Stoddart argues, though, that the circus is not

Mamzelle Dotty
© *Monika Marion*

a carnivalesque space; when we look, we are evidently spectators engrossed in the voyeuristic pleasures of watching this 'low' Other, who performs death-defying acts or balances precariously on horseback in a sequined leotard. In *Circus Bodies: Cultural Identity in Aerial Performance* (2005), however, Peta Tait argues that stepping into a big top was a suspension of social laws, as these circus bodies were seen to 'contravene social categories of gender'.[4] For her, circus can be seen as 'inheriting the Bakhtinian site of the carnivalesque'.[5] Using this argument, stepping through the opening of a circus tent was akin to stepping into a space where the spectator would feel the thrill of the unknown; of pushing boundaries and being in a space where bodies could act otherwise.

Tait argues that female aerial performers were doubly gendered, and that their androgynous spirit affected the spectator. Their freedom of movement inspired in the viewer an imagined transgression. Yet the audience themselves were not transgressing as such. They felt the vicarious thrill of danger, but their sense of transgression came from stepping into a temporary travelling space which seemed to operate outside of social and cultural laws and rules. The excitement, thrill and edginess of being in the same physical space as these performers, who were seen as both physically and mentally free, would momentarily give the spectator an exhilarating sense of life beyond social conventions. However, these performers were still perceived as 'Other' and 'low' – and therefore 'freak' – in this arrangement. It was still a hierarchical structure where the spectator paid for a voyeuristic 'kick', a vicarious experience of the 'low', before going back to normality.

According to Tait, the circus experience was a popular pastime because of its transgression of gender norms. Not only did these circus bodies perform outside prescribed boundaries for their sex, but in the case of (for instance) the trapeze performer, they also defied natural laws of gravity. The pleasure of watching these performers came from this voyeuristic awe of the outsider. The big top became a space of curiosity, and the circus ring a voyeuristic thrilling space of transgression which was safely cordoned off from real life. In this experience of bodies that were unrestrained, the 'freak' remained safely 'Other'.

Watching the artistes perform at Burly Q, though, we are entertained by their skill or quirkiness without creating a hierarchical

Mamzelle Dotty
© Riksh Upamaya

Mister Joe Black
© Scott Chalmers

distance between stage and audience. We are filled with wonder; yet the curiosity that is provoked is not one characteristic of the freak show. For what is piqued in us is a sense of our shared language. They are performing the language of the audience's own exploratory and experimental gender or sexual ambiguity and self-invention. And it is this element of creative spectatorship and inclusion that defines the Burly Q cabaret space differently. This is the aspect that is most intriguing, for it is the audience's flamboyant participation that moves this event from a temporary release into something more politically potent. As in the circus, we are being given licence to stare. But this is a different kind of gaze.

My experience in Derby of another cabaret event, Hurly Burly, made the different kinds of gazes distinctly apparent, and this is pertinent to my discussion of a creative rather than divisive spectatorship. On that evening in March 2012, it was the erratic, unpredictable and anarchic behaviour of Mister Joe Black that finally gave the audience something that had been sorely missing in this event and in most of the acts that preceded his. The missing element was the engagement and involvement of the audience.

Mister Joe Black dressed as a lovable Victorian Gothic rogue, with thick black eyeliner, tall top hat, piercing eyes and a wiry body, which was always in motion. His risqué Dickensian sense of the immoral and 'low' engaged the audience via humour, entertainment and the thrill of danger. His act kept us on our toes and at the edge of our seat. We felt beads of sweat at the speed of his act – his singing, his music-making, his darting eyes – and also from the tension of knowing that he could potentially do anything.

With Mister Joe Black's act there was a Victorian sense of the freak show, with a performative twist. He pushed boundaries of acceptability, like the acrobatic doubly gendered aerial acts spoken about by Tait and Stoddart. His act here was edgy, and similarly queered up in terms of sexuality and gender, but there was also a death-defying speed to his act, which made the electricity in the auditorium palpable. His fast-paced singing, offbeat, close-to-the-bone lyrics and physical humour were pleasurably shared subversion. But, unlike the sense of transgression experienced by the circus spectator, with Black there was much more uncertainty, wariness and tension. This was a sense of the 'Other' that was not securely cordoned off. We did not feel safely separate; the trepidation and danger were threatening our subjective integrity. This was exhilarating.

With his wry smile (which was utterly disarming) we found ourselves pulled in by an incredibly likeable and empathetic entertainer. Black was an attractive character, and we wanted to be led astray: to think the unthinkable, hear the unmentionable, visualize the unconventional. And we laughed and smiled wryly back at the shocking explosive energy, expletives and fast and frenetic behaviour. With his jerky uncontrollability – physically and mentally – and the sparkle in his constantly darting eyes we took a sharp intake of breath as we got a sense of a performer who moved too fast to be pinned down. He could not be trapped, could not be categorized. It was like something had been untethered in all of us, and we felt exhilarated as it ran amok in the room. We did not want it to stop – it felt creative, irreverent, dynamic and fresh.

With the other acts, however, there was a feeling of voyeurism, and this just did not work; they did not provoke empathy and joy in the same way. Instead what was created was a narcotic safeness, which rankled. The auditorium did not help. When the audience sits in tiered seating, which darkens the spectators and lights up the stage, the atmosphere and power dynamic is divisive from the start. In one act we were subjected without any sense of irony or collective pleasure to watching a woman dancing erotically. This was not pushing boundaries but strengthening them, along with cultural rules and conventions. What was entertaining here? What was different? Perhaps a sexualized pleasure for some, but it certainly didn't feel liberating; instead it felt awkward and voyeuristic, and perhaps even insulting. This sort of act was supporting the status quo, and there was some feminist antagonism amongst the women I attended this event with, who were quite offended at being party to this spectatorial distance and control. For them, it felt like coerced visual violation. It was discomfort, not pleasure, that we experienced.

And indeed burlesque as a peep show tradition came from this idea of licensed and validated voyeurism for all classes. These tent 'booths' were later developed into 'turns' on the stage. This was a fairground tradition[6] where the body was there to pique the curiosity about real bodies – where the spectator paid to be allowed to stare. This evidently highlighted Victorian England's blatant contradictions with regard to the sexual and moral hypocrisy of the time. And indeed these sexualized female bodies were allowed to be framed in this way because they were seen as 'low' and 'Other': 'low' in that they were working class, but also 'low' in that the fair was a popular entertainment, outside of 'culture', lacking sophistication. It was not art; it was crass and inappropriate. The sexual titillation and pleasure consolidated binaries. They were allowed to be different because they were 'low', popular and unsophisticated – sluttish, even. This is where these sort of inappropriate 'loose' titillating bodies and women resided.

It is relevant at this point to discuss an example which questions this categorization and the control of bodies, and which legitimizes 'high' and 'low' culture. Marisa Carnesky is a contemporary showwoman who puts herself on display to reveal the limitations and restrictions of this kind of categorization. Roger Malbert argues in his essay 'Exaggeration and degradation: grotesque humour in contemporary art' that – as a tattooed woman who is also Jewish – Carnesky creates a spectacle of her body in the 'low' arena in order to show how bodies are looked at and how they are framed.[7] This is the expected arena for these bodies as 'Other', yet to categorize them as 'low' is to dismiss them out of hand.

In one performance that is discussed by Malbert, entitled *The Jewess Tattooess* (1999), Carnesky mixes the circus 'freak' show with Yiddish theatre and ends the show by having a tattoo of a Star of David inscribed on her thigh. Malbert argues that tattoos cast her as a freak and outsider in the 'real' world, where she is seen as a permanent 'freak'. To tattoo her body, as a woman, is to violate bourgeois beauty conventions and ideals by permanently scarring her youthful female skin. However, being Jewish, tattooing her body is also a cultural and religious violation, for this sort of practice is forbidden by the Torah. So by making a spectacle out of this transgression, Carnesky is also marking herself as an outsider from the categories set out for her as Jewish and as a woman; categories which are equally as scarring. As a performer who chooses to display her thoughtful transgressive body in a 'low' arena, Carnesky is therefore evading the categories of art and the 'high', instead choosing to display this out-of-place body in the 'low' arena of the circus or the fairground.

Thoughtful, questioning transgression is usually framed as 'art', and is not usually framed within the 'low' or the popular. The 'low' arena of the circus or the fairground has traditionally been there to accommodate 'freaks' who have become entertainment, or entertain because of not fitting in. The spectacle of their difference as 'Other' is what attracts the spectator. The spectator can pay to stare and take pleasure from this category of life outside of the norm, thus consolidating those divisions and categories. 'High' art also frames deviance as acceptable as long as it remains within the framework of the art and the artist. A body that puts on show its intelligence, subversiveness and agency is allotted to 'art'. Titillation, sexualized display and inappropriate, misappropriated bodies are allotted to the 'low' and the popular. Carnesky questions these distinctions and categorizations, and questions the ways that bodies are framed by culture. And this is what is so incredibly exciting about her practice as well as other new burlesque and cabaret acts who collapse the boundaries between the 'low' or popular, and the 'high'.

Roger Malbert argues that what Carnesky presents us with is 'the treacherous distinction between art and life'.[8] Carnesky (and indeed Mister Joe Black) put on a different kind of show, which is popular and entertaining. And it is within that very slippery nature of their 'show' that the display of their deviance becomes so dangerous. They are sanctioning the pleasure of looking at different bodies which have penetrated 'life'. This is a movement away from the institutionalized framing of 'freakery', which is legitimized within the category of art. In the concluding remarks to his essay 'The social construction of freaks', Robert Bogdan states that: '"Freak" is a frame of mind', 'people filtered through stories and world views. To study deviance is to look at those in charge [...] telling us who deviants are and what they are like.'[9]

Mister Joe Black and Marisa Carnesky's invention of bodies create empathy through a creative collapse of the 'low' and the 'high', and of art and life. They are the subjects of a 'freakery' that doesn't fit into categories. By making a 'show' of their difference as the subject of their own transgression they are making visible different kinds of identities, but these are identities that are free to roam in 'life' outside the framework of art. They perform in the 'low' popular arena in order to not move outside of 'life'. Their bodies invite the gaze to share and empathize and find pleasure in their perversion of categorization within an arena, which seeks to make a spectacle of that difference and freakery through spectatorial distance and control. This is a critique and rebellion through the body.

And it is this idea of a critical body which was so lacking in the erotic dance that I watched at the Hurly Burly event that I discussed earlier. Rather than evading categorization, the female dancer was replicating pre-existing stereotypes of the sexualized female body. This 'low' body was dancing for an audience who watched from a darkened auditorium. It felt awkward and uncomfortable because of the spectatorial distance and control that was akin to slaves dancing for their masters. This was legitimizing and validating the display of a docile body and making this 'low' body into an 'art' form. By so readily accepting boundaries, it enacted the 'treacherous' boundary between art and life. This was a performance that was allowing 'easy' viewing, so readily disposed to fit in.

Carnesky's display, however, is not so 'easy', and that is its pleasure and entertainment. This disorderly body that sits within and outside of

Leggy Pee and Charles M. Montgomery
© Ian Sloan

'rules' therefore works creatively in terms of spectatorship. It becomes politicized entertainment.

Burly Q was also refreshing because it expanded out of the categorization and distance that limits bodies and our creative imagination. They were 'freaks' in terms of performing stunts or turns such as fire- and sword-swallowing and juggling, stripping or behaving eccentrically (or zanily even, if we include Leggy Pee, who performs with her puppet, Charles M. Montgomery). This was also about curiosity, of course: a curiosity that finds the wondrous in the visual, the new and the 'deviant'. It opens up rather than closes down understanding. There is an intersubjective shared sense of our politicized bodies and their potential for imagination and creativity rather than them being used to elevate oneself and consolidate one's status and position as better in some way from the exotic or the erotic, which thrives on distance. What marks this space out as different is in the event's fusion of magic, communal play and curiosity.

There was in Burly Q a magical sense of moving beyond and the discovery of new, unseen things. It was open, incomplete and a magical celebration of creative spectatorship. We still watched as spectators, yet there was visual communication on both sides of the stage throughout the performance. Following on from their essay 'Narrativizing visual culture', Ella Shohat and Robert Stam would term this 'Carnivalization', as it was 'an extraordinary flexible form of artistic visualization, a peculiar sort of heuristic principle making possible the discovery of new and as yet unseen things'.[10] The acts initiated a playful starting point, which was then played out by the spectators as a collective site of invention, experimentation and fun as this creation of new bodies and realizations moved into the everyday: constantly shifting, changeable and organic. And it is this subject of magic and the unseen which the final section of this chapter seeks to wrap up.

THE MIND AS MAGICAL FAIRGROUND

Chanel's fashion show for 2013 took place in the round. At the centre of the excited audience, who sat waiting in anticipation for the show to begin, was a large, covered cylindrical shape. The music began, sounding much like when one winds up a musical box, and the cover was slowly hoisted up – to the astonishment and awe of the audience. For what was revealed was a life-size fairground carousel ride with models poised side-saddle on painted horses as it began to rotate. This was the fantasy and pleasure of the fairground as popular spectacle and amusement, which figures largely in new burlesque shows and imagery where one can see Dita von Teese (for instance) posing or stripping aboard these painted rides.

The attraction of the fairground comes from its whirligig of visual pleasure that overwhelms the senses. This is poignantly expressed in an essay written by Henry Warren, 'A note on fairs', in which he narrates the experience of being seduced by the fair: 'Then at last the roundabout gave shrill summons and we mounted wooden horses with lips of vivid red. Under the painted, curly canopy we rode, clutching at the twisted rods of brass.'[11] Warren explains that the fair, like the circus, was traditionally an exhilarating release from the relentless harshness of daily working life. When the travelling circus or fair pitched up in your local town or village, it was a temporary escape into the out-of-the-ordinary. 'Time deals gently with side-shows [...] They belong to the days before cinema and the radio, when a magic lantern could create a stir.'[12]

These are simple pleasures, where 'joy' is differentiated from 'pleasure'. 'Joy', for Warren, is a feeling of freedom and happiness, as opposed to 'pleasure', which is purely about sensual satiation. The fair, as an exhilarating synaesthetic surge of excess, saturates and seduces the body with the frenetic and the chaotic. Colour, smell, touch, speed, taste, sound and the crowds create a dizzy overstimulated sense of pleasure. It caters to the 'low' pleasures of the body in order to replicate the 'joy' of what is missing. As Warren states, '[e]ach emotion that is starved in real life finds a stimulus at the fair'.[13] Dreams and imaginings wake up and beckon us with what life could be and feel like. However, when our heads are in the clouds without our feet being on the floor, we float aimlessly – it becomes a narcotic release, a release grounded in illusions. We give over our money to pay for a taste of freedom.

Yet the bubble will burst. For what begins as pleasure can soon become nausea. As Warren states, this pleasurable overstimulation soon leads to a drunken stupor, with the fair-goers in days gone by sleeping it off in ditches.[14] Pleasure and joy are therefore intertwined but not the same: the joy which is induced by various carnal pleasures can soon turn to hell. The carousel ride, the English dobby horse or the merry-go-round performs this repetitive feeling of merriment, creating a perpetual state of being joyful. A merry-go-round – on which painted horses take us on a journey to nowhere – enacts a life in transition where sensual intoxication makes tangible our physical journey into our dreams. This creates feelings of elation and freedom, as the visual sense of magic and awe at the sweet bright colours, rhythm, movement and shapes induces a euphoric sense of elation that there may be something more, something else aside from the mundane, the predictable and the ordinary.

The adrenaline of the climax soon plummets from pleasure to nausea; from excitement to disappointment. Pleasure becomes dizziness. Your perception is askew; you lose your footing and fall and fall, spiralling downwards. Your visual perception and your physical bearing in the world are out of kilter; you become disorientated, yet to reorientate your being in the world is to make the world stop spinning and to reinstate 'normality'. Pleasure does not turn into joy. It is a reminder of the possibility of joy, but does not create it. It is not permanent. The repetition and the whirligig of the merry-go-round soon turns into boredom and frustration, much like New Year's Eve, for the bells chime in the anticlimax that reveals that life has not changed and that the saliva of anonymous kisses does not on the whole lead to wild sex, nor does it bring new beginnings, and we go home disappointed, disillusioned and the worse for wear.

As we all know, we can never achieve a perpetual state of being merry, for intoxication always moves us over the edge from the sensual to the sickly. What then disappears? And what is it that lures us in? There is evidently a need for a sense of wonder, of magic, of the conjuring trick, of inexplicable acts, enchantment, fairy tales and otherworldly fictions. In *Mythologies* (1973) Roland Barthes discusses the visual in relation to the magical when he states 'touch is the most demystifying of all the senses, unlike sight, which is the most magical.'[15] The showman's ability is to lure the fair-goer in through the manipulation of this most magical sense of the visual, tempting us through this spectacle into wanting to see more. And this spectacle reflects the times. In 2013, walking around Nottingham Goose Fair (which has purportedly been running for approximately 700 years) I could see the signposts to past eras in the artwork on the rides. As Geoff Weedon and Richard Ward state in their book, 'fairground art will continue to act like a mirror to society.'[16]

I noticed on the sides of rollercoasters 1980s-style painted depictions of buxom bikini-clad Amazonian women, sexually charged dominatrices: Wonder Woman; six-foot Sigourney Weaver in *Alien*; supermodels Naomi Campbell, Linda Evangelista and Helena Christensen. This was fetishized pleasure distilled from the commercial landscape and popular imagination. And from our current era were slick, photorealist images of Abercrombie and Fitch-style older teenagers and early twenty-somethings dancing with sensual abandon – the women in bikinis and the men in shorts – indicative of new millennium Ibiza party-style hedonism and 'ideal' Photoshopped bodies.

This is a trade in pleasure – the commerce of pleasure, of images and sensations lifted from the mainstream, everyday public commercial arena. This is the high gloss, high energy narcotics of the moment. And indeed Nottingham's Goose Fair began its life around 700 years ago as a market to sell poultry. At the edge of the market, as a 'sideshow', it also became a market for prostitutes to show their wares as well as a way for farm maids or servants to sell their services. However, it soon became simply about pleasure, and the showman's job was to lure people in. By way of the spectacular, he would give them a tantalizing 'show' of what had disappeared from their daily life via a highly visual spectacle and 'show' of what was most visible. It was a sexual licence for the excesses of the now. To part with our money, though, we need to feel that we have been immersed in a fully loaded expression of what it means to be alive, what it feels like to really be living life to the full.

However, this is the rub. Can the image tell us everything? The fairground imagery is mirroring what is spelt out for us every day. It is spelling out what matters: the known visual quality that is seen everywhere, as everything, in our contemporary arena. There is no intrigue or mystery – the subjects are flattened out so they become a known quantity, without invention. We are looking for Wonderland, for curious acts of wonder and magic, in amusement which replicates the wonder-less and charmless. We are trying to conjure up dormant pleasures out of the mundane.

Showmen show us the spectacle of gendered heteronormative bodies performing in an expected way in order to induce magic and joy. We need therefore to consider what constitutes 'pleasure' and understand how this pleasure takes on a gendered position in term of power and politics. 'Joy' – a sense of unquantifiable mental and bodily freedom – is nevertheless being quantified through visual pleasure determined by a culture that asserts a particular way of seeing. The 'showman' re-inscribes the known of our visual culture (and therefore re-inscribes a strictly codified way of being visual), and equates this with 'joy'. But how could this creative spectacle be used to link the pleasure of this 'low' form with the female body, pleasure and politics? What would it mean to have a contemporary showwoman? It was Marisa Carnesky's *Carnesky's Ghost Train* which attracted me the most in relation to this question.

The ride was permanently constructed in 2010 near Blackpool's Pleasure Beach, which Carnesky stated was its spiritual home. At the entrance to the amusement park are black-and-white photographs showing the park through the decades from its Art Deco beginnings. Until April 2014 (when the attraction was closed due to high maintenance costs), next to the Pleasure Beach on the south promenade, you could find the ghost train, where the 'high' of performance art was interspersed with the 'low' of the fairground attraction, and pleasure was linked into the politics of the visual. This was an attraction which figured real bodies that inhabited the dark recesses of the ghost train's tunnel – there to embody the ghosts of the disappeared. The performers, young men and women dressed in bedraggled Gothic Victoriana styles, enticed and heckled the 'punters' as we strolled by along the Pleasure Beach. Intrigued, of course, we would approach these characters slightly hesitantly, and pay up at the kiosk.

As part of the *Carnesky's Ghost Train* experience, a heavy, dusty curtain was pulled back and we were taken into a room to wait. Inside there were pictures of those people who had disappeared – and it was their ghosts who inhabited the niches and crevices of the tunnel we would soon enter. More paying customers joined us as the excitement and anticipation mounted. Soon we were chivvied through another curtain and instructed to quickly get aboard the train. The tunnel was dark and the ride jolted, much like a traditional funfair ghost train, whose clichés we were well aware of. However, this felt more unexpected; we were on red alert. The characters appeared and disappeared from view all around us, danced and moved near us and behind us, jumped out at us. The carriage moved through a series of trapdoors and revolving spaces, and mock cobwebs touched our faces. The 'ghosts' performed separately in niches, and appeared and disappeared through revolving doors. And as a finale to the show, a curtain was raised, a voice-over began, and the figures performed a strange incarnation of a remembrance ceremony – a dance for the disappeared – and then we were jolted back outside into the light, the show now being over.

As we regained our footing on the Pleasure Beach, the idea of 'pleasure' was again brought to my attention by horse-drawn pink princess carriages which were intermittently riding past *Carnesky's Ghost Train*. There was of course an unintended irony in the appearance of this candyfloss-caked popular rendition of gender. But it was a blatant, disembodied visual trope which I enjoyed, having immediately come paired with the contradiction of the embodied disappearance of lost female souls in the attraction I had just visited.

In one way the Day of the Dead festival in Mexico is an appropriate parallel with this contradiction. Mexico's popular celebration of the lost souls of the dead is enacted via the sweet confectionery of skulls and other metaphors of death. The festival is a positive remembrance of the life of the dead by eating a sweet metaphor of their deathly residue. Death and life are intermingled – the memory of the dead is evoked through visual pleasure and the disappeared body becomes physically embodied into the popular body. Remembering who has disappeared is imaged, in this popular cultural celebration, by way of visual, sometimes edible, objects.

The eating of sickly sweet candyfloss on Blackpool's Pleasure Beach becomes an embodied visual signifier of frivolous fun and the pink Barbie carriage becomes a signifier of the happy-ever-after femininity of Barbie movies. It is a popular pastiche of what is seen as successful in terms of a gendered female body and the pleasure that can be gained from following this as embodied practice. By contrast, in *Carnesky's Ghost Train,* female bodies as subjects made an eerie appearance and became a trigger to what was not there. The visual signifiers in our popular imagination to demonstrate what *was* there therefore jarred with that which was evidently not.

As Peggy Phelan has argued, perception is performative because it moves into our imagination; it is interactive, not passive.[17] This was a spectacle of 'real' bodies in a popular fairground attraction where the ride relied on the expectation of being scared of the unknown and the unseen. The ghost train is usually situated amongst the adrenaline and rush, thrill and buzz of big dippers, rollercoasters and death-defying drops that take us beyond our comfort zone. And we feel the thrill of these rides whilst simultaneously being immersed in visual sexual references heralding the parameters of our cultural 'real' in terms of bodies, sexuality, pleasure and hedonistic licentiousness. Images are not neutral. The fantasy of the fairground and its representations therefore becomes a performative idea of 'freedom' where sensual abandonment is aligned with what our popular culture has forwarded as an 'ideal' gendered visual pleasure.

This plays with the fair-goers' own experience and perception of their bodies. These experiences disappear into their own perceptions as they hurtle towards an anticlimactic showdown; they are pushing against the edges of what constitutes freedom, yet this freedom is already inflexibly framed within the already marked and the already visible. And we rotate around and become merry in our longing to quench our desires beyond the fast climax of the big-breasted blondes or the prescribed order of the candyfloss-pink world. And the idea of the 'pleasure' in 'Pleasure Beach' still resonates in my imagination as well as the question of what has 'disappeared' from our commercial landscape and popular imagination.

Carnesky's creative spectacle worked with this question of 'disappearance' and pleasure. The pleasure disappeared, as Peggy Phelan would argue, into the audience's own imagination, where it continued to perform.[18] It played with this idea of pleasure as a politicized gesture, for it left a critical and reflective residue; it was performative.

Marisa Carnesky, as contemporary showwoman, seduced and lured us, the 'punters', in by the spectacle of her extravagant show.

What did Carnesky bring to the fair that was different? This was entertainment that brought the embodied memory of fictive female subjects with their lived narratives and significance back into our memories as a politicized performative gesture. It was not based on fact, but neither is the imagery that surrounds us every day. It nevertheless brought female bodies back into our memory and into the political memory. Indeed, the pleasure of these bodies who had now 'disappeared' disappeared into our memory, with the picture of them in the foyer still in our brain and the visual evocation of remembering poetically embodied in the choreographed moves and gestures performed for us in the attraction. They were women with a history and a narrative created through these haunting, dancing gothic bodies performing the ghosts of those who have disappeared.

To conclude, let us rotate ourselves smoothly around to the fashion show and the Chanel merry-go-round ride that began this section. And in turn let us consider this the last ride we sit astride before stepping into the conclusive remarks of this book as a whole.

The Chanel ride was indeed a visual spectacle of splendid fairytale enchantment: the excitement of the fair brought into the fantasy of fashion. But what did that mean in terms of cultural significance? The excitement that tingled through my body initially was the magical performative potential produced by the merry-go-round. But the magic, which at first produced a sharp intake of breath, soon turned into boredom and frustration. There was the magical expectation and excitement set in motion by the visual extravaganza, but this was not satisfied by these (expected) fashionable bodies who stepped off the ride and washed into the foreground. What was important about that initial frisson was the possibility that something magical was being conjured up in our imagination. The spectator was stepping aboard the ride, and it was taking on the shape of our invention. This was creative spectatorship, and the fantasy of that pleasure became the residue.

Mamzelle Dotty
© *Silvia Cruz*

CONCLUSION

NOW YOU SEE ME...

So, what do I mean by being gorgeous?

This book started off as a way of exploring certain strands of contemporary culture which were flamboyantly celebrating the body and its presentation as object. This was not in my opinion a rejection of feminism. It was still embracing mainstream expectations regarding imagery, but there was something exceeding these expectations that made this imagery defiantly pleasurable: there was both pleasure and a sardonic bite. My last publication, *The Happy Stripper: Pleasures and Politics of the New Burlesque*, opened up a can of worms for me. I began that book with one main question: why did women still feel the need to strip off their clothes? I needed to ask why this still seemed to be the key to social and cultural success. The fascination with new burlesque, however, was that it seemed to be putting the issue of objectification and sexual commodification centre stage – the stripping acted as a critique of the bland bevy of naked female bodies that we have become accustomed to in our daily lives.

I began writing this book quite a few years ago, and as I draw my enquiry to an end I am still surrounded by an utter overload of sexy and sexualized images of women. Questioning this imagery, this visual excess, is still a pressing concern. Popular music, fashion, television and the internet proclaim the exposed female body as the key to upward mobility and popularity. I am therefore intrigued by and would like to understand the way in which women feel and react to this barrage of imagery that comes at them from every angle and at almost every moment of their lives, images which on the whole seem to nullify pleasure and complexity. We are also now saturated with an abundance of 'selfies' which present us with young women voluntarily pouting for the camera – again scantily clad, appearing always ready to please.

In her book *Porn Chic* (2012), Annette Lynch questions whether this kind of imagery is objectification or 'sexual subjectification'.[1] She looks at cyber-identities and argues that this may be a way in which young women assert their sexual power. This is evidently a complex argument which would merit further exploration, and Lynch then goes on to discuss the issue further at the end of her book in relation to the SlutWalk, which began in 2012 in Toronto. The criticism of this activism by people like the American Black Community – Black Women's Blueprint, Inc. as well as scholars such as Gail Dines and Wendy J. Murphy is that it plays to sexualized stereotypes, for women are openly parading their scantily clad bodies in a provocative manner. The SlutWalk, of course, is about this kind of freedom: women are demonstrating their right to dress however they want. To dress as a 'slut' in a short revealing skirt or with your cleavage on show – or even with your breasts completely naked – does not mean that you are inviting sexual abuse.

The SlutWalk began its life as a direct reaction against comments made by a Toronto police officer when speaking to women who had enrolled on a self-defence class who had said that 'women should avoid dressing like sluts in order not to be victimized'.[2] Participants in the SlutWalk argued that the word 'slut' was always used to 'wound', 'so we're taking it back. "Slut" is being re-appropriated'.[3] However, it could be argued that these women are again showing that their identities all boil down to their bodies and what is sexually on show. And indeed I would argue that that is exactly what they are exposing.

Young women on these walks are taking to task the fact that the relentless wallpaper of sexually ready women, waiting to satisfy, has created a diseased landscape of sexual inequality. Boys can get porn in school at the touch of a button, and expect girls to 'perform' accordingly.

We could ask what else we can expect when young people grow up to see this kind of sexual imbalance of visual power blatantly played out in the public arena as 'normal'. The everyday mainstream world in which we go to school or work or leisure corroborates this visual expectation: the female body is there to be exploited, for anybody, anywhere, anytime. The idea that all women are 'asking for it' and therefore 'deserve it' has now moved into the everyday cultural arena. It is quite shocking that this has become normalized as part of our 'civilized' twenty-first century visual culture.

In a 2014 review of the book *Everyday Sexism* by Laura Bates, journalist Eleanor Mills writes how she found the content of the posts drawn together by Bates, especially those about university life, 'shocking' and 'chilling':

> The posts describe a culture where every fancy-dress event involves women dressing as 'slags' or 'hoes' and 'lads' banter about rape and revel in humiliating their conquests. Female students are encouraged by boys, porn and magazines to look 'hot'.[4]

Young women believe that this is the way to be, and young men grow up seeing that women's sexuality is about their need to please a man at all cost. This idea of being 'hot', of being the starlet of a porn movie – which of course has moved into the mainstream – means that women's sexual purpose appears to be that they are there just to pose explicitly for men, have 'cum' on their face and be 'fucked'. There is no sense of women's satisfaction in this; they are there solely to satisfy men. An object has no feelings and doesn't matter. And this is the way porn chic has penetrated our lives.

With fashion mirroring the contemporary landscape, fashion glossies are competing with this idea of 'porn chic': Terry Richardson's soft-porn high-fashion shoots being a 'cutting-edge' example of this. Many young intelligent women that I come across, several of them fashion students, are appalled and angry at the disappearing boundaries between pornography and life. High art, of course, also shows this kind of nudity, and this is perhaps the point of Richardson's erotica: it is not pretending to be otherwise. It is painted as risqué and rebellious, a rejection of the sleekly polished sexualized body. But the problem that arises with Richardson's photography is when we consider the question of control and power. Who is in control of these shots? Are they exploitative, or are the many women (including those who are famous in their own right) in charge of this sexploitation?

Words such as 'slutty' and 'smutty' come to mind when looking at the imagery; the same ones that come to mind when discussing soft porn and the 'Readers' Wives' genre of photography. Yet I believe that I come to these issues with my own feminist prejudices. So with my questioning, irritation and anger comes a nagging undercurrent of self-doubt about my own perspective. Should I be looking at this differently, less judgmentally?

One of the key issues that threads its way through my discussion, of course, is the issue of class: a subject which is now also rearing its head in academia. A rigorous discussion about class, the gaze, pleasure and feminism is very much needed. The key objection to the SlutWalks comes from the 'slutty' flesh-revealing outfits. And similarly what Mills finds 'chilling' about the posts in Laura Bates' book about sexism is that young female students are dressing up as 'sluts' and 'hoes'. They are encouraged by men to dress this way as there is an expectation that women who dress like that condone free play and allow men access 'who want to do unspeakable things to them'.[5]

The SlutWalk protest is not just about some 'body' or just any free-for-all body; it is a collective dissenting body. It is also not about sexual 'subjectification' – which of course the media's discussion is trying to make it remain – but about controlling what this 'sluttiness' means visually. As such it takes to task what is being stereotyped, and shifts the context from within the frame. The female activists who dress as 'sluts' and 'hoes' are questioning what is being framed and how it is being framed. This therefore is more complicated and more problematic, and actually more profound in its challenge. Class-based stereotypes are simplified ways in which women can be categorized and sexually and visually controlled. They can be perceived as easily 'knowable' and definable by sight, where 'sight' and being on show, showing everything, equates to open access and a dissolution of ethical boundaries and social responsibility: choosing to wear that kind of clothing means you are *that* kind of woman, and being 'loose' somehow strips you of your right to agency, intelligence or power.

*　　*　　*

What is clearly evident is the paradox of contemporary culture. This is a confused social panorama which safeguards sexual fantasy as a commodified version, emptied of life. There is a perverted sense of sexual agency, where sexual agency is seen as 'slutty' and 'low' whilst the 'classy' and commodified ideal is passive (yet is also 'asking for it'). This is not a sexual subject, but an object to be acted upon. Sexual subjects are advertised as prizes to be bought or won – commodities. To have sexual subjectivity, however, is punished as 'low' and whorish. Sexual freedom is inappropriate: these are bodies out of control.

The rise in popularity of such television shows as *Geordie Shore*, *Big Brother* and docusoaps of girls 'out on the town' reveals the way in which the audience sympathizes with this excessive resistance to homogenized restrictive notions of how women should behave. When we see female media celebrities who wet the bed, drink themselves into oblivion, soil themselves, fart and belch, curse loudly and flash their breasts and buttocks, a televised spectacle is being made of their inappropriate femininity. It is car-crash TV. However, what we also see in this instance is the carnivalesque idea of the 'grotesque' body that is challenging correct 'femininity'. It does a 'moonie' to middle-class feminism and its ideals of appropriate values and ways of thinking and imaging itself. The girls out on the town are certainly making a spectacle out of themselves, forgoing restraint for anarchic excess and, what's more, having a laugh. Being crude and vulgar is highly effective resistance and an instant means by which one can disobey and trounce.

The pleasures of being crude and vulgar in terms of corporeality are effective and create immediate impact, and they divide along class lines. But they open up yet more questions. My support of new burlesque performers could be seen as skewered feminism in terms of this class conflict. Burlesque is – is it not? – mainly middle-class white young(ish) girls taking their clothes off. Why is it all right to do this if it is seen as an 'art', and therefore thinking/intelligent and 'clean' performance? For me, burlesque offers a refreshing perspective, for it sits in between the 'low' and the 'high' as both performance art and amateur stripping, between the artist and the artiste. It refuses to be pinned down as 'high', yet is evidently creative and provocative, and it refuses to be pinned down as 'feminist', yet undeniably puts the thinking spectacle of woman's body centre stage. What it is refusing, therefore, is hegemonic control over its meaning, framework and significance.

Burlesque on the whole does not use excess to debase the body, however. The work I discuss in this book is not necessarily 'obscene' if we think about Lynda Nead's ideas of sitting outside the frame, or 'scene', of art.[6] Nead's concept of 'obscenity' as outlined in her book *The Female Nude* (1992) is raw matter which is transformed by culture into the submissive Nude. Obscenity is raw sexual flesh that stands 'outside of cultural representation'.[7] The images and performances that I have discussed in this book do not stand outside of the frame, but instead reconstitute and re-appropriate what is inside. They are also not 'grotesque' if we consider Mary Russo's concept of bursting loudly and 'monstrously' out of conventional expectations in terms of being too fat, too old or too 'lairy'.[8] The dangerous identities reside within the frame of 'femininity' yet somehow shift the context, and by doing this somehow implode the image and expectations. This is a different kind of everyday aesthetics of the body whose sympathy finds resonance with Caitlin Moran's popular feminist text, *How to be a Woman*, which was published in 2011. The book kicks off with the idea of dangerous identities, bodies that don't fit in, and Moran describes a scene where she is running away from boys who are throwing stones at her: 'The Princess of Wales is feminine, Kylie Minogue is feminine: I'm femi-none. So I understand the Yobs' confusion.'[9] She doesn't fit and therefore has to be destroyed or humiliated. She has to disappear; her appearance is offensive, a subcultural challenge of the frame of the popular, the normal, the everyday. Being not conventionally feminine means being a lesbian, a 'bloke' or a 'bummer'.[10]

What interests me is imagery made on the whole by women which explores the body otherwise. It is not obscene as such, but still exceeds the rules of the game from within the conventions of the frame. The artists and artistes that I have explored in this book challenge the framework which legitimizes particular bodies, images and transgressions by reframing and revising the 'aesthetics' of the female body. Something usually confined to the 'high' is now hovering over a non-discriminatory array of 'low' and 'high' art forms in order to reconfigure and open up, as well as violate, the frame from within the frame. By imploding rather than exploding out of the frame, it reconstitutes what is inside. As Roger Malbert argues: 'The frame that legitimizes art is imaginary'.[11] So what about all these other imagined and constructed frames? What are their purposes? Who is being suppressed, oppressed and controlled by them, and to what ends?

What is offered up in this book is a politics of aesthetics rather than a politics of the grotesque. This is imagery that uses excess to reveal an anarchic and mischievous sensibility. It unravels the complexity of the subject from within the image. This is visual pleasure which challenges a limited representation of the female gendered body as subject, and it does this by way of fabric, colour and painterly concerns. What is revealed is a richer aesthetic which moves across a wider affective register. The artists and artistes that I have focused on in this book use the canonical body or 'nude' and contaminate this traditional 'painting' with other elements of pain, the brash use of colour, the vulgar 'low' sensual pleasures of food and the 'feminine' practices of fashion and fabric, playing with various 'class-based' meanings considered insignificant or frivolous. This is a broader idea of aesthetics and the pleasure of the everyday, which has been edited out of the representation of female bodies. It is the recomposition of the pictorial form, whether that be by way of violence or masturbation, piercing the body or licking one's lips over a tremendous mountain of trifle and hundreds and thousands. This is the 'high' of the 'ideal', the nude and aesthetics which has moved into the 'low' of the insignificant and the unworthy.

...AND NOW YOU DON'T

What is tantalizingly evident in the art and cabaret examples in this book is that they react with relish to the excess of an already over-populated visual sexualized arena by stepping into these images in order to subvert and implode them from within. But what is also plainly evident is the performance of a magical pleasure in what one cannot see. The artists and artistes reveal a body-in-process, of objects not quite beautiful, not fully visible, a body and subject not completely revealed or exposed. By way of crystal balls, puppets, trapdoors and flamboyant dressing up, identities are performed which give us the potential for creative imagining. The fascinating insights offered by Frenchy Lunning in *Fetish Style* (2013) can help us perhaps to more succinctly situate the final section of this book within the context of the present moment.

Towards the end of this text, Lunning quotes Ulrich Lehmann in her idea that masks can make 'the mysterious become manifest'.[12] And indeed this intrigue of masks in fashion caught my attention in 2012–13 with Rick Owens and Maison Martin Margiela. The sheer exuberance of the theatrical disguise, concealment and underplay through theatricality was what I found intensely engaging. For Rick Owens, masks fully covered the head in knitted or crocheted balaclava-like black 'beanies' with large gaps created in the pattern to partially show the face, and with Maison Martin Margiela the balaclava fully masked the face with bold pinks, turquoise and jade-coloured jewels and sequins which dramatically caught the light. In this collection just the nape of the neck was revealed, making this area incredibly attractive and sensual. The identity of the face had disappeared in order to reveal something else which was far more open and did not pin the body's identity down so easily. This of course also has an element of violence as it annihilates the visual characteristics and identity of the female subject; however, it is through this fully visible knowledge that categories are able to be immediately discerned and controlled. This is the way that one is perceived by being mapped onto stereotyped genres of the perfect 'look', or judged by one's variations from the 'ideal'. By shielding the gaze, one can control what one allows the spectator to see. It also allows one to have some kind of creative ownership over an identity which is commodified and objectified.

In a culture that sanctions visual display as power and a means to control, artists and artistes can expose the ways in which violence is inflicted upon the subject by disappearing behind creative boundaries. But it also becomes a means by which the subject can reconfigure their own objecthood. Identity is seen to be easy to decipher through the visual, where the body is simplified and understood. In this way our visual culture promotes the idea that we have complete and utter knowledge over female bodies, which we have permission to see.

Therefore to be excessively visible is to pervert expectations; but equally, I would argue, so is to be invisible. Within the glut of the visual a reaction is to find magic and pleasure in what we can't see and to disappear into our imagination. What this evidently reveals is the ambivalent and complex relationship with the other's gaze, which can be an invitation but also a violation of the subject's boundaries. The use of masks to guard the self also reveals the way in which the body sits on a knife's edge between peekaboo fantasy, which is playful and surprising, and other forms of sexualized control.

Masks can of course in our 'pornified' society be yet another form of sexual fetishization, for our culture clings to the sexual objectification and commodification of the female body. The fragmentation of the body as object through masking can play up to the thirst for exposure of pornographic visibility. Masks evoke the idea of 'kinkiness', with the word 'kinky' describing the sense of performing a 'kink' in one's sexual identity. The word 'kinky', used to describe a woman, though, also implies being 'easy'. Her deviancy equates to her promiscuity, and is thus a fortuitous opportunity for sex on a plate. Killing Kittens, Britain's first sex club for women, which started in Covent Garden, London in 2005 but has since spread to other cities, illustrates the manner in which 'kinkiness' clings to convention. One goes to Killing Kittens to partake in orgies or watch one happening. Men must come with an invite, and everybody is required to wear a mask for the first hour after having disrobed.

In a 2014 article in *The Sunday Times Magazine* entitled 'The women's room',[13] Tanya Gold discusses the masks used by the people who frequent the club (which the founder, Emma Sayle, argues is for the 'sexual elite'[14]). Indeed, to be interviewed and reviewed by *The Sunday Times* is to be accepted perhaps as part of a 'high' exclusive polite cultured society. This could be seen as a chance for 'posh' girls to temporarily break away from daddy's respectability: the wild days of being naughty before settling down with stories to tell.

This is again a point about class, but one could say that the mask, as a method of disguise and dissimulation in order to sexually 'slum it', is being used in a similar way to the glamour used by working-class or underclass women as a means to upward mobility. Emma Sayle's published memoir is entitled *Behind the Mask*, and the idea of the mask being a wall that guards one's shame is a good starting point in trying to understand what the mask as a boundary is doing. Her idea for the club came from the time when she was at an Ibiza party watching a 'world-famous' actress having group sex and loving it. She argued that there was 'no sense of exploitation or shame'.[15] The idea of donning a mask to temporarily evade the judging eye of the Other is therefore interesting, as it becomes a sexual licence. It means that the young women can partake without shame in free and easy sexual activity or in watching naked beautiful bodies having sex. This is all about sex and – more evidently – all about the gaze.

The mask is an exterior object worn over the eyes which conceals the face. It enables, guards against, fields, deflects or obfuscates the gaze. When there is such an exclusive vetted group of young women in terms of attractiveness, youth and social cachet, one wonders what they have to be ashamed of. They are at the peak of perfection in terms of what is deemed to be successful in our social and visual order and hierarchy.

What is the issue with being known? There is a sense of social power, for visual knowledge brings you back sharply to act as a reminder of your 'real self', much like sitting on a boy's knee at a disco as a teenager and having your dad walk in: it gives you a reality check. Feelings of shame become the social chastity belt of your cultural order and make you aware of your own ethical and moral boundaries – your own world view. And this is what the young women at the club want to bypass temporarily whilst remaining rank-and-file members of society. Covering our eyes gives us respite from sight, a release from scrutiny and thus the anxieties of the gaze. It gives us a feeling of anonymity, and therefore a sense of freedom.

Wearing a mask whilst being completely naked allows you to therefore be shameless without leaving the mark of shame on your respectability, which controls the way that you are perceived – for you want to go back to being respected after the pleasurable interlude. You want to remain in control of how you are perceived, and you want to maintain your integrity. The accessory of the mask therefore is a halfway house mediating one's relationship as object and subject, enabling one to 'act' out fantasies whilst shielding the eyes against the paralysis of the gaze. The Killing Kittens events are described as a 'feminist orgy'[16] because the women cannot be approached or touched without permission, and men cannot attend without an invite from a woman. The mask becomes a point of mediation, a tacit agreement that you are giving the Other licence to look and permission to pleasure.

At this point it would be useful to return to Frenchy Lunning's discussion of masks in *Fetish Style* where she refers to fashion designers such as Thierry Mugler, Gareth Pugh and Junya Watanabe from 2007 to 2011 in order to argue that the mask in these collections

> has an object identity juxtaposed with a human body that eternally pivots in a nanosecond's time – from object to human, from human to object – under which is a human who created the objects they enliven and who, as a subject of fashion and an identity as a fashion model, generates her condition as an object.[17]

Therefore if we consider the mask in relation to Lunning's comment, the interplay between the object and the woman is very intriguing. The woman uses the mask to reveal how she 'generates her condition as object'. The mask gives agency into objecthood. As active objects, we are sanctioning the use of our body for pleasure. We implicate ourselves in our own objecthood. The mask highlights this transparency of power; this is sanctioned play. The mask as an inanimate object is being used to let us see the female subject who has implicated herself in her own objecthood. She is playing with her object status through control and play. And the mask becomes a signifier of this consent. But ultimately it is also a shield which seals off and mediates the body from the cruelty and control of the gaze in order to give one the space for play.

I have referred therefore to the mask because theoretically this can allow us to consider the way in which objects can be used to highlight and play with the paradoxical condition of 'being gorgeous'. Accessories and other objects are not used purely because of their capacity for facilitating escape in terms of role play. They also act as a means by which one can both shield and entice the gaze. These are objects which represent seduction and violation. Clothing and accessories allow one to play with one's pleasurable objectification. For one can seal oneself up as a glittering self-pleasuring object much like a dildo or a smooth golden vibrator – a self-enclosed orgasm-making package – or this object can act much like a violent, jewel-encrusted dagger, where one's objecthood can be used to harm. Objects can thus be used to signify women's paradoxical body as receptor of both pleasure and violence.

As spectacle, one is an object of the gaze and of capitalist commodification, but this is also the state under which one gains recognition, validation and a sense of pleasure and wholeness as a sensual and sexual subject. What is so present in the images explored in this book is that the artists and artistes play with this objecthood by disappearing behind and into objects. Their overdetermined and 'marked' appearance makes the idea of disappearance that much more endearing, for as a woman one is overdetermined in terms of age, race, shape, weight, class, 'prettiness' or 'ugliness'. Objects such as costume, dressing up, eyelashes, pink wigs and green jelly allow the self to reconfigure and creatively expand into the environment. This more sensitively embellishes the subject and allows one to hide yet dance in the dark: enigmatic yet blatantly visual. This is a play with visual pleasure without the obstacles and parameters of cultural restriction.

Objects mediate the gaze and shield the body and self from an excess of vision, but also enable one to be deflected into their textures, shapes and intriguing crevices. Gaynor Kavanagh argues that

we project our thoughts and feelings onto objects [...] The transference of emotion and memory on to the concreteness of an object separates that object from the run of the mill and appears to invest it with something almost magical.[18]

Fairs, crystal balls, puppets or eyelashes allow for the 'marked' female subject to express a more complex relationship to her environment and the Other. This relationship with objects allows for porosity and a subject that doesn't stop at the skin but also performs more widely via other elements: smell, touch, sound, humour, history and memory. This is a body and a self that makes and leaves an impression.

Objects can become a way of disorientating the gaze, performing the subject by rerouting that gaze. One can make one's mark, rather than being quite so violently and rigidly marked and anchored. They allow the subject to pull up the anchor and express one's identity and personality, sensuality and sexuality, gender and beauty as revealed through the flamboyance of fabric and pattern, conjuring tricks and the objects which one uses every day. The subject therefore is revealed as a process, and not something that is fully understood and known. Rather than be marked out as fully delineated and cut and pasted, this is more about a suggestion, a faint impression, a sensual evocation. It is about multiplicity and complexity, connectivity and collectivity. With wide-open eyes, one can anticipate a subject in the process of invention and creation. It is a creative process and a shared creativity.

And spectatorship is creative in this process as it mobilizes the imagination into a political collective aesthetic endeavour. For what is being envisaged in the imaginative connection between the spectator and the performer is an empathy and a collective, positive fun imagining. Being conjured up before our eyes is a visual pleasure which delights, refreshes, invigorates and uplifts the spirits. Smiling, this sleight of hand bypasses commodification and plays with vision, with our perceptions, with our expectations and presumed knowledge and power over the image: over what we believe we see. These are visual tricks which dodge, deflect and befuddle the drudgery of habitual representation with a spectacle which enlivens, not deadens.

This becomes therefore a playful critique of the glare of the homogenized gaze which beats down on the female sexualized body. We make contact with the subject who disappears into objects, wallpaper and crystal balls. This is about evoking what one can't see through the magic of playing with what one has creatively imagined oneself to be.

And it is couched within this idea of magic that I would like to draw this book to a close. The artists and artistes that I have explored in this text have been shown to disappear behind a shield in order to reappear in the cut glass of many-faceted guises and narratives. Emotions, aesthetics, memories, histories, ideas, humour, pain, creativity and intelligence have been performed via crystal balls, puppets, dancing ghosts, melting bubbling bath bombs and a smear of foundation on a bathroom cabinet doorknob. The gaze has been dispersed in the flutter of eyelashes or the multicoloured sparkle of a ring; and this also becomes a means by which one can disperse the complexity of the subject in all its effervescent glitter and glare to catch the eye obliquely or delight the unaware.

NOTES

INTRODUCTION

1 Originally published in *Screen* 16/3 (1975).
2 Mulvey, Laura, 'Visual pleasure and narrative cinema', in Amelia Jones (ed.), *The Feminism and Visual Culture Reader* (London and New York: Routledge, 2003), p. 47.
3 Ibid., p. 52.
4 Ibid.
5 Ibid., p. 47.
6 Zurcher, Anthony, 'Are viewers the "abusers" in celeb photo leak?', *BBC News*, 2 September 2014. Available at http://www.bbc.co.uk/news/blogs-echochambers-28992328 (last accessed 15 January 2015).
7 Betterton, Rosemary (ed.), *Unframed: Practices and Politics of Women's Contemporary Painting* (London and New York: I.B.Tauris, 2004), p. 5.
8 Jenni Murray's interview with Lorella Zanardo, 'Women on Italian television', *Woman's Hour*, BBC Radio 4, 21 May 2010.
9 HollaBackLDN is the UK arm of the American organization. The London Anti-Street Harassment campaign (LASH) was set up in 2011 by Vicky Simister.
10 Mulvey: 'Visual pleasure', p. 45.
11 Paglia, Camille, 'Lady Gaga and the death of sex', *The Sunday Times Magazine* [website], 12 September 2010. Available at http://www.thesundaytimes.co.uk/sto/public/magazine/article389697.ece (last accessed 15 January 2015).
12 Bruzzi, Stella, 'Tempestuous petticoats: costume and desire in *The Piano*', *Screen* 36/3 (1995), p. 259.
13 Bruzzi, Stella, *Undressing Cinema: Clothing and Identity in the Movies* (London and New York: Routledge, 1997), p. xiii.
14 Ibid.
15 Butler, Judith, *Gender Trouble: Feminism and the Subversion of Identity* (New York and London: Routledge, 1990), p. 179.
16 I must thank Dr Vanessa Brown, Design and Visual Culture Team Leader at Nottingham Trent University, for making me aware of this publication.

17 Feldman, Jessica, R., *Gender on the Divide: The Dandy in Modernist Literature* (Ithaca, NY, and London: Cornell University Press, 1993), p. 3.
18 Butler: *Gender Trouble*, p. 178.
19 O'Reilly, Sally, *The Body in Contemporary Art* (London: Thames & Hudson, 2009), pp. 17–18.
20 Ibid., p. 83.

Chapter 1. Drop Dead Gorgeous

1 Spector, Nancy, 'Only the perverse fantasy can save us', in *Matthew Barney: The Cremaster Cycle* (New York: Guggenheim Museum, 2002), p. 14.
2 Bonami, F. (ed.), *Matthew Barney* (Milan: Mondadori Electa, 2007), p. 10.
3 Ibid.
4 Spector: 'Only the perverse fantasy can save us', p. 14.
5 Feldman, Jessica R., *Gender on the Divide: The Dandy in Modernist Literature* (Ithaca, NY, and London: Cornell University Press, 1993), p. 3.
6 Ibid., p. 5.
7 Gamman, Lorraine, 'If looks could kill: on gangster suits and silhouettes', *Museum of the Moving Image: Source* [website] (8 May 2012). Available at http://www.movingimagesource.us/articles/if-looks-could-kill-20120508 (last accessed 15 January 2015).
8 Gamman, Lorraine, 'On gangster suits and silhouettes', in Marketa Uhlirova (ed.), *If Looks Could Kill: Cinema's images of Fashion, Crime and Violence* (London: Koenig, 2008), p. 218.
9 Baudelaire, Charles, *The Painter of Modern Life and Other Essays* [trans. and ed. Jonathan Mayne] (London: Phaidon Press Limited, 1964), p. 9.
10 Ibid., p. 2.
11 Ibid., p. 8.
12 Ibid., p. 9.
13 Senelick, Laurence, *The Changing Room: Sex, Drag and Theatre* (London and New York: Routledge, 2000), p. 504.
14 Schor, Mira, *Wet: On Painting, Feminism, and Art Culture* (Durham and London: Duke University Press, 1996), p. vii.
15 Ibid.
16 Ibid., p. 155.
17 Ibid., p. 154.
18 Martin Harrison quoted in Jennifer Craik, *The Face of Fashion: Cultural Studies in Fashion* (London and New York: Routledge, 1994), p. 78.

19 Baudelaire: *Painter of Modern Life*, p. 30.

20 LaChapelle, David, *Hotel LaChapelle* (New York and Boston, MA: Bulfinch Press, 1999), pp. 8–9.

21 Mercurio, Gianni, in Thomas Osterkorn, *Fotografie: David LaChapelle, Portfolio No. 51* (Dusseldorf: teNeues, 2008), p. 10.

22 Ibid.

23 Evans, Caroline, 'The enchanted spectacle', in *Fashion Theory* 5/3 (2001).

24 Dior collection, *Vogue* (September 2013), pp. 10–11.

25 Baudelaire: *Painter of Modern Life*, p. 31.

26 Ibid., p. 33.

27 Lloyd-Evans, Jason, and Pithwa, Sudhir, 'Charm school', *Vogue* (September 2013), p. 167.

28 Baudelaire: *Painter of Modern Life*, p. 33.

29 Feldman: *Gender on the Divide*: p. 138.

30 Nietzsche, Friedrich, *Beyond Good and Evil: Prelude to a Philosophy of The Future*, trans. R.J. Hollingdale (London: Penguin, 1973 [originally published 1886]), p. 13.

31 Céline collection, photographer Jürgen Teller, in *Vogue* UK (September 2013), pp. 67–9.

32 Schor: *Wet*, p. 155.

33 Ibid.

34 Tseëlon, Efrat, *The Masque of Femininity: The Presentation of Woman in Everyday Life* (London; Thousand Oaks, CA; New Delhi: Sage Publications, 1995), p. 39.

35 Vasseleu, Cathryn, *Textures of Light: Vision and Touch in Irigaray, Levinas and Merleau-Ponty* (London and New York: Routledge, 1998), p. 75

Chapter 2. Skin Deep

1 Vivid, Franky, 'We're turning two years old!', *Naked Girls Reading*, 5 February 2011. Available at http://nakedgirlsreading.com/2011/02/05/were-turning-two-years-old/ (last accessed 15 January 2015).

2 For more on these salons, see Goodman, Dena, 'Enlightenment salons: the convergence of female and philosophic ambitions', *Eighteenth-Century Studies* 22/3 (Special Issue: The French Revolution in Culture) (1989), pp. 329–50, and Beasley, Faith E., *Salons, History, and the Creation of Seventeenth-century France: Mastering Memory* (Farnham, Surrey: Ashgate Ltd, 1996).

3 'OBJECT: women not sex objects'. Available at http://www.object.org.uk/about-us (last accessed 15 January 2015).

4   Jane Garvey interview with Julia Long and Ophelia Bitz, 'Burlesque: emancipation or exploitation?', *Woman's Hour*, BBC Radio 4, 6 December 2010.

5   Kilbourne, Jean, *Can't Buy My Love: How Advertising Changes the Way We Think and Feel* (London: Touchstone, 2000), p. 260. I would like to thank my fashion students at Nottingham Trent for making me aware of this interesting book.

6   Cochrane, Kira, 'The X Factor final: call this family viewing?', *Guardian G2* (14 December 2010), p. 2.

7   Wolff, Janet, 'Reinstating corporeality: feminism and body politics', in Janet Wolff, *Feminine Sentences: Essays on Women and Culture* (Cambridge; Oxford: Polity Press, 1990), pp. 120–1.

8   Epley, Nathan Scott, 'Pin-ups, retro-chic and the consumption of irony', in Susanna Paasonen, Kaarina Nikunen and Laura Saarenmaa (eds), *Pornification: Sex and Sexuality in Media Culture* (Oxford and New York: Berg, 2007), p. 56.

9   Hutcheon, Linda, *Irony's Edge: The Theory and Politics of Irony* (London: Routledge, 1994), p. 27. Discussed by Epley in 'Pin-ups', ibid.

10 Buszek, Maria Elena, *Pin-Up Grrrls: Feminism, Sexuality, Popular Culture* (Durham and London: Duke University Press, 2006), p. 3.

11 Epley in Paasonen, Nikunen and Saarenmaa (eds): *Pornification*, p. 57.

12 Quoted in Buszek: *Pin-Up Grrrls*, p. 1.

13 Solomon-Godeau, Abigail, 'The other side of Venus: the visual economy of feminine display', in Victoria de Grazia and Ellen Furlough (eds), *The Sex of Things: Gender and Consumption in Historical Perspective* (Berkeley; Los Angeles; London: University of California Press, 1996), p. 115.

14 Lilley, Ed, 'Art, fashion and the nude: a nineteenth century realignment', *Fashion Theory* 5/1 (2001), p. 57.

15 Ibid., p. 59.

16 Twain, Mark, *Extracts from Adam's Diary* (New York: Harper & Brothers, 1897).

17 Buszek: *Pin-Up Grrrls*, p. 3.

18 Kale, Steven, *French Salons: High Society and Political Sociability from the Old Regime to the Revolution of 1848* (Baltimore, MD: Johns Hopkins University Press, 2004), p. 18.

19 Ibid.

20 Craik, Jennifer, *The Face of Fashion: Cultural Studies in Fashion* (London and New York: Routledge, 1994), p. 1.

21 Ibid., p. 12.

22 Kale: *French Salons*, p. 18.

23 This second part of Chapter 2 was adapted into a conference paper

entitled 'False eyelashes: with a flutter, our gaze is dispersed', delivered at Sheffield University's *Dressed Bodies: A Symposium* (17 July 2013).

24 Wilson, Elizabeth, *Adorned in Dreams* (London and New York: I.B.Tauris, 2005 [originally published in 1985 by Virago Press]), p. 246.

25 Walters, Ben, 'Burlesque: The daily grind', *Guardian G2* (14 December 2010), pp. 19–21.

26 Roach, Catherine M., *Stripping, Sex and Popular Culture* (Oxford and New York: Berg, 2007), p. 109.

27 Leader, Darian, 'Cut-outs', in Dawn Woolley, *Visual Pleasure* (Cardiff: Ffotogallery, 2010), p. 7.

28 Ibid.

29 Entwistle, Joanne, *The Fashioned Body: Fashion, Dress and Modern Social Theory* (Cambridge and Malden, Oxford: Polity Press, 2000), p. 185.

30 Sawchuk, Kim, 'A tale of inscription/fashion statements', in Malcolm Barnard, (ed.), *Fashion Theory: A Reader* (London and New York: Routledge, 2007), p. 476.

31 Entwistle, Joanne, 'The dressed body', in Joanne Entwistle and Elizabeth Wilson (eds), *Body Dressing: Dress, Body, Culture* (Oxford and New York: Berg, 2001), p. 36.

32 Doane, Mary Ann, 'Woman's stake: filming the female body', *October* 17 (1981), p. 25. Quoted in Jane Gaines' essay 'Fabricating the female body', in Jane Gaines and Charlotte Herzog (eds), *Fabrications: Costume and the Female Body* (London and New York: Routledge, 1990), p. 7.

33 Gaines, Jane, 'Fabricating the female body', in Gaines and Herzog: *Fabrications*, p. 6

34 Dyhouse, Carol, *Glamour: Women, History, Feminism* (London and New York: Zed Books, 2010), p. 3.

35 Ibid.

36 Jackson, Rosemary, *Fantasy: The Literature of Subversion* (London and New York: Routledge, 1981), pp. 40–1.

37 Tickner, Lisa, *The Spectacle of Woman: Imagery of the Suffrage Campaign, 1907–14* (London: Chatto & Windus, 1987), p. xi.

38 Ibid.

39 Sawchuk: 'A tale of inscription/fashion statements', in Barnard: *Fashion Theory*, p. 479.

40 Hurly Burly was a cabaret and vaudeville event which took place at the Déda theatre in Derby on 3 March 2012.

41 You can read this discussion in Lee Wright's essay 'Objectifying gender: the stiletto heel', in Barnard: *Fashion Theory*.

42 Dyhouse: *Glamour*, p. 2.

43 Jackson: *Fantasy*, p. 40.

CHAPTER 3. CRINOLINE AND CUPCAKES:
DANGEROUS IDENTITIES

1   Lee, Nathan, 'Pretty vacant: the radical frivolity of Sofia Coppola's Marie Antoinette', *Film Comment* 42/5 (2006), p. 25.
2   Waters, Darren, 'Coppola's period drama falls flat', *BBC News*, Wednesday 24 May 2006. Available at http://news.bbc.co.uk/1/hi/entertainment/5012530.stm (last accessed 15 January 2015).
3   Lee: 'Pretty vacant', p. 26.
4   Zevin, Alexander, 'Marie Antoinette and the ghosts of the French Revolution', *Cineaste* 32/2 (2007), pp. 32–5.
5   Ibid., p. 26.
6   Kennedy, Todd, 'Off with Hollywood's head: Sofia Coppola as feminine auteur', *Film Criticism* 35/1 (2010), p. 48.
7   Arnold, Rebecca, conference report: 'The art of dress', *Textile History* 40/2 (November 2009), pp. 240–1. Courtauld History of Dress Association Annual Conference (CHODA), Courtauld Institute of Art, London, 26–7 June 2009.
8   James, Nick, 'American decadence and other tales: Cannes', *Sight and Sound* 16/7 (2006), pp. 18–20, p. 22.
9   Ibid.
10 McGill, Hannah, 'Marie Antoinette', *Sight and Sound* 16/11 (2006), p. 68.
11 Lee: 'Pretty vacant', p. 26.
12 Zevin, 'Marie Antoinette and the ghosts of the French Revolution', p. 35.
13 McGill: 'Marie Antoinette', p. 68.
14 Gundle, Stephen, *Glamour: A History* (Oxford and New York: Oxford University Press, 2008), p. 28.
15 Ibid., p. 27.
16 Hunt, Lynn, 'The many bodies of Marie Antoinette: political pornography and the problem of the feminine in the French Revolution', in Lynn Hunt (ed.), *Eroticism and the Body Politic*, (Baltimore, MD and London: Johns Hopkins University Press, 1991), p. 112.
17 Ibid.
18 Ibid.
19 Ibid., p. 113. Lynn Hunt references three essays here: Paul Hoffmann, *La Femme dans la pensée des lumières* (Paris: Éditions Ophrys, 1977) pp. 324–446; Joan Landes, *Women and the Public Sphere in the Age of the French Revolution* (Ithaca, NY: Cornell University Press, 1988); and Outram, '"Le langage male de la vertu": women and the discourse of the French Revolution", in Peter Burke and Roy Porter (eds), *The*

Social History of Language (Cambridge: Cambridge University Press, 1987), pp. 120–35, p. 125.

20 Barthes, Roland, *The Pleasure of the Text*, trans. Richard Miller (New York: Hill and Wang, 1975), [originally published in 1973 by Éditions du Seuil, Paris], p. 12.

21 McGill: 'Marie Antoinette', p. 69.

22 Hoffmann, 'Museum of the streets', in Douglas Kahn and Diane Neumaier (eds), *Cultures in Contention* (Seattle: Real Comet Press, 1989), p.136.

23 Boyd, Andrew, 'Irony, meme warfare, and the extreme costume ball', in Benjamin Shepard and Ronald Hayduk (eds), *From ACT UP to the WTO: Urban Protest and Community Building in the Era of Globalization* (London and New York: Verso, 2002), p. 246.

24 Ibid., p. 248.

25 Duncombe, Stephen, 'Stepping off the sidewalk: reclaim the streets/ NYC', in Shepard and Hayduk: *From ACT UP to the WTO*, p. 228.

26 Krupskaya, Nadezdha, *Memories of Lenin*, trans Martin Lawrence (London: Panther, 1970), p. 53. Quoted in Elizabeth Wilson, *Bohemians: The Glamorous Outcasts* (London and New York: I.B.Tauris, 2000), p. 209.

27 Debord, Guy, 'Report on the Construction of Situations and on the International Situationist Tendency's Conditions of Organization of Action', in Ken Knabb (ed.) *Situationist International Anthology*, (Berkeley: Bureau of Public Secrets, 1981), p. 19.

28 Vaneigem, Raoul, 'Basic banalities II', *Internationale Situationniste*, Jan, 1963 and *Situationist International Anthology*, p. 124.

29 Zevin: 'Marie Antoinette and the ghosts of the French Revolution', p. 35.

30 Lloyd-Evans, Jason, and Pithwa, Sudhir, 'Charm school', *Vogue* (September 2013), p. 168.

31 Lee: 'Pretty vacant', p. 26.

32 The Wallace Collection online, 'Jean-Honoré Fragonard, *The Swing*'. Commentary available at http://wallacelive.wallacecollection.org/eM useumPlus?service=ExternalInterface&module=collection&object Id=65364 (last accessed 15 January 2015).

33 Ibid.

34 Westwood, Vivienne, 'From art to fashion'. This short video can be found on the lively blog *Making History Tart & Titillating*, available at http://lifetakeslemons.wordpress.com/2011/07/13/fashion-at-versailles-vivienne-westwood-more/ (last accessed 15 January 2015).

35 Cook, Pam, 'Portrait of a Lady: Sofia Coppola', *Sight & Sound* 16/11 (2006), p. 38.

36 Ibid.

37 Westwood, 'From art to fashion'. Available at http://lifetakeslemons. wordpress.com/2011/07/13/fashion-at-versailles-vivienne-westwood-more/ (last accessed 15 January 2015).

38 Silverman, Debora, *Art Nouveau in Fin-De-Siècle France: Politics, Psychology and Style* (Berkeley, CA; Los Angeles; London: University of California Press, 1989), p. 74.

39 Silverman, Debora, 'The "new woman" in fin-de-siècle France', in Lynn Hunt (ed.), *Eroticism and the Body Politic* (Baltimore, MD and London: Johns Hopkins University Press, 1990), p. 147.

40 Ibid., p. 152.

41 de Fourcaud, Louis, 'Les Arts de la femme au Palais de L'Industrie', *La Grande Dame* 1 (1893), pp. 27–8, in Silverman: 'The "new woman"'; p. 152.

42 Silverman: 'The "new woman"', p. 154.

43 Lee: 'Pretty vacant', p. 26.

44 Ibid.

45 Westwood, Vivienne, 'Active resistance to propaganda'. Available at www.activeresistance.co.uk/getalife, p. 3 (last accessed 15 January 2015).

46 Ibid., p. 19.

47 Haywood, Susan, *Key Concepts in Cinema* (London and New York: Routledge, 1996), p. 54.

48 Buscombe, Edward, 'Sound and colour', *Jump Cut* 17, p. 25, in Stephen Neale, *Cinema and Technology: Image, Sound, Colour* (London and Basingstoke: Macmillan Education Ltd, 1985), p. 146.

49 Kristeva, Julia, *Desire in Language* (New York: Columbia University Press), p. 221. In Neale: *Cinema and Technology*, p. 158.

50 Kristeva: *Desire in Language*. In Neale: *Cinema and Technology*, p. 219.

51 Ibid., p. 158.

52 Kennedy: 'Off with Hollywood's head', p. 48.

Chapter 4. Powder Puffs and Beauty Spots: Spectacular Objecthood

1 This first section of Chapter 4 was adapted as a paper entitled 'The Beauty Manifesto' for the *Gender, Race and Representation in Magazines and New Media* conference at Cornell University, Ithaca, New York, USA on 25–7 October 2013.

2 'Positive Beauty Manifesto', *Psychologies* (June 2011), pp. 114–5.

3 Vogue, Tricity, 'Our manifesto', *Blue Stocking Society* [website] (2011)

(published online 2011). Available at https://bluestockingssociety.
wordpress.com/about/ (last accessed 15 January 2015).

4   Ibid.

5   'Girls' attitudes explored... role models'. *Girl Guiding UK* [website].
Available at http://www.girlguiding.org.uk/news/girls%E2%80%99_
attitudes_explored%E2%80%A6.aspx (last accessed 15 January 2015).

6   Quoted by Cadwalladr, Charlotte, in review of Charlotte Chandler,
'The girl who walked home alone' [(London: Simon & Schuster, 2006),
published in the *Observer*, 18 June 2006, available at http://www.
theguardian.com/books/2006/jun/18/biography.features1 (last accessed
15 January 2015)], in Carol Dyhouse, *Glamour: Women, History,
Feminism* (London and New York: Zed Books, 2010), p. 75.

7   Tseëlon, Efrat, *The Masque of Femininity: The Presentation of Woman
in Everyday Life* (London; Thousand Oaks, CA; New Delhi: Sage
Publications, 1995), p. 39.

8   Ibid.

9   Scott, Linda M., *Fresh Lipstick: Redressing Fashion and Feminism* (New
York and Houndsmills, Basingstoke, Hampshire: Palgrave Macmillan,
2005), p. 11.

10   Ibid., p. 12.

11   Radcliffe Richards, Janet, *The Sceptical Feminist: A Philosophical
Enquiry* (Harmondsworth: Penguin, 1982), p. 239. Quoted in Pamela
Church Gibson, 'Redressing the balance: patriarchy, postmodernism and
feminism', in Stella Bruzzi and Pamela Church Gibson (eds), *Fashion
Cultures: Theories, Explorations and Analysis* (London and New York:
Routledge, 2000), p. 352.

12   Walter, Natasha, *Living Dolls: The Return of Sexism* (London: Virago
Press, 2010), p. 67.

13   Greer, Germaine, *The Female Eunuch* (London: Paladin, 1972), pp. 58–9.
Quoted in Church Gibson: 'Redressing the balance', p. 350.

14   Ahmed, Sara, *The Cultural Politics of Emotion* (New York: Routledge,
2004), p. 173.

15   Riviere, Joan, 'Womanliness as masquerade', in Victor Burgin, James
Donald and Cora Caplan (eds), *Formations of Fantasy* (London: Methuen,
1986).

16   Hanson, Julie, 'Drag kinging: embodied acts and acts of embodiment',
Body and Society 13/1, (Los Angeles, CA; London; New Delhi; Singapore:
Sage Publications, 2007), p. 73.

17   Ibid.

18   Ibid.

19   Ibid.

20 Berlant, Lauren, *The Female Complaint: The Unfinished Business of Sentimentality in American Culture* (Durham and London: Duke University Press, 2008), p. viii.

21 The images that I have included in this section are from a different Dr. Sketchy event to the one I attended (which unfortunately was not photographed). The photographs still clearly evoke the same ambience, 'drag', and politics of inclusion and fun. These images include the cabaret host Dusty Limits and artistes Bettsie Bon Bon and Tricity Vogue.

22 Robinson, Hilary, 'Border crossings: womanliness, body, representation', in Katy Deepwell (ed.), *New Feminist Art Criticism: Critical Strategies* (Manchester and New York: Manchester University Press: 1995), p. 138.

23 Grosz, Elizabeth, *Volatile Bodies: Towards a Corporeal Feminism* (Bloomington and Indianapolis, IN: Indiana University Press, 1994), p. 82.

24 Warwick, Alexandra, and Cavallaro, Dani, *Fashioning the Frame: Boundaries, Dress and the Body* (London and New York: Berg, 1998), p. 140.

25 Nead, Lynda, *The Female Nude: Art, Obscenity and Sexuality* (London and New York: Routledge, 1991).

26 Joselit, David, 'Notes on surface: toward a genealogy of flatness', *Art History* 23/1 (2000), p. 32.

27 Ibid.

28 Mackenzie, Catriona, 'Imagining oneself otherwise', in Catriona Mackenzie and Natalie Stoljar (eds), *Relational Autonomy: Feminist Perspectives on Autonomy, Agency, and the Social Self* (New York and Oxford: Oxford University Press, 2000), p. 144.

29 Deleuze, Gilles and Guattari, Felix, *A Thousand Plateaus: Capitalism and Schizophrenia* (Minneapolis, MN: University of Minnesota Press, 1987), p. 175.

30 Ibid, p. 178.

31 Joselit: 'Notes on surface', p. 27.

32 Ibid.

33 Deleuze and Guattari: *A Thousand Plateaus*, p. 187.

34 Ibid., p. 188.

35 Zagala, Stephen, 'Aesthetics: a place I've never seen', in Brian Massumi (ed.), *A Shock to Thought: Expression after Deleuze and Guattari* (London and New York: Routledge, 2002), p. 21.

36 Ibid.

37 A contemporary example of women's desire to dissolve this gap between the artist, the art and the spectator was demonstrated in an

art performance I contributed to at Chelsea School of Art and Design. It was entitled *Performance Dinner No. 5*: 'Woman as image, man as bearer of the look', where guests, invited by the Subjectivity and Feminisms Research Group based at Chelsea, were asked to contribute a performance as a response to Laura Mulvey texts. The event took place on 29 April 2013.

38 Carr, Alison J. [PhD candidate at Sheffield Hallam University], 'Glamour: the embodied surfaces of the showgirl', paper presented at *Dressed Bodies: A Symposium*, University of Sheffield, 17 July 2013.

39 Braidotti, Rosi, *Transpositions: On Nomadic Ethics* (Cambridge, UK and Malden, MA: Polity Press, 2006), p. 153.

40 Ibid.

41 Butler, Judith, *Bodies that Matter: On the Discursive Limits of 'Sex'*, (New York and London: Routledge, 1993), p. 234.

42 Freud, Sigmund, 'A note upon the "mystic writing-pad"', in *The Ego and the Id and Other Works*, Vol. XIX (1923–5) (London: Hogarth Press, 1961), p. 227.

43 Derrida, Jacques, *Of Grammatology* (Baltimore, MD and London: Johns Hopkins University Press, 1976 [Originally published by Les Éditions de Minuit, 1967]), p. 66.

44 Ahmed: *The Cultural Politics of Emotion*, p. 179.

CHAPTER 5. THE PARADOXICAL BODY

1 Schneider, Rebecca, *The Explicit Body in Performance* (London and New York: Routledge, 1997), p. 92.

2 Ibid.

3 Ibid.

4 Ibid., pp. 92–3.

5 Evans, Caroline, 'The enchanted spectacle', in *Fashion Theory* 5/3 (2001), pp. 271–310.

6 Debord, Guy, *The Society of the Spectacle* (London: Zone Books, 1994), para 1. Discussed by Evans in 'The enchanted spectacle', p. 272.

7 Solomon-Godeau, Abigail, 'The other side of Venus: the visual economy of feminine display', in Victoria de Grazia with Ellen Furlough (eds), *The Sex of Things: Gender and Consumption in Historical Perspective* (University of California Press: Berkeley, CA; Los Angeles, CA; London, 1996), p. 113.

8 Ibid.

9 Mulvey, Laura, *Fetishism and Curiosity* (Bloomington and Indianapolis, IN: Indiana University Press, 1996), p. 4.

10 Ibid., p. 8.

11 Baudrillard, Jean, 'The ideological genesis of needs/fetishism and ideology', in Malcolm Barnard, *Fashion Theory: A Reader* (London and New York: Routledge, 2007), p. 459.

12 Miller, Daniel, *The Dialectics of Shopping* (Chicago, IL, and London: University of Chicago Press, 2001), p. 186.

13 Reekie, Gail, *Temptations: Sex, Selling and the Department Store* (Sydney: Allen and Unwin, 1993), p. 119.

14 Lancaster, Bill, *The Department Store: A Social History* (London and New York: Leicester University Press, 1995), p. 175.

15 Woodhead, Lindy, *Shopping, Seduction & Mr Selfridge* (London: Profile Books, 2007), p. 5.

16 Ibid.

17 Leach, William, *Land of Desire* (1993), p. 57, in Lancaster: *The Department Store*, p. 175.

18 Baudrillard, Jean, 'The ideological genesis of needs', p. 454.

19 Evans: 'The enchanted spectacle', p. 272.

20 Doyle, Jennifer, *Sex Objects: Art and the Dialectics of Desire* (Minneapolis, MN, and London: University of Minnesota Press, 2007), p. 131.

21 Swiffen, Amy, and Kellogg, Catherine, 'Pleasure and political subjectivity: fetishism from Freud to Agamben', in *Theory & Event* 14/1 (2011).

22 Probyn, Elspeth, *Blush: Faces of Shame* (Minneapolis, MN: University of Minnesota Press, 2005).

23 Ibid., p. 34–5.

24 Swiffen and Kellogg: 'Pleasure and political subjectivity'.

25 Lancaster: *The Department Store*, p. 175.

26 Vasseleu, Cathryn, *Textures of Light: Vision and Touch in Irigaray, Levinas and Merleau-Ponty* (London and New York: Routledge, 1998), p. 38.

27 Von Teese, Dita, *Burlesque and the Art of the Teese/Fetish and the Art of the Teese* (New York, NY: Regan Books, 2004).

28 The key texts in this tradition being Descartes' *Meditations* (1637), Hobbes' *Leviathan* (1651) and La Mettrie's *Man in the Machine* (1748).

29 Grosz, Elizabeth, *Volatile Bodies: Toward a Corporeal Feminism*. (Bloomington and Indianapolis, IN: Indiana University Press, 1994), p. 3.

30 Muehl, Otto, 'Material Action Manifesto' (1964), in Malcolm Green (ed.), *Brus, Muehl, Nitsch, Schwarzkogler: Writings of the Vienna Actionists* (London: Atlas Press, 1999), p. 17.

31 Nitsch, Hermann, *6-Tage-Spiel in Prinzendorf 1998* (Vienna: Museum Moderner Kunst Stiftung Ludwig, 1999), p. 14, in Green (ed.): *Brus, Muehl, Nitsch, Schwarzkogler*, p. 17.

32 Grosz: *Volatile Bodies*, p. viii.
33 Ibid., p. 191.
34 Ibid., p. 192.
35 Ibid., p. 95.
36 Ibid., p. 189.
37 Bataille, Georges, *Visions of Excess: Selected Writings, 1927–39* (Minneapolis: University of Minnesota Press, 1994 [originally published in 1985 by the University of Minnesota]).
38 O'Dell, Kathy, *Contract with the Skin: Masochism, Performance Art and the 1970s* (Minneapolis, MN: University of Minnesota Press, 1998).
39 Gatens, Moira, 'Towards a feminist philosophy of the body', in Barbara Caine, Elizabeth A. Grosz and Marie de Lepervanche (eds), *Crossing Boundaries: Feminisms and the Critique of Knowledges* (Sydney; Wellington; London; Boston, MA: Allen & Unwin, 1988), p. 60.
40 Gorton, Kristyn, *Theorizing Desire: From Freud to Feminism to Film* (Houndmills, Basingstoke, Hampshire: Palgrave Macmillan, 2008), p. 124 quoting Constable (2004), p. 692.
41 Marks, Laura U., *Touch: Sensuous Theory and Multisensory Media* (Minnesota, MN: University of Minnesota Press, 2002), p. xvi.
42 This reference can be found in Leo Bersani's 'Is the rectum a grave?', in Douglas Crimp (ed.), *AIDS: Cultural Analysis, Cultural Activism* (Cambridge: MIT Press, 1988), p. 206.
43 Marks, *Touch*, p. xvi.
44 Ibid.

CHAPTER 6. THE SEXUAL BODY

1 Paglia, Camille, *Sex, Art, and American Culture* (New York: Vintage Books, 1992).
2 Williams, Linda, 'A provoking agent: the pornography and performance art of Annie Sprinkle', in Carol J. Clover and Roma Gibson (eds), *Dirty Looks: Women, Pornography, Power* (London: BFI Publishing, 1993), p. 178.
3 Ibid., p. 179.
4 Ibid., p. 189.
5 Birringer, Johannes, *Theatre, Theory, Postmodernism.* (Bloomington and Indianapolis, IN: Indiana University Press, 1991), p. 215.
6 Annie Sprinkle, quoted in Andrea Juno and Vivian Vale (eds) *Angry Women* (San Francisco, CA, and London: Re/Search Publications, 1991), p. 34.
7 *Dressed Bodies: A Symposium*, Interdisciplinary Centre of the Social

Sciences, University of Sheffield (17 July 2013). My paper for this was entitled 'False eyelashes: with a flutter our gaze is dispersed' (adapted from Chapter 2 of this book).

8 Nicholls, Emily, '"Harsh, bright and in your face": (in)appropriate feminine dress and identities on a "girls' night out"' (2013). Paper given at *Dressed Bodies: A Symposium*, as above.

9 Finel Honigman, Ana, 'Overwhelming life', *Artnet.com* [website] (23 March 2006). Available at http://www.artnet.com/magazineus/features/honigman/honigman3-29-06.asp (last accessed 15 January 2015).

10 Le Duc, Frank, 'Brighton MP ordered to cover up during Page 3 debate', *Brighton and Hove News* [website]. Available at http://www.brightonandhovenews.org/2013/06/12/brighton-mp-ordered-to-cover-up-during-page-3-debate/21818 (last accessed 15 January 2015).

11 Ibid.

12 *Purple Fashion*, Anniversary Edition, Fall/Winter 2012–13.

13 Poyner, Rick, *Obey the Giant: Life in the Image World* (Basel; Boston, MA; Berlin: Birkhauser, 2001), p. 97.

14 One of my second-year fashion students at Nottingham Trent University in 2012 found it incredulous that these soft porn images had found their way into credible fashion magazines: this became the subject of her third-year dissertation.

15 Buck-Morss, Susan, *The Dialectics of Seeing: Walter Benjamin and the Arcades Project*, p. 184. Quoted in Rebecca Schneider, 'After us the savage goddess: feminist performance art of the explicit body staged, uneasily, across modernist dreamscapes', in Elin Diamond (ed.), *Performance and Cultural Politics* (London and New York: Routledge: London and New York, 1996), p. 158.

16 Schneider: 'After us the savage goddess', p. 160.

17 Cumming, Laura, 'Tracey Emin: love is what you want', *Observer*, 22 May 2011. Available at http://www.theguardian.com/artanddesign/2011/may/22/tracey-emin-love-hayward-review (last accessed 15 January 2015).

18 O'Reilly, Sally, *The Body in Contemporary Art* (London: Thames & Hudson, 2009), p. 84.

19 Ibid., p. 85.

20 Dumas, Marlene, *Sweet Nothings* (1993). Quoted in Adrian Searle, 'I am a dirty woman. That's why I paint', *theguardian.com* [website] (30 March 1999). Available at http://www.theguardian.com/theguardian/1999/mar/30/features11.g2 (last accessed 15 January 2015).

21 Schumacher, Rainald, 'Marlene Dumas: yes we can!', *Flash Art* (March/April 2009), p. 53.

22 Ibid.
23 Searle: 'I am a dirty woman'.
24 Paasonen, Susanna, *Carnal Resonance: Affect and Online Pornography* (Cambridge, MA; London, England: MIT Press, 2011) p. 202.
25 Wright, Lee, 'Objectifying gender: the stiletto heel', in Malcolm Barnard (ed.), *Fashion Theory: A Reader* (London and New York: Routledge, 2007), p. 197.
26 Ibid., p. 203.
27 Ibid.
28 Ibid., p. 202.
29 Irigaray, Luce, *Sexes et Parenté* (Paris: Les Éditions de Minuit, 1987), [Translation modified in *Sexes and Genealogies* (New York: Columbia University Press, 1993)], p. 112.
30 Ibid., p. 113. In Robinson, Hilary, *Reading Art, Reading Irigaray: The Politics of Art by Women* (London and New York: I.B.Tauris, 2006), p.129
31 Irigaray, Luce, *Sexes et Parenté* (Paris: Les Éditions de Minuit, 1987), p. 112. Translation modified in *Sexes and Genealogies* (New York: Columbia University Press, 1993), pp. 97–8. In Robinson: *Reading Art*, p. 129.
32 Massumi, Brian, 'Notes on the translation', in Gilles Deleuze and Felix Guattari, *A Thousand Plateaus: Capitalism and Schizophrenia* (Minneapolis: University of Minnesota Press, MI, 1987 [original 1980]), p. xvi.
33 Braidotti, Rosi, *Transpositions: On Nomadic Ethics* (Cambridge, UK; Malden, MA: Polity Press, 2006), p. 154.

CHAPTER 7. PLEASURE, VIOLENCE AND THE SENSUAL SPECTACLE

1 Black, Karla, *TateShots*, Turner Prize (Gateshead: Baltic Centre for Contemporary Art, 2011).
2 Kusama, Yayoi, *Obliteration Room* (London: Tate Modern, 9 February–5 June 2012).
3 Random International [art group founded in 2005 by Hannes Koch, Florian Ortkrass and Stuart Wood], *The Rain Room* (London: Barbican, 4 October 2012–3 March 2013).
4 *Light Show* (London: Hayward Gallery, Southbank Centre, 30 January–6 May 2013).
5 Ibid. Available at http://www.haywardlightshow.co.uk (last accessed 15 January 2015).

6   Welsh, Katharine, 'Karla Black', in *Turner Prize 2011 Catalogue* (Gateshead: Baltic Centre for Contemporary Art in association with Tate Publishing, 2011), p. 11.

7   Highmore, Ben, 'Bitter after taste: affect, food and social aesthetics', in Melissa Gregg and Gregory J. Seigworth, *The Affect Theory Reader* (Durham and London: Duke University Press, 2010), p. 121.

8   Eagleton, Terry, *The Ideology of the Aesthetic* (Oxford: Blackwell, 1990), p. 13. In Highmore: 'Bitter after taste', p. 121.

9   Highmore: 'Bitter after taste', p. 123.

10 Black, Karla, quoted in Welsh: 'Karla Black', p. 11.

11 Ibid.

12 Black: *TateShots*.

13 Highmore: 'Bitter after taste'.

14 Welsh: 'Karla Black', p. 11.

15 Seremetakis, C. Nadia, *The Senses Still: Perception and Memory as Material Culture in Modernity* (Boulder, CO; San Francisco, CA; Oxford: Westview Press, 1994), p. 14.

16 Ibid., p. 13.

17 Bergson, Henri, *Matter and Memory* (Mineola, NY: Dover Publications, 2004), p. 89.

18 Ibid., p. 173.

19 Seremetakis: *The Senses Still*, p. 9.

20 O'Reilly, Sally, *The Body in Contemporary Art* (London: Thames & Hudson, 2009), p. 86.

21 Lane, Rebecca, 'Guilty pleasures: Pipilotti Rist and the psycho/social tropes of video', *Art Criticism* 18/2 (2003), p. 30.

22 Phelan, Peggy, 'Opening up spaces within spaces: the expansive art of Pipilotti Rist', in Phelan, Peggy, Hans-Ulrich Obrist and Elisabeth Bronfen, *Pipilotti Rist* (New York and London: Phaidon, 2001), pp. 59–62. In Lane: 'Guilty pleasures', p. 29.

23 Rush, Michael, 'Wadsworth Atheneum/Hartford Caravaggio and his Italian followers', and 'Pipilotti Rist: ever is over all', *Art New England* 19/5 (1998), p. 35.

24 Rist, Pipilotti, 'Interview with Rochelle Steiner', in *Wonderland* [catalogue] (Saint Louis, MO: The Saint Louis Museum of Art, July 1–24 September 2000), p. 90. In Lane: 'Guilty pleasures', p. 29.

25 Rist, Pipilotti, as quoted in Elisabeth Bronfen, *(Entlastungen) Pipilottis Fehler [(Absolutions) Pipilotti's mistakes]*, in Peggy Phelan, *Pipilotti Rist*, p. 90. In Lane: 'Guilty pleasures', p. 22.

26 Schwabsky, Barry, 'Plastic surgery', *Art Review* 55/7 (2004), p. 78.

27 Ibid., p. 79.

28 Burn, Gordon, 'The encounter with reality', *Parkett* 70 (2004), p. 111.
29 Augé, Marc, *Non-Places: Introduction to an Anthropology of Supermodernity* (London and New York: Verso, 1995), p. 103.
30 Ibid.
31 Shohat, Ella, and Stam, Robert, 'Narrativizing visual culture: towards a polycentric aesthetics', in Nicholas Mirzoeff (ed.), *Visual Culture Reader* (London: Routledge, 2013), p. 36.
32 Shohat and Stam: 'Narrativizing visual culture', p. 35.

CHAPTER 8. CREATIVE SPECTATORSHIP AND THE POLITICAL IMAGINATION

1 Dreadful, Penny, *No. 101, The Wonderful World of Burly Q* [cigarette cards]. Photograph by Dave Glossop, imaging by Darkstar.
2 Dotty, Mamzelle, *No. 99, The Wonderful World of Burly Q* [cigarette cards]. Photograph by Monika Marion.
3 Stoddart, Helen, *Rings of Desire: Circus History and Representation* (Manchester and New York: Manchester University Press, 2000), p. 166.
4 Tait, Peta, 'Feminine free fall: a fantasy of freedom', *Theatre Journal* 48/1 (1996), p. 30, in Stoddart: *Rings of Desire*, p. 173.
5 Ibid.
6 See my last book, *The Happy Stripper: Pleasures and Politics of the New Burlesque* (London and New York: I.B.Tauris, 2009), for more details on this (and indeed the history of burlesque as a phenomenon).
7 Malbert, Roger, 'Exaggeration and degradation: grotesque humour in contemporary art', in Timothy Hyman and Roger Malbert, *Carnivalesque* (London: Haywood Gallery Publishing, 2000).
8 Ibid., p. 96.
9 Bogdan, Robert, 'The social construction of freaks', in Rosemarie Garland Thomson (ed.), *Freakery: Cultural Spectacles of the Extraordinary Body* (New York: New York University Press, 1996), p. 35.
10 Shohat, Ella, and Stam, Robert, 'Narrativizing visual culture: towards a polycentric aesthetics', in Nicholas Mirzoeff (ed.), *Visual Culture Reader* (London: Routledge, 2013 [revised: originally published in 2002]), p. 36.
11 Warren, C. Henry, 'A note on fairs', in M. Willson Disher, *Fairs, Circuses and Music Halls* (London: W. Collins, 1942), p. 9.
12 Ibid., p. 19.
13 Ibid., p. 14.
14 Ibid.

15 Barthes, Roland, *Mythologies* (London: Random House, 2000) [originally published in 1972 by Jonathan Cape, London], p. 90.

16 Weedon, Geoff and Ward, Richard, *Fairground Art* (London: New Cavendish Books, 2004), p. 267.

17 Phelan, Peggy, *Unmarked: the politics of performance* (London: Routledge, 1993), p. 147. Helena Rickett also referenced Peggy Phelan's idea of 'disappearance' in relation to art in her 'performance' at Chelsea School of Art entitled *Performance Dinner No. 5*: 'Woman as image, man as bearer of the look' (29 April 2013), where guests, invited by the Chelsea-based Subjectivity and Feminisms Research Group were asked to contribute a performance as a response to Laura Mulvey texts.

18 Referred to by Peggy Phelan as 'transformative becoming' in her book *Unmarked*, p. 11.

Conclusion

1 Lynch, Annette, *Porn Chic: Exploring the Contours of Raunch Eroticism* (London and New York: Berg, 2012), p. 11.

2 SlutWalk Toronto, 'Why' (http://www.slutwalktoronto.com/about/faqs/) (n.d.), quoted in Lynch: *Porn Chic*, p. 186.

3 Ibid.

4 Mills, Eleanor, 'Equality? What equality?', *The Times Culture Magazine* (13 April 2014), p. 50.

5 Ibid.

6 Nead, Lynda, *The Female Nude: Art, Obscenity and Sexuality* (London and New York: Routledge, 1992).

7 Ibid., p. 14.

8 For these ideas please refer to Russo, Mary, *The Female Grotesque: Risk, Excess and Modernity* (New York and London: Routledge, 1994), and Russo's 'Female grotesques: carnival and theory', in Katie Conboy, Nadia Medina and Sarah Stanbury (eds), *Writing on the Body: Female Embodiment and Feminist Theory* (New York: Columbia University Press, 1997), pp. 318–36.

9 Moran, Caitlin, *How to be a Woman* (St Ives, Cornwall: Ebury Press, 2011), p. 2.

10 Ibid., p. 3.

11 Malbert, Roger, 'Exaggeration and degradation: grotesque humour in contemporary art', in Timothy Hyman and Roger Malbert, *Carnivalesque* (London: Haywood Gallery Publishing, 2000), p. 96.

12 Lehmann, Ulrich, *Tigersprung: Fashions in Modernity* (Cambridge; MA: MIT Press, 2000), p. 354. Quoted in Frenchy Lunning, *Fetish*

Style (London; New Delhi; New York; Sydney: Bloomsbury, 2013), p. 117.

13 Gold, Tanya, 'The women's room', in *The Sunday Times Magazine* (13 April 2014), pp. 12–19.

14 Sayle, Emma, quoted ibid., p. 12.

15 Ibid.

16 Ibid.

17 Lunning, Frenchy, *Fetish Style* (London; New Delhi; New York; Sydney: Bloomsbury, 2013), p. 117.

18 Kavanagh, Gaynor, *Dream Spaces: Memory and the Museum* (London: Leicester University Press, 2000) p. 22.

BIBLIOGRAPHY

INTERNET LINKS

Gamman, Lorraine, 'If looks could kill: on gangster suits and silhouettes', *Museum of the Moving Image: Source* [website] (8 May 2012). Available at http://www.movingimagesource.us/articles/if-looks-could-kill-20120508 (last accessed 15 January 2015).

Madame Jojo's, 'Bête-Noire line-up', 2011. Available at http://web.archive. org/web/20110716202807/http://www.madamejojos.com/cabaret/bete-noire/line_up/ (last accessed 15 January 2015).

Mamzelle Dotty, 'Karine Friez'. Available at http://www.karinefriez.com/home. htm (last accessed 11 February 2015).

'OBJECT: women not sex objects'. Available at http://www.object.org.uk/ about-us (last accessed 15 January 2015).

Paglia, Camille, 'Lady Gaga and the death of sex', *The Sunday Times Magazine* [website], 12 September 2010. Available at http://www.thesundaytimes.co.uk/ sto/public/magazine/article389697.ece (last accessed 15 January 2015).

Searle, Adrian, 'I am a dirty woman. That's why I paint', *theguardian.com*, 30 March 1999. Available at http://www.theguardian.com/theguardian/1999/ mar/30/features11.g2 (last accessed 15 January 2015).

Vivid, Franky, 'We're turning two years old!', *Naked Girls Reading*, 5 February 2011. Available at http://nakedgirlsreading.com/2011/02/05/were-turning-two-years-old/ (last accessed 15 January 2015).

Vogue, Tricity, 'Our Manifesto', *Blue Stocking Society*, 28 February 2011. Available at http://bluestockingssociety.wordpress.com/about/ (last accessed 15 January 2015).

Waters, Darren, 'Coppola's period drama falls flat', *BBC News*, Wednesday 24 May 2006. Available at http://news.bbc.co.uk/1/hi/entertainment/5012530. stm (last accessed 15 January 2015).

Zurcher, Anthony, 'Are viewers the "abusers" in celeb photo leak?', *BBC News*, 2 September 2014. Available at http://www.bbc.co.uk/news/blogs-echochambers-28992328 (last accessed 15 January 2015).

TELEVISION/FILM/RADIO

'Burlesque: emancipation or exploitation?' [Jane Garvey interview with Julia Long and Ophelia Bitz], *Woman's Hour*, BBC Radio 4, 6 December 2010.

'Women on Italian television' [Jenni Murray interviews filmmaker Lorella Zanardo], *Woman's Hour*, BBC Radio 4, 21 May 2010.

BOOKS, ESSAYS AND ARTICLES

Ahmed, Sara, *The Cultural Politics of Emotion* (New York: Routledge, 2004).

Anderson, Melissa (2006) 'The Sun Queen', *Film Comment* 42/5 (2011), pp. 27–8, 30.

Arnold, Rebecca, 'The art of dress' [conference report, *Textile History* 40/2, pp. 240–1 (November 2009)], Courtauld History of Dress Association Annual Conference (CHODA), Courtauld Institute of Art, London (26–7 June 2009).

Banyard, Kat, *The Equality Illusion: The Truth about Men and Women Today*, (London: Faber & Faber, 2010).

Barthes, Roland, *Mythologies* (London: Random House, 2000) [originally published in 1972 by Jonathan Cape, London].

—— *The Pleasure of the Text*, trans. Richard Miller (New York: Hill and Wang, 1975) [originally published in 1973 by Éditions du Seuil, Paris].

Bataille, Georges, *Visions of Excess: Selected Writings, 1927–1939.* (Minneapolis, MN: University of Minnesota Press, 1994 [originally published in 1985 by the University of Minnesota]).

Bates, Laura, *Everyday Sexism* (London: Simon & Schuster, 2014).

Baudelaire, Charles, *The Painter of Modern Life and Other Essays* [trans. and ed. Jonathan Mayne] (London: Phaidon Press Limited, 1964).

Baudrillard, Jean, 'The ideological genesis of needs/fetishism and ideology', in Malcolm Barnard, *Fashion Theory: A Reader* (London and New York: Routledge, 2007).

Bergson, Henri Louis, *Matter and Memory* (Mineola, NY: Dover Publications Inc., 2004).

Berlant, Lauren, *The Female Complaint: The Unfinished Business of Sentimentality in American Culture* (Durham and London: Duke University Press, 2008).

Bersani, Leo, 'Is the rectum a grave?', in Douglas Crimp (ed.), *AIDS: Cultural Analysis, Cultural Activism* (Cambridge, MA: MIT Press, 1988).

Betterton, Rosemary, (ed.) *Unframed: Practices and Politics of Women's Contemporary Painting* (London and New York: I.B.Tauris, 2004).

Birringer, Johannes, *Theatre, Theory, Postmodernism* (Bloomington and Indianapolis, IN: Indiana University Press, 1991).

Black, Karla, *TateShots*, Turner Prize (Gateshead: Baltic Centre for Contemporary Art, 2011).

Bogdan, Robert, 'The social construction of freaks', in Rosemarie Garland Thomson, *Freakery: Cultural Spectacles of the Extraordinary Body* (New York: NYU Press, 1996).

Bonami, Francesco (ed.), *Matthew Barney* (Milan: Mondadori Electa, 2007).

Boyd, Andrew, 'Irony, meme warfare, and the extreme costume ball', in Benjamin Shepard and Ronald Hayduk (eds), *From ACT UP to the WTO: Urban Protest and Community Building in the Era of Globalization* (London and New York: Verso, 2002).

Braidotti, Rosi, *Nomadic Subjects: Embodiment and Sexual Difference in Contemporary Feminist Theory* (New York; Chichester, West Sussex: Columbia University Press, 1994).

—— *Transpositions: On Nomadic Ethics* (Cambridge, UK and Malden, MA: Polity Press, 2006).

Brooks, Mary M., and Backhouse, Clare, 'The art of dress', *Textile History* 40/2 (2009) pp. 240–1.

Bruzzi, Stella, 'Tempestuous petticoats: costume and desire in The Piano', *Screen* 36/3 (1995), pp. 257–66.

—— *Undressing Cinema: Clothing and Identity in the Movies* (Routledge: London and New York, 1997).

Buckley, Réka and Gundle, Stephen, 'Flash trash: Gianni Versace and the theory and practice of glamour', in Stella Bruzzi and Pamela Church Gibson (eds), *Fashion Cultures: Theories, Explorations and Analysis* (London and New York: Routledge, 2000), pp. 331–48.

Buck-Morss, Susan, *The Dialectics of Seeing: Walter Benjamin and the Arcades Project* (Cambridge, MA: MIT Press, 1989).

Burn, Gordon, 'The encounter with reality', *Parkett* 70 (2004).

Buscombe, Edward, 'Sound and colour', in Stephen Neale, *Cinema and Technology: Image, Sound, Colour* (London and Basingstoke: Macmillan Education Ltd., 1985).

Buszek, Maria Elena, *Pin-Up Grrrls: Feminism, Sexuality, Popular Culture* (Durham and London: Duke University Press, 2006).

Butler, Judith, *Bodies that Matter: On the Discursive Limits of 'Sex'* (New York and London: Routledge, 1993).

—— *Gender Trouble: Feminism and the Subversion of Identity* (New York and London: Routledge, 1990).

Calefato, Patrizia, *The Clothed Body* [trans. Lisa Adams] (Oxford and New York: Berg, 2004).

Carson, Fiona, and Pajaczkowska, Claire (eds), *Feminist Visual Culture* (Edinburgh: Edinburgh University Press, 2000).

Church Gibson, Pamela, 'Redressing the balance: patriarchy, postmodernism and feminism', in Stella Bruzzi and Pamela Church Gibson (eds) *Fashion*

Cultures: Theories, Explorations and Analysis (London and New York: Routledge, 2000), pp. 349–362.

Cochrane, Kira, 'The X Factor final: call this family viewing?', *Guardian G2* (14 December 2010), p. 2. Also available at http://www.theguardian.com/tv-and-radio/2010/dec/13/x-factor-final-family-viewing (last accessed 15 January 2015).

Cook, Pam, 'Portrait of a lady: Sofia Coppola', *Sight & Sound* 16/11, (2006), pp. 36–40.

Craik, Jennifer, *The Face of Fashion: Cultural Studies in Fashion* (London and New York: Routledge, 1994).

Cumming, Laura, 'Tracey Emin: love is what you want', *Observer* (22 May 2011). Available at http://www.theguardian.com/artanddesign/2011/may/22/tracey-emin-love-hayward-review (last accessed 15 January 2015).

Debord, Guy, *The Society of the Spectacle* (London: Zone Books, 1994).

Deleuze, Gilles, and Guattari, Felix, *A Thousand Plateaus: Capitalism and Schizophrenia* (Minneapolis, MN: University of Minnesota Press, 1987).

Derrida, Jacques, *Of Grammatology* (Baltimore, MD, and London: Johns Hopkins University Press, 1977 [originally published by Les Éditions de Minuit, 1967]).

Diamond, Elin (ed.), *Performance and Cultural Politics* (London and New York: Routledge, 1996).

Disher, M. Willson, *Fairs, Circuses and Music Halls* (William Collins: London, 1942).

Doyle, Jennifer, *Sex Objects: Art and the Dialectics of Desire* (Minneapolis, MN, and London: University of Minnesota Press, 2007).

Duncombe, Stephen, 'Stepping off the sidewalk: reclaim the streets/NYC' in Benjamin Shepard and Ronald Hayduk (eds), *From ACT UP to the WTO: Urban Protest and Community Building in the Era of Globalization* (London and New York: Verso, 2002).

Dyhouse, Carol, *Glamour: Women, History, Feminism* (London and New York: Zed Books, 2010).

Eagleton, Terry, *The Ideology of the Aesthetic* (Oxford: Wiley-Blackwell, 1990).

Entwistle, Joanne, *The Fashioned Body: Fashion, Dress and Modern Social Theory* (Cambridge; Malden, Oxford: Polity Press, 2000).

Entwistle, Joanne, and Wilson, Elizabeth (eds), *Body Dressing: Dress, Body, Culture* (Oxford and New York: Berg, 2001).

Epley, Nathan Scott, 'Pin-ups, retro-chic and the consumption of irony', in Susanna Paasonen, Kaarina Nikunen and Laura Saarenmaa (eds), *Pornification: Sex and Sexuality in Media Culture* (Berg: Oxford; New York, 2007), p. 56.

Evans, Caroline, 'The enchanted spectacle', *Fashion Theory* 5/3 (2001), pp. 271–310.

Freud, Sigmund, 'A note upon the "mystic writing-pad", in *The Ego and the Id and Other Works* XIX (1923–5) (London: The Hogarth Press, 1961).

Feldman, Jessica R., *Gender on the Divide: The Dandy in Modernist Literature* (Ithaca, NY, and London: Cornell University Press, 1993).

Gamman, Lorraine, 'On gangster suits and silhouettes', in Marketa Uhlirova (ed.), *If Looks Could Kill: Cinema's images of Fashion, Crime and Violence* (London: Koenig, 2008).

Gaines, Jane, 'Fabricating the female body', in Jane Gaines and Charlotte Herzog (eds), *Fabrications: Costume and the Female Body* (London and New York: Routledge, 1990).

Gatens, Moira, 'Towards a feminist philosophy of the body', in Barbara Caine, E. A. Grosz and Marie de Lepervanche (eds), *Crossing Boundaries: Feminisms and the Critique of Knowledges* (Sydney; Wellington; London; Boston, MA: Allen & Unwin, 1988).

Gold, Tanya, 'The women's room', in *The Sunday Times Magazine* (13 April 2014), pp. 12–19.

Gorton, Kristyn, *Theorizing Desire: From Freud to Feminism to Film* (Houndmills, Basingstoke, Hampshire: Palgrave Macmillan, 2008).

Green, Malcolm (ed.), *Brus, Muehl, Nitsch, Schwarzkogler: Writings of the Vienna Actionists* (London: Atlas Press, 1999).

Grosz, Elizabeth, *Volatile Bodies: Towards a Corporeal Feminism* (Bloomington and Indianapolis, IN: Indiana University Press, 1994).

Gundle, Stephen, *Glamour: A History* (Oxford and New York: Oxford University Press, 2008).

Hall-Duncan, Nancy, *The History of Fashion Photography* (New York: Alpine Book Company Inc., 1979).

Hamilton, Sean, and Samson, Pete, 'Ga Ga: I'm no piece of meat (…er you bloody well look like one)', *The Sun* (14 September 2010), pp. 1, 5.

Hanson, Julie Louise, 'Drag kinging: embodied acts and acts of embodiment', *Body and Society* 13/1 (Los Angeles, CA; London; New Delhi; Singapore: Sage Publications, 2007).

Haywood, Susan, *Key Concepts in Cinema Studies* (London and New York: Routledge, 1996).

Heathfield, Adrian, *Live: Art and Performance* (London: Tate Publishing, 2004).

Heuring, David, 'A lonely throne', *American Cinematographer* 87/10, (2006), pp. 64–70, 72–3.

Highmore, Ben, 'Bitter after taste: affect, food and social aesthetics', in Melissa Gregg and Gregory J. Seigworth (eds), *The Affect Theory Reader* (Durham and London: Duke University Press, 2010).

Hunt, Lynn, 'The many bodies of Marie Antoinette: political pornography and the problem of the feminine in the French Revolution', in Lynn Hunt (ed.), *Eroticism and the Body Politic* (Baltimore, MD, and London: Johns Hopkins University Press, 1991).

Irigaray, Luce, *Sexes et Parentés* (Paris: Les Éditions de Minuit, 1987 [translation modified in *Sexes and Genealogies* (New York: Columbia University Press, 1993)]).

Jackson, Rosemary, *Fantasy: The Literature of Subversion* (London and New York: Routledge, 1981).

James, Nick, 'American decadence and other tales: Cannes 2006', *Sight & Sound* 16/7 (2006), pp. 18–20, 22–3.

Joselit, David, 'Notes on surface: toward a genealogy of flatness', *Art History* 23/1 (2000).

Juno, Andrea and Vale, Vivian (eds), *Angry Women* (San Francisco, CA, and London: Re/Search Publications, 1991).

Kale, Steven, *French Salons: High Society and Political Sociability from the Old Regime to the Revolution of 1848* (Baltimore, MD: Johns Hopkins University Press, 2004).

Kavanagh, Gaynor, *Dream Spaces: Memory and the Museum* (London: Leicester University Press, 2000).

Kennedy, Todd, 'Off with Hollywood's head: Sofia Coppola as feminine auteur', *Film Criticism* 35/1 (2010).

Kilbourne, Jean, *Can't Buy My Love: How Advertising Changes the Way We Think and Feel* (London: Touchstone, 2000).

Knox, Kristin, *Alexander McQueen: Genius of a Generation* (London: A & C Black Publishers Ltd., 2010).

Kristeva, Julia, *Desire in Language* (New York: Columbia University Press, 1980).

LaChapelle, David, *Hotel LaChapelle* (New York and Boston, MA: Bulfinch Press, 1999).

Lancaster, Bill, *The Department Store: A Social History* (London and New York: Leicester University Press, 1995).

Lane, Rebecca, 'Guilty pleasures: Pipilotti Rist and the psycho/social tropes of video', *Art Criticism* 18/2 (2003).

Lee, Nathan, 'Pretty vacant: the radical frivolity of Sofia Coppola's Marie Antoinette', *Film Comment* 42/5 (2006), pp. 24–6.

Lehmann, Ulrich, *Tigersprung: Fashions in Modernity* (Cambridge, MA: MIT Press, 2000).

Lilley, Ed, 'Art, fashion and the nude: a nineteenth-century realignment', *Fashion Theory* 5/1 (2001), pp. 57–78.

Lloyd-Evans, Jason, and Pithwa, Sudhir, 'Charm school', *Vogue* (September 2013).

Lunning, Frenchy, *Fetish Style* (London; New Delhi; New York; Sydney: Bloomsbury, 2013).

Lynch, Annette, *Porn Chic: Exploring the Contours of Raunch Eroticism* (London and New York: Berg, 2012).

Mackenzie, Catriona, 'Imagining oneself otherwise', in Catriona Mackenzie and Natalie Stoljar (eds), *Relational Autonomy: Feminist Perspectives on Autonomy, Agency, and the Social Self* (New York; Oxford: Oxford University Press, 2000).

Malbert, Roger, 'Exaggeration and degradation: grotesque humour in contemporary art', in Timothy Hyman and Roger Malbert, *Carnivalesque* (London: Haywood Gallery Publishing, 2000).

Marks, Laura U., *Touch: Sensuous Theory and Multisensory Media* (Minneapolis, MN: University of Minnesota Press, 2002).

Massumi, Brian, 'Notes on the translation', in Gilles Deleuze, and Felix Guattari, *A Thousand Plateaus: Capitalism and Schizophrenia* (Minneapolis: University of Minnesota Press, 1987 [original 1980]).

McGill, Hannah, 'Marie Antoinette', *Sight & Sound* 16/11 (2006), pp. 68–9.

Miller, Daniel, *The Dialectics of Shopping* (Chicago, IL, and London: University of Chicago Press, 2001).

Mills, Eleanor, 'Equality? What equality?', *The Times Culture Magazine* (13 April 2014).

Moran, Caitlin, *How to be a Woman* (St Ives, Cornwall: Ebury Press, 2011).

Morice, Jacques, 'Qu'on leur coupe la tête', *Beaux Arts Magazine* 264 (2006), p. 20.

Mulvey, Laura, *Fetishism and Curiosity* (Bloomington and Indianapolis: Indiana University Press, 1996).

—— 'Visual pleasure and narrative cinema', in Jones, Amelia (ed.), *The Feminism and Visual Culture Reader* (London and New York: Routledge, 2003).

Nead, Lynda, *The Female Nude: Art, Obscenity and Sexuality* (London and New York: Routledge, 1992).

O'Dell, Kathy, *Contract with the Skin: Masochism, Performance Art and the 1970s* (Minneapolis, MN: University of Minnesota Press, 1998).

O'Reilly, Sally, *The Body in Contemporary Art* (London: Thames & Hudson, 2009).

Osterkorn, Thomas, *Fotografie: David LaChapelle, Portfolio No. 51* (Dusseldorf: teNeues, 2008).

Paasonen, Susanna, *Carnal Resonance: Affect and Online Pornography* (Cambridge, MA; London: MIT Press, 2011).

Paasonen, Susanna, Nikunen, Kaarina and Saarenmaa, Laura (eds),

Pornification: Sex and Sexuality in Media Culture (Oxford and New York: Berg).

Paglia, Camille, *Sex, Art, and American Culture* (New York: Vintage Books, 1992).

Phelan, Peggy, Obrist, Hans-Ulrich and Bronfen, Elisabeth, *Pipilotti Rist* (New York and London: Phaidon, 2001).

Plant, Sadie, *The Most Radical Gesture: The Situationist International in a Postmodern Age* (London: Routledge, 1992).

Poyner, Rick, *Obey the Giant: Life in the Image World* (Basel; Boston, MA; Berlin: Birkhauser, 2001).

Probyn, Elspeth, *Blush: Faces of Shame* (Minneapolis, MN: University of Minnesota Press, 2005).

Radcliffe Richards, Janet, *The Sceptical Feminist: A Philosophical Enquiry* (Harmondsworth: Penguin, 1982).

Rappaport, Erika Diane, *Shopping for Pleasure: Women in the Making of London's West End* (Princeton, NJ, and Oxford: Princeton University Press, 2000).

Reekie, Gail, *Temptations: Sex, Selling and the Department Store* (Sydney: Allen & Unwin, 1993).

Riviere, Joan, 'Womanliness as masquerade', in Victor Burgin, James Donald and Cora Caplan (eds), *Formations of Fantasy* (London: Methuen, 1986).

Roach, Catherine M., *Stripping, Sex and Popular Culture* (London and New York: Berg, 2007).

Robinson, Hilary, 'Border crossings: womanliness, body, representation', in Katy Deepwell (ed.), *New Feminist Art Criticism: Critical Strategies* (Manchester and New York: Manchester University Press: 1995).

—— *Reading Art, Reading Irigaray: The Politics of Art by Women* (London and New York: I.B.Tauris, 2006).

Russo, Mary, *The Female Grotesque: Risk, Excess and Modernity* (New York and London: Routledge, 1994).

—— 'Female grotesques: carnival and theory', in Katie Conboy, Nadia Medina and Sarah Stanbury (eds), *Writing on the Body: Female Embodiment and Feminist Theory* (New York: Columbia University Press, 1997).

Sawchuk, Kim, 'A tale of inscription/fashion statements', in Malcolm Barnard (ed.), *Fashion Theory: A Reader* (London and New York: Routledge, 2007), pp. 475–88.

Schor, Mira, *Wet: On Painting, Feminism, and Art Culture* (Durham and London: Duke University Press, 1997).

Schneider, Rebecca, *The Explicit Body in Performance* (London and New York: Routledge, 1997).

Schroeder, Jonathan E., *Visual Consumption* (London and New York: Routledge, 2002).

Schumacher, Rainald, 'Marlene Dumas: yes we can!', *Flash Art* (March/April 2009).

Schwabsky, Barry, 'Plastic surgery', *Art Review* 55/7 (2004).

Scott, Linda M., *Fresh Lipstick: Redressing Fashion and Feminism* (New York; Houndmills, Basingstoke, Hampshire: Palgrave Macmillan, 2005).

Senelick, Laurence, *The Changing Room: Sex, Drag and Theatre* (Routledge: London and New York, 2000).

Seremetakis, C. Nadia, *The Senses Still: Perception and Memory as Material Culture in Modernity* (Boulder, CO; San Francisco, CA; Oxford: Westview Press, 1994).

Shohat, Ella, and Stam, Robert, 'Narrativizing visual culture: towards a polycentric aesthetics', in Nicholas Mirzoeff (ed.), *Visual Culture Reader* (London: Routledge, 2013).

Silverman, Debora L., *Art Nouveau in Fin-de-Siècle France: Politics, Psychology and Style* (Berkeley, NY, and Los Angeles, CA: University of California Press, 1989).

—— 'The "new woman", feminism, and the decorative arts in fin-de-siècle France', in Lynn Hunt (ed.), *Eroticism and the Body Politic* (Baltimore, MD, and London: The John Hopkins University Press, 1991), pp. 144–8.

Solomon-Godeau, Abigail, 'The other side of Venus: the visual economy of feminine display', in Victoria de Grazia with Ellen Furlough (eds), *The Sex of Things: Gender and Consumption in Historical Perspective* (Berkeley; Los Angeles, CA; London: University of California Press, 1996).

Spector, Nancy, *Matthew Barney: The Cremaster Cycle* (New York: Guggenheim Museum, 2002).

—— 'Only the perverse fantasy can save us', in Nancy Spector, *Matthew Barney: The Cremaster Cycle* (New York: Guggenheim Museum, 2002).

Stoddart, Helen, *Rings of Desire: Circus History and Representation* (Manchester and New York: Manchester University Press, 2000).

Swiffen, Amy, and Kellogg, Catherine, 'Pleasure and political subjectivity: fetishism from Freud to Agamben', in *Theory & Event* 14/1 (2011).

Tait, Peta, *Circus Bodies: Cultural Identity in Aerial Performance* (London and New York: Routledge, 2005.

—— 'Feminine free fall: a fantasy of freedom', *Theatre Journal* 48/1 (1996).

Tickner, Lisa, *The Spectacle of Woman: Imagery of the Suffrage Campaign, 1907–14* (London: Chatto & Windus, 1987).

Topping, Alexandra, 'A cut above? Lady Gaga's new line in evening wear', *Guardian* (14 September 2010), p. 11. Also available at http://www. theguardian.com/music/2010/sep/13/lady-gaga-meat-dress-vmas (last accessed 15 January 2015).

Tseëlon, Efrat, *The Masque of Femininity: The Presentation of Woman in Everyday Life* (London; Thousand Oaks, CA; New Delhi: Sage Publications, 1995).

Valenti, Jessica, *Full Frontal Feminism* (Berkeley, CA: Seal Press, 2007 [revised 2nd edition, 2014]).

—— *He's a Stud, She's a Slut* (Berkeley, CA: Seal Press, 2008).

Vasseleu, Cathryn, *Textures of Light: Vision and Touch in Irigaray, Levinas and Merleau-Ponty* (London and New York: Routledge, 1998).

Von Teese, Dita, *Burlesque and the Art of the Teese/Fetish and the Art of the Teese* (New York, NY: Regan Books, 2004).

Walter, Natasha, *Living Dolls: The Return of Sexism* (London: Virago Press, 2010).

Walters, Ben, 'Burlesque: The daily grind', *Guardian G2* (14 December 2010), pp. 19–21. Also available at http://www.theguardian.com/stage/2010/dec/13/burlesque-dita-von-teese-christina-aguilera (last accessed 15 January 2015).

Warren, C. Henry, 'A note on fairs', in M. Willson Disher, *Fairs, Circuses and Music Halls* (London: W. Collins, 1942).

Warwick, Alexandra, and Cavallaro, Dani, *Fashioning the Frame: Boundaries, Dress and the Body* (Berg: London and New York, 1998).

Welsh, Katharine, 'Karla Black', in *Turner Prize 2011 Catalogue* (Gateshead: Baltic Centre for Contemporary Art in association with Tate Publishing, 2011).

Weedon, Geoff and Ward, Richard, *Fairground Art* (London: New Cavendish Books, 2004).

Wilson, Elizabeth, *Adorned in Dreams* (London and New York: I.B.Tauris, 2005 [originally published in 1985 by Virago Press]).

—— *Bohemians: The Glamorous Outcasts* (London and New York: I.B.Tauris, 2000).

Williams, Linda, 'A provoking agent: The pornography and performance art of Annie Sprinkle', in Pamela Church Gibson and Roma Gibson (eds), *Dirty Looks: Women, Pornography, Power* (London: BFI Publishing, 1993).

Willson, Jacki, *The Happy Stripper: Pleasures and Politics of the New Burlesque* (London and New York: I.B.Tauris, 2008).

Wolff, Janet, 'Reinstating corporeality: feminism and body politics', in Janet Wolff, *Feminine Sentences: Essays on Women and Culture* (Cambridge; Oxford: Polity Press, 1990).

Woodhead, Lindy, *Shopping, Seduction & Mr Selfridge* (London: Profile Books, 2007).

Woolley, Dawn, *Visual Pleasure* (Cardiff: Ffotogallery, 2010).

Wright, Lee, 'Objectifying gender: the stiletto heel', in Malcolm Barnard (ed.), *Fashion Theory: A Reader* (London and New York: Routledge, 2007).

Zagala, Stephen, 'Aesthetics: a place I've never seen', in Brian Massumi (ed.), *A Shock to Thought: Expression after Deleuze and Guattari* (London and New York: Routledge, 2002).

Zevin, Alexander, 'Marie Antoinette and the ghosts of the French Revolution', *Cineaste* 32/2 (2007), pp. 32–5.

INDEX